# YEOVIL

# KILL THE
# TIGER

## OPERATION RIMAU AND THE BATTLE
## FOR SOUTHEAST ASIA

**PETER THOMPSON & ROBERT MACKLIN**

First Published by Hodder Australia in 2002.
This edition published in 2007 by Maverick House Publishers.

Maverick House, Main Street, Dunshaughlin, Co. Meath, Ireland.
Maverick House SE Asia, 440 Sukhumvit Road, Washington Square, Klongton, Klongtoey, Bangkok 10110, Thailand.

info@maverickhouse.com
http://www.maverickhouse.com

ISBN: 978-1-905379-39-2

5 4 3 2

Printed by CPD.

The paper used in this book comes from wood pulp of managed forests. For every tree felled, at least one tree is planted, thereby renewing natural resources.

# CONTENTS

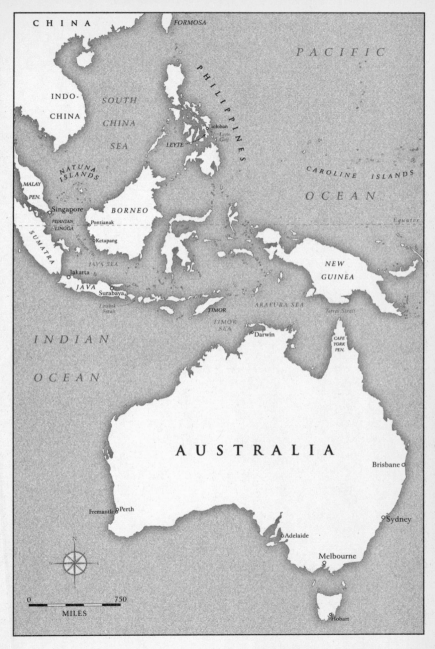

*Australia and Singapore environs.*

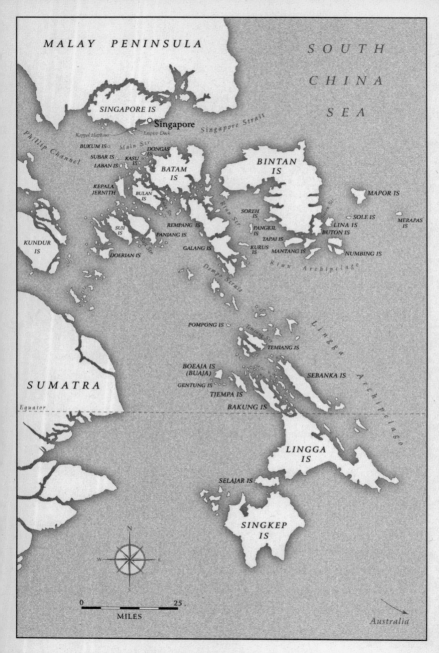

*Singapore and the islands of the Riau Archipelago.*

# AUTHORS' NOTE

DURING OUR collaboration on *The Battle of Brisbane* we became thoroughly familiar with the war in the Pacific up to the end of 1942. This formed the background to the drama detailed in that book. We also learned of some of the behind-the-lines activities of the Allied Special Forces.

We knew, for example, of the adventures of the *Krait* when a commando team sailed the old scow from Australia far into hostile territory to attack Singapore Harbour in 1943.

But the Rimau Raid of 1944—in which many of the same personnel participated—first came to our attention when Peter received a letter from his friend John Parker, chronicler of the Special Boat Service. It contained some intriguing research material—compiled by an enthusiastic amateur—and John suggested there was a cracking story to be told.

Peter brought it to Australia from his London base during the launch of *The Battle of Brisbane*. And since there was a rare chance for us to work in physical proximity—Robert being based in Canberra—we made a number of forays at the Australian War Memorial. We were soon chasing a range of fascinating leads.

Rimau had a publishing history. Some excellent groundwork had been done, particularly by Tom Hall of Sydney, to retrace the steps of the raiders. But we were utterly unprepared for the new material that we were able to uncover as gradually we found ourselves dealing with the most ambitious and heroic commando operation of the Pacific War.

Moreover, at a crucial point in our investigation we lucked upon a document which laid bare the determination of the highest levels of the British Establishment to develop and deploy Operation Rimau at all cost.

Suddenly much of the obfuscation which for half a century had puzzled and frustrated researchers was swept away.

And as we followed the brave men of Rimau on their extraordinary mission we became ever more conscious of the dark and terrible forces drawn into the unfolding saga.

We were also extraordinarily fortunate to discover two people for whom the events of Rimau in 1944 and 1945 still reverberate—Clive Lyon in England and Roma Page in Australia. They became our guides and our companions as we strove to lay bare the story beneath the story.

We, like all who have been touched by this heroic episode amid the horror of war, are greatly in their debt.

Peter Thompson
Robert Macklin

# THE LONELIEST MAN

MERAPAS ISLAND is a speck on the map, a tiny outcrop of black volcanic rock and coconut palm that barely causes a ripple in the jade waters of the South China Sea. It lies one hundred kilometres east of Singapore on the fringes of the Riau Archipelago, between the tip of the Malay Peninsula and the equator, an infinitesimal link in the chain of 'a thousand islands' that stretches down to Sumatra and Java. For twenty years, rarely a night had passed when Walter Chapman, formerly a major in the Royal Engineers, hadn't revisited that lonely shore and relived the terror.

He had been a few months short of his thirtieth birthday when the submarine HMS *Tantalus* dropped him at Merapas Island at one o'clock on the night of 22 November 1944—a Wednesday—yet, in his nightmares, while he had grown older with each succeeding year, the scenario had remained terrifyingly the same.

Drenched with sweat, slime and sea-spray, he was forever scrambling over the slippery black boulders at Dead Coral Beach, falling, hurting himself, then sneaking through the coconuts to the Hammock Tree, or climbing Wild Cat Hill to the banana plantation on top, fearing that every movement—a dislodged stone—would be followed by a shout, a shot and searing pain. And all the time he was searching for the twenty-three men he had been sent to find, the British and Australian commandos of Operation Rimau, the boldest sabotage venture of the Pacific War, but finding nothing except tantalising traces of their existence.

With the passage of time, those brave men had become spectral figures who stood over him like ghosts on Judgment Day because, at war's end, Walter Chapman had learned that his incompetence had left most of them at the mercy of their Japanese enemies. Through bad soldiering, Chapman had bungled the vital rendezvous that steamy November night and his report to the submarine's imperious captain, Lieutenant Commander Hugh 'Rufus' Mackenzie, that the men were nowhere to be seen guaranteed there would be no return visit, no second chance.

On 5 May 1964, the troubled engineer parked his car on the road outside the district hospital in the leafy, provincial town of Amersham, Buckinghamshire, took a small, black, Bakelite capsule from his pocket and extracted the pill that was contained inside. A few days earlier he had been interviewed by a war historian about his role in the Rimau rescue operation and it was only a matter of time before his incompetence was revealed. His conscience must have weighed heavily and that, coupled with the fear of imminent exposure, apparently tipped the balance of his mind.

The loneliest man on earth may have sat there for some time, contemplating that his last act might go some way to expiating his guilt, or he may have acted quickly to kill the fear once and for all. But at some time that day Walter Chapman slipped the pill into his mouth and within seconds he was dead. In a macabre tribute to the heroes, it was the same cyanide pill he had been given twenty years earlier at the outset of Operation Rimau on the opposite side of the globe in Australia.

Chapman's last thoughts may have been that, culpable though he was, he was far from being the only guilty one. Rufus Mackenzie, for one, should have borne much of the ignominy but he had been promoted to Vice Admiral and was therefore an untouchable member of the navy hierarchy. And Mackenzie wasn't the only one. The chain of betrayal of the Rimau heroes ran right to the top of the Allied high command.

# CHAPTER 1
# THE EMPIRE STRIKES BACK

WAR-WEARY LONDONERS would have taken heart had they been privy to the plans of the tall, tanned soldier striding down Oxford Street on a crisp March morning in 1944. It had been a miserably cold winter in the wartime capital, with icy winds whipping off the Thames and freezing fog adding an impenetrable cloak to the blackout. Today, however, the first blossoms of spring were on show in Hyde Park, daffodils were blooming in the squares and Lieutenant Colonel Ivan Lyon of the Gordon Highlanders symbol-ised the spirit of a great British regeneration.

It was not before time.

Civilian morale in the battered capital was still high but the Luftwaffe had returned and the city was in the grip of 'the Little Blitz' in which hundreds of people would be killed, thousands of houses destroyed and, to rub it in, the windows of 10 Downing Street blown in.

News vendors swathed in 'WAR LATEST' placards grinned at Ivan Lyon's jauntiness and passengers trundling past in a freshly painted red double-decker bus nodded appreciatively. His deep tan told them he had come from some far-flung battlefield, the Middle East or the Mediterranean, or perhaps even further afield in India or Asia, and the MBE on his tunic attested to distinguished active service in defence of the king's realm.

Ivan Lyon, twenty-nine, a character from the world of British derring-do, returned their greetings with a ready smile of his own. They would have been astonished had the immaculate officer opened his shirt and revealed the huge head of a Malayan tiger which was tattooed on his chest in vivid scarlet, black and yellow. And they would have been even more astonished had they known that his latest mission—Operation Jaywick in Occupied Singapore— had been one of the most stunning coups ever perpetrated against the enemy.

With a group of British and Australian commandos, Lyon had sailed 3500 kilometres from Western Australia to Singapore in a Japanese fishing boat, the *Krait*. Once within striking distance, he and his team had climbed into two-man canoes, or folboats (folding boats), and penetrated heavily guarded Singapore Harbour. Dodging air patrols and the naval *Kempei Tai*, the fearsome Japanese water police, they had attached magnetic limpet mines to seven enemy ships, then paddled away without the loss of a single man. Ivan Lyon's team had sunk almost 50 000 tons of shipping under the very noses of the Japanese.

That joint Anglo-Australian mission in September 1943, still a closely guarded secret as Lyon walked down Oxford Street six months later, had been carried out despite an American attempt to sabotage it. The United States was in total charge of the war in the Pacific, where their carrier-led fleets had seized air and sea superiority in monumental battles with the Japanese following the debacle of Pearl Harbor.

It was no secret that, for political reasons, victory in the Pacific had to be an American affair, with America's British, Australian and Dutch allies playing subordinate roles. When Japan was defeated, as she must be, the far-sighted Roosevelt, Churchill's wartime friend and collaborator, was opposed to Britain regaining her Eastern empire. After Pearl Harbor, America was never going to lose control of the Pacific again.

From his Australian headquarters, the Supreme Commander of the South-West Pacific Forces, General Douglas MacArthur, had his own agenda. His intelligence chief, Brigadier General Charles Willoughby, knew there was to be only one conquering hero in the Pacific—Douglas MacArthur—and it was the duty of his minions to ensure that he had no competition from the more unorthodox branches of the Australian and British military forces. All the glory had to attach itself to Willoughby's egotistical boss: that wasn't fanciful thinking, it was authorised policy. Willoughby had studied the Jaywick plan and blithely turned it down.

But Lyon, Jaywick's co-author as well as its chief activator, proved to be as persistent as he was audacious. Enlisting the support of the Governor-General of Australia, Lord Gowrie, and the head of Australian Land Forces, General Sir Thomas Blamey, he had taken Jaywick to its triumphal climax without any official American assistance whatsoever.

3

Shortly after he had returned from Singapore Lyon had been granted an audience with MacArthur, who had become aware that something fairly spectacular had taken place. He congratulated Lyon on the phenomenal success of his mission and pledged support for future sorties in the same region, noting that the effects of such attacks on the enemy's war effort 'are greater here than any other theatre'.

In truth, the former British colonies meant little to him. MacArthur was obsessed with the Philippines, which he had promised to liberate after being driven out by the Imperial Japanese Army in March 1942. 'I shall return,' he had declared on reaching Australia and nothing was going to divert him from that righteous, not to say self-righteous, cause. No matter how high the cost, he would make good on the flamboyant promise with which his name was so closely associated. And when the time arrived he would re-enact it several times.

MacArthur was still a long way from Manila when Ivan Lyon headed for England to present an even bolder plan than Jaywick to Combined Operations, Britain's joint army–navy–air command, and to her clandestine warfare agency, the Special Operations Executive (SOE). He had just been promoted from major to lieutenant colonel and was to about to be recommended for the Victoria Cross.

At that time, London was the hub of great excitement as thousands of combat troops poured into bases in southern England in the build-up to Operation Overlord, the Allied invasion of France. 'The hour of our greatest effort is approaching,' Winston

Churchill told his people in a radio broadcast and they thrilled at the prospect.

Ivan Lyon had already been awarded the MBE for his bravery in helping refugees to escape during the fall of Singapore and he wore the decoration pinned to the chest of his Gordons khaki jacket. The jacket's silver buttons were engraved with the cross of Saint Andrew and two of the regiment's most famous battle honours—the royal tiger of India and the Sphinx of Egypt. Lyon wore a kilt of Gordon tartan—dark green with yellow stripes—and a Sam Browne belt. On his head was a glengarry cap with the regimental silver badge of stag's head and ducal coronet ringed by ivy leaves, with the regiment's motto written in Gaelic: BYDAND— 'Be watchful'.

Uniforms in the throng streaming down Oxford Street that March morning told the shape of things to come: green berets for British commandos, maroon for British paratroopers, dark blue for Free Poles, the tricolour of de Gaulle's Free French, but mostly the uniforms were American khaki. General Dwight D. 'Ike' Eisenhower's headquarters was in 20 Grosvenor Square, and US servicemen in the Grand Alliance fanned out from there throughout the West End, with the greatest numbers to be found in the 24-hour canteen at Piccadilly Circus.

It was said the Yanks were 'over-paid, over-sexed and over here', to which one wit had replied that the British 'were under-paid, under-sexed and under Eisenhower'.

Ivan Lyon had met plenty of American soldiers in the Pacific but it was London town that he wanted to see. He was visiting his homeland for the first time in seven years and the capital of an empire on which the sun never set had changed dramatically. Barrage balloons hovered over the Houses of Parliament and, at night, the sound of anti-aircraft batteries assailed the ears from every direction.

Much of the damage inflicted by the 1940 Blitz had been cleared away but there were huge gaps between buildings and gardens of wild flowers and weeds had sprung up in the bombsites. Many shops were almost bare of merchandise, rationing was strict and there were few private cars puttering down Oxford Street.

Near Oxford Circus, the John Lewis department store had been completely gutted and its stock incinerated, while at the western end of the street a banner for War Bonds was strung across the face of Marble Arch, originally planned as a monument to the great British victories at Trafalgar and Waterloo.

It was the loss of empire that rankled most deeply with those in high places. Being kicked out of Malaya, Singapore, Hong Kong and Burma by the Japanese in just three months, with the possibility of losing even India, had dealt a devastating blow to British prestige. At the highest levels of British society—in Whitehall, Westminster and Buckingham Palace itself—there was an utter determination to retake the colonies and, if possible, rebuild the Empire.

Ivan Lyon understood these objectives. He was from a respected military family who shared an ancestor with the Queen, the former Lady Elizabeth Bowes-Lyon, and he was prepared to play his part in restoring British pride in South-East Asia. Furthermore, the breathtaking plan he was carrying in his head would not only eclipse the magnificent Jaywick mission but re-establish Britain's claim to her old colonies in the eyes of their subject peoples and, just as importantly, the Americans.

The risks were enormous, the stakes incalculably high.

AS LUCK would have it, Lord Louis 'Dickie' Mountbatten, the king's cousin, had been appointed Supreme Allied Commander in South-East Asia by Churchill, with President Roosevelt's approval, just a month before Jaywick. An old 'special ops' man himself, Mount-batten applauded Lyon's success. His previous posting had been Chief of Combined Operations Command, where his brief from Churchill had been to mastermind commando raids on Occupied Europe, culminating in preparations for the amphibious landings at Normandy in early summer 1944.

Churchill's first directive to the new supreme commander ordered him to liberate all colonial territories lost by Britain, France and the Netherlands. Mountbatten's planners at South-East Asia Command in New Delhi quickly came up with an adventurous scheme to launch an amphibious assault to capture the northern tip of Sumatra, with Singapore as the main target. But when Operation Culverin, as it was called, was presented to the British chiefs of staff early that year it had been rejected on the grounds that it would deplete the Allies' supply of landing craft. Churchill favoured the plan, but refused to overrule his commanders.

The US High Command in Washington also vetoed Culverin after Mountbatten's disloyal deputy, Joseph W. Stilwell, the American general known as 'Vinegar Joe' because of his acerbic tongue, sent a team to the capital to badmouth it, just as Willoughby had badmouthed Jaywick.

The line of demarcation between Mountbatten and MacArthur's commands ran through Saigon, capital of French Indochina, which meant that Singapore fell into Britain's strategic domain. Despite the failure of Mountbatten's own plan to get the go-ahead, he urged Ivan Lyon's outfit, the Services Reconnaissance Department (SRD) —cover name for Special Operations Australia (SOA)—to seek American assistance for further raids against the former British island fortress, as well as an attack on Saigon.

The success of Jaywick had already inspired India Mission, the Indian office of SOE, to conceive a plan to unleash a team of saboteurs against the Japanese from a base inside the perimeter of occupied islands in the South China Sea. Asked to provide the manpower, Ivan Lyon and his Australian comrades had developed Operation Hornbill, a complete program of sabotage and subversion for the whole of 1944.

The first step would be the establishment of a base in the Natuna Islands, three hundred miles north-east of Singapore, for a virtual pirate fleet of commandos in six motorised replica Chinese junks which would spearhead raids on shipping in Bangkok and Saigon.

At a later date, with up to sixty of these 'Country Craft' operating in the China Sea, guerrillas would be landed in Malaya, Thailand and French Indochina to harass the enemy. Of special interest to the British was that part of the plan which would infiltrate agents into the Riau Archipelago, just south of Singapore, in advance of an Allied invasion.

The pièce de résistance, however, was Lyon's plan for another strike in the very heart of the former colonial bastion. Revisiting Singapore Harbour with a British–Australian force including

Commander Donald Davidson, his second-in-command (2IC) on Jaywick, and another Jaywick veteran, the brilliant young Captain Robert Page, nephew of an Australian prime minister, he would smash sixty ships at anchor and leave the harbour itself a smoking ruin.

This attack, ultimately named Rimau (the Malay word for tiger and inspired by the tiger's head on Ivan Lyon's chest) would be of a much greater magnitude than Jaywick. It would let the Japanese know that their days as an imperial power were numbered. It would be a signal to the thousands of British and Australian servicemen rotting in barbarous conditions inside Japanese prison camps that help was on its way. And most significantly it would let the world know that British power would be re-established in South-East Asia once the war was over.

If anyone was equal to the task it was Ivan Lyon, a man who might well have leapt the centuries from the first Elizabethan age. He was a buccaneer in the mould of Sir Walter Raleigh or Sir Philip Sidney, an adventurer with a record of solid success.

As he approached Selfridges, its display windows boarded up and the red flag of Soviet Russia flying defiantly from its rooftop, Lyon executed a sharp turn into Orchard Street, a short thoroughfare which ran into Portman Square and thence into Baker Street, Marylebone. His destination was 64 Baker Street, not far from Sherlock Holmes's mythical lodgings, and headquarters of the SOE.

Compared with the streets in stylish neighbouring Mayfair, Baker Street was an austere boulevard of dull business premises and unimaginative apartment blocks. Lyon discovered that SOE headquarters was a solid, grey, six-storey office building whose sombre appearance belied the high drama enacted daily within its walls.

SOE had been formed in 1941 when Hugh Dalton, Britain's Minister of Economic Warfare, was instructed by Churchill to 'set Europe ablaze'. Its directive was 'to co-ordinate all action by way of subversion and sabotage against the enemy overseas'. Normally referred to outside the highest circles as the vaguely academic-sounding Inter-Services Research Bureau, the SOE's main function at the beginning of the war was dropping Allied agents into Occupied Europe, but as the war progressed its quota of aircraft, arms and explosives was dramatically increased and it expanded its area of operations to South-East Asia and Australia.

SOE sections were scattered about the Marylebone area, some in buildings such as Michael House, home of Marks & Spencer, and others in mews cottages and apartment blocks. Violette Szabo, heroine of the book and feature film *Carve Her Name With Pride*, was in the signals directorate at Montagu Mansions, an apartment block off Baker Street, learning the codes for her first mission in France. Australian Nancy Wake, who had trained with Violette, had been parachuted into France at the end of February and was distributing British arms and ammunition to Resistance fighters.

SOE WAS RUN by Major General Sir Colin Gubbins who was about to depart on a tour of SOE's overseas outposts, including Australia where he was due to meet General MacArthur in an attempt to breathe some life into Britain's moribund relationship with America in South-East Asia. Ivan Lyon was introduced to the Earl of Selborne, a friend of Churchill's who had replaced Dalton as

Minister of Economic Warfare. Both Selborne and Gubbins were a head shorter than Lyon, but their lack of stature was deceptive. Lord Selborne was shrewd and tough despite a stooping, inoffensive manner, while Gubbins was a World War I hero who had studied guerrilla warfare in Ireland and Russia.

Lyon also renewed his acquaintance with Colonel Egerton G. Mott, an SOE veteran who had established SOE's first Australian mission in April 1942. Mott had discussed Jaywick with Ivan Lyon in Melbourne and had given it his complete support, but he had returned to London in April 1943 while the Jaywick components were still being assembled. He was delighted to be able to pass on his congratulations.

Once the pleasantries were over, Lyon set to work with Major Walter Chapman of the Royal Engineers, a tall, thin, bespectacled man with a bristling handlebar moustache whose speciality was providing tailor-made equipment for SOE's covert operations. A peacetime major in the Territorial Army, Chapman had served with Special Operations in North Africa before being posted to Burma. Invalided home suffering from a gastrointestinal infection, he had found a congenial billet with the SOE Research Station at Aston House, Knebworth, working on various devices. It was from there that he had gone to meet Ivan Lyon in London.

Chapman listened intently as Lyon outlined his requirements for Operation Hornbill and chipped in when Lyon mentioned a new invention for underwater travel which he had heard about through India Mission. Chapman knew all about the new one-man submersible canoe. Its codename was 'Sleeping Beauty' (SB).

The SB had been developed by Major 'Blondie' Hasler of the Royal Marines for Combined Operations in Mountbatten's time after the Admiralty had dismissed it as 'impracticable'. Working in conjunction with speed ace Sir Donald Campbell, Hasler had modified the design slightly and the first SBs were now rolling off the production line.

Ivan Lyon listened with mounting enthusiasm as Chapman reeled off a list of the vessel's capabilities: the motor submersible canoe was 3.9 metres (12 feet 8 inches) long, with a 68.6 centimetre (27 inch) beam and was made of mild steel and aluminium. Driven by a silent electric motor powered by four car batteries, it could travel fifty kilometres to a target area at a top speed of four and a half knots, then be submerged for a limpet mine attack on enemy shipping at a speed of three and a half knots.

The pilot, clad in a rubber diving suit equipped with breathing apparatus, stretched out in a cockpit with his nose almost level with the rim and controlled the SB by manoeuvring a joystick. After flooding two ballast tanks and diving, he could travel wholly under water and navigate with the use of an underwater compass, or have his head protruding above the surface for better visibility. A third method of travel was 'porpoising' to the surface every fifty metres or so to get his bearings.

The SBs were also unaffected by high winds, virtually impossible to capsize, had no giveaway paddles and could carry an adequate supply of limpet mines or other high explosives. They were clearly superior to the more fragile rubber and wood folboats used in Jaywick and Lyon was impatient to see one of them in action. A few days later he and Chapman drove to Staines reservoir beside the Thames to test the revolutionary new craft.

The test pilot was a nineteen-year-old Scottish sublieutenant named Gregor Riggs and Lyon marvelled at the manner in which he could manoeuvre the gleaming silver fish, weighing two hundred and seventy kilograms, through the reservoir's freezing waters, ducking and diving at will and even performing an underwater loop-the-loop. Donning a wetsuit himself, Lyon was permitted to test-drive the SB, but not before Riggs warned him that a man had drowned in January while being trained to use one of the same breathing sets. Lyon listened carefully to instructions and was soon handling the craft with some measure of skill.

A further demonstration was arranged at Portsmouth, the scene of feverish activity in the run-up to Operation Overlord, where Riggs showed how easy it was to approach naval ships unseen and to attach dummy mines to their hulls in almost complete silence. Lyon was ecstatic. The SB was the perfect vehicle for delivering explosives to the ships in Singapore Harbour. He wanted to ship fifteen back to Australia as quickly as possible for members of the Jaywick team to start practising with for their new mission.

Donald Davidson, his 2IC, was a master canoeist and Lyon could imagine the look on his long, lantern-jawed face when confronted with this sophisticated new mode of transport. He anticipated a similar reaction from the other members of the Jaywick team who would be taking part in the new adventure: Able Seaman 'Poppa' Falls, a big, rugged man, deadly calm in times of danger; 'Happy' Huston, a banana farmer from Queensland, slim as a sapling but utterly single-minded; and 'Boofhead' Marsh, a cabinet-maker's apprentice in civilian life, stocky and quick, with great powerful shoulders and a fierce desire to engage the enemy.

While he was still in London, Lyon was invited to the War Office to meet Britain's top soldier, Field Marshal Sir Alan Brooke, Chief of the Imperial General Staff. Brooke noted in his diary for 6 April 1944, 'had interview with Lyon who is back from a very bold penetration to Singapore where he blew up seven Japanese ships. He is now just off on a new mission on a larger scale.' As Brooke was involved in heated discussions about strategy with Churchill over his enthusiasm for Mountbatten's dangerous Sumatran mission, and with Mountbatten himself over the faltering Burma campaign, as well as planning Operation Overlord with Eisenhower and Montgomery, the fact that he saw Lyon at all was a measure of the Gordon Highlander's standing with Britain's top brass. Brooke also knew from intelligence intercepts that the Japanese Imperial Navy had moved its main base to Singapore in February and that a commando attack on shipping in that area would be most desirable.

With this high-powered backing, Lyon did not have long to wait for an answer. He was informed in mid-April that SOE and Combined Operations had given Operation Hornbill the thumbs-up. He would be supplied with fifteen SBs which would be ferried to Australia by the Royal Navy as deck cargo. It had been realised, however, that the craft were too big to be carried north to the target area in the projected junks and would have to be moved there in special containers attached to the hull of a submarine.

For that task, the Navy nominated the biggest submarine in the British fleet, HMS *Porpoise*, commanded by Lieutenant Commander

Hubert Marsham. *Porpoise* was already fitted with a mine-laying casing which ran the length of her hull and it was hoped to adapt this to accommodate each SB in a special, watertight container.

It was a complex operation and Lyon and Chapman spent many hours with naval commanders attempting to sort out the specifications and logistics. On 20 April the RAF cheered everyone up by dropping a record 4500 tons of bombs on Germany in a single raid to celebrate Hitler's fifty-fifth birthday. But time was now Ivan Lyon's enemy. The raid on Singapore had to be carried out before the monsoon started in November, which meant that the SBs and their special containers had to be shipped to Australia within a matter of weeks. Furthermore, the Jaywick team had to be more than doubled in size and the men trained to a high degree of proficiency with the new craft.

Lyon and Chapman dashed to Glasgow in the last few days of April to see *Porpoise* for the first time while she was taking on stores and fuel for the long voyage to Australia. They only just made it. There was barely enough time to inspect the huge submarine before she slipped her moorings and vanished down the Clyde.

Ivan Lyon spent the final day of his leave with his father, General Francis Lyon, and mother Jane at their home in Surrey. He was a married man but his wife Gabrielle and baby son Clive had disappeared in the Indian Ocean after setting sail from Perth in the SS *Nankin* in May 1942. He had since discovered that their ship had been attacked by the German raider *Thor* and that they had been shipped to Japan, but he had heard nothing about them for fourteen months.

On May Day, with barely six months remaining until he returned to Singapore to sink sixty Japanese ships, Ivan Lyon hitched a lift in a RAF plane bound for Australia via Cairo, Delhi and Colombo. Just an hour after take-off, his family received word from the Red Cross. His wife and son were both alive and well and being held in the Fukushima internment camp, three hundred kilometres north of Tokyo. All of Ivan Lyon's dreams were coming true.

# CHAPTER 2
# THE SCOTTISH TIGER

IVAN LYON'S family, a collateral branch of the Strathmores, one of Scotland's most illustrious dynasties, were warriors to the hilt. The Lyons shared a common Strathmore ancestor with King George VI's consort—Queen Elizabeth, the former Lady Elizabeth Bowes-Lyon—in David Lyon of Baky and Cossins, second son of John, third Lord Glamis. The medieval Thanes of Glamis were descended from Robert II, King of Scotland from 1371 to 1390, whose daughter Princess Jean married his chamberlain, Sir John Lyon, in 1376. Sir John's estates included Glamis Castle, home of Macbeth in the eleventh century, and he was styled by the king as 'Our dear son John Lyon'.

David Lyon was killed in the Battle of Flodden on 9 September 1513 when the Scots suffered a shattering defeat at the hands of the English. King James IV, nine earls, thirteen barons and an archbishop were among the 10 000 Scottish dead. Undeterred,

David Lyon's descendants provided generations of soldiers for Britain's future adventures in foreign fields.

Ivan Lyon's grandfather, Francis, was an officer in the prestigious Horse Artillery, but the family's fortunes suffered a serious reversal when a high-explosive shell blew up during an experiment in Kent and he was mortally wounded. Ivan's father, also Francis, was brought up with very little money and there was no question of his going into the Horse Artillery as this was an elite formation with close connections to the cavalry. Instead, he went straight into the Royal Field Artillery, where he rose to the rank of brigadier general. On the way up he served as aide-de-camp to Field Marshal Sir George White in the siege of Ladysmith during the Boer War. Badly wounded, he had been awarded the DSO.

'He was a great friend and admirer of Sir George, a very famous Gordon Highlander who had won the Victoria Cross in the Afghan War,' says his grandson, Clive Lyon.

Ivan Lyon was born on 17 August 1915—at the height of the Gallipoli campaign—and was surrounded by soldiery from birth. His mother, Jane, a niece of Lord Borwick, delivered her eldest son at Boar's Hill, just outside Oxford, while General Lyon was fighting on the Western Front.

When peace returned in 1918 the general's last posting was as British military *attaché* in Brussels and he took his wife and four young children—Susan, Ivan, Paul and Anne—with him.

'My father learned to speak good French,' says Clive Lyon. 'His parents travelled a lot and he picked it up.'

After Brussels, General Lyon retired, eventually settling at Farnham, thirty kilometres from Winchester, where Ivan was dispatched to West Downs prep school. In 1929 he was accepted by Churchill's old school, Harrow, and over the next four years grew into a striking young man, a touch under six feet tall, with blue eyes, sandy hair and a lean, wiry build. When Roma Page, wife of his comrade-in-arms Captain Robert Page, met him in Australia, she was impressed. 'He was quietly spoken but he was a very forceful man,' she says. 'He spoke with a nice English accent. He was not as tall as Bob but, in his Scottish rig, very dashing.'

Ivan also possessed two other assets that would serve him well in his turbulent life: an incurable sense of humour and a talent for making mischief.

While at Harrow, he learned to sail with the encouragement of one of the masters, a Mr Gannon, and once took a boat single-handed across the North Sea. 'He was not an academic,' says Clive Lyon, 'but he had a lively brain and excelled at athletics, particularly cross-country running.'

Ivan's first love was the navy but on leaving school he failed to impress the Naval Board as officer material and, deciding to follow his ancestors into the army, went to the Royal Military College, Sandhurst. After graduating as a second lieutenant in 1935, he was commissioned in the Gordon Highlanders. Curiously, although he came from one of the great military families of Scotland, he was the first Lyon to go into a Highland regiment.

The Gordons had been considered by Churchill as second to none during the Boer War and were still highly rated.

'Grandfather was a great friend of Sir Ian Hamilton, commander of the British forces at Gallipoli,' says Clive Lyon. 'Sir Ian was a Gordon and Grandfather was supposed to have said to my father,

"You have a choice: you either go into the artillery and use your brain or you can go into the Gordons and be smart.'" Ivan joined the 1st battalion, Gordon Highlanders, at Redford Barracks, Edinburgh.

The war drums were beating loudly all over Europe and Asia but the Gordons' newest officer spent an uneventful year at Redford, with nothing more taxing than cross-country running to push him to the limits of endurance. Thirsting for adventure, he volunteered for overseas service with the regiment's 2nd battalion which was based in Singapore. In the winter of 1936, he embarked in the troop ship *Dorchester* and his life took an irrevocable turn towards the East.

SINGAPORE, founded by Sir Stamford Raffles in 1819, was the thriving heart of British interests in the Far East, a vital bastion and trading post strategically situated on the sea route between China and India. Raffles might have acquired the island for his employer, the East India Company, but a Sumatran prince had already provided the name: he called the ramshackle settlement on its swampy southern shores Singapura—'Lion City'. The symbolism would not have been lost on Ivan Lyon when he arrived for an extended tour of duty at the end of 1936.

Geographically, Singapore, a crown colony since 1867, was tucked into the toe of the Malay Peninsula, just one hundred and thirty-seven kilometres above the equator. The island itself measured forty-two kilometres by twenty-three kilometres and was linked to Malaya by a causeway spanning the Straits of Johore. To the south, the Straits of Malacca separated it from Sumatra, Java and the multitude of other islands that formed the Dutch East Indies, later Indonesia. As a sign of its importance as an entrepot, the Roads outside Keppel Harbour, where ships waited their turn to come into port, were among the most congested in the East.

Raffles had stamped a British colonial character on Singapore City by levelling one of the hills south of the Singapore River to form a new commercial district—Raffles Place—and erecting government buildings around Fort Canning Hill on the north bank. There was a fine city green, the Padang, where Europeans disported themselves, and elegant, grey-stone buildings and churches where they conducted business and prayed to their Christian God.

Despite his company's dominance over trade, Raffles depended heavily on the Royal Navy to maintain law and order in the unruly Straits Settlement, as it was first called. There was a curious paradox here: on the one hand, a prosperous opium farm on Singapore Island attested to the Empire's reputation as the world's leading state-run drug cartel, while on the other hand the rule of law and the Royal Navy represented the bulwarks of British civilisation. No wonder the locals were sceptical about their lords and masters.

The opium farm had disappeared by the time Ivan Lyon arrived, but opium dens were still doing a roaring trade in Chinatown. As he walked down the narrow, twisting lanes, his senses were assailed by the sounds and smells of the Orient, coupled with the reassuring thunder of imperial cannon as the guns at Changi artillery base indulged in some target practice.

Rickshaws plied for hire in the sweltering heat, the aroma of spices masked the stink of bad sanitation, the click of mah-jong tiles echoed from the verandas and the babble of dozens of different dialects ebbed and flowed on the ethnic tide. Many groups inhabited this equatorial melting pot. The Chinese, for instance, consisted of Hokkien, Hakka, Cantonese, Teochew and Straits-born Peranakan, all of whom spoke their own languages, had their own political aspirations and belonged to their own *kongsi*, or secret societies.

Lyon discovered that the various groups were divided into kampongs, or villages, with Europeans living mainly to the northeast of the government offices or in the spacious western garden suburbs, Chinese around the mouth of the Singapore River, Indians in Kampong Kapor and Serangoon Road, Muslims in the Arab Street area, Tamil Muslims in Market Street and Malays on the northern fringes of the city.

Rigid social segregation was also enforced among the European community. The expatriate elite—a few thousand planters, bankers, shipping executives and civil servants—lived a life of leisured ease playing tennis, cricket or bridge, or dancing, or just drinking at Raffles Hotel and the Tanglin Club, both of which admitted officers but were off-limits to other ranks. Chinese and Malays were totally forbidden.

Although he was socially well-connected, Ivan Lyon preferred the rough and tumble of Chinatown bars to the more salubrious watering holes. It was here, after consuming large quantities of Tiger beer, that he had a tiger's head tattooed on his chest in brilliant scarlet, black and yellow. He called it Rimau—pronounced *reem-ow*, the Malay word for tiger—and revelled in the sensation he caused among the local population whenever he stripped off to go swimming. Man-eating tigers were still known to attack the

occupants of remote Malayan villages and were widely ⟨
Singapore.

'I suspect he and the other officers had all had a good deal to drink,' says Clive Lyon. 'All the others had tiny little tattoos but my father, being my father, had to have something bigger. The tiger was on offer and he just took it. It stayed with him for the rest of his life. It was enormous and he was very proud of it. He had no inhibitions about it.'

THE IMPERIAL Japanese Army had been at war on the Chinese mainland since 1931 when they invaded the rich industrial province of Manchuria and converted it into a Japanese possession named Manchukuo. Six years later wave after wave of Japanese bombers dropped incendiary bombs on Shanghai and a Japanese fighter pilot contemptuously machine-gunned the British ambassador to China, Sir Hughe Knatchbull-Hugessen, even though his limousine was flying the Union Jack. Fortunately, he survived.

When Ivan Lyon arrived in Singapore the British commander in Malaya was Major General William Dobbie, one of the few realists who took the threat of Japanese expansionism seriously. He discovered that the Japanese secret service had recruited thousands of local Japanese photographers, barbers and merchants in the name of their emperor–deity Hirohito to gather intelligence about the colony's military capabilities. They had infiltrated all levels of society: the official photographer at Singapore Naval Base was later identified as Colonel Nakajima of Japanese Intelligence. Dobbie was determined to end this blatant abuse of British hospitality and had Lieutenant Colonel Francis Hayley Bell, an old China hand

whose daughter Mary later married the actor (Sir) John Mills, appointed as Defence Security Officer.

This was a War Office MI5 appointment and Hayley Bell, who had been born in Shanghai and understood the Eastern psyche better than most Europeans, could have expected to enjoy the co-operation of the Singapore Special Branch in tracking down enemy agents and deporting them. But although Japanese spies were thick on the ground, he found himself in conflict with an old adversary, Major Kenneth S. Morgan, head of the Singapore Special Branch's Japanese Section. There had been bad blood between the two men in China in the twenties and Morgan still harboured a grudge. He refused to allow Hayley Bell to see any of his files.

The pragmatic Hayley Bell, who worked from an office in police headquarters, immediately took steps to set up an intelligence network of his own. He travelled the length of the Malay Peninsula to find suitable recruits, taking his two beautiful daughters with him as cover. One of the men he seconded to his small team of intelligence officers was Ivan Lyon. 'He was a natural for that sort of job,' says Clive Lyon. Hayley Bell found him immensely capable, a mercurial figure, self-effacing yet charismatic, with a wry smile and the ability to see every obstacle as a challenge rather than a hindrance.

His new counterespionage team quickly penetrated the Japanese spy ring and learned that the Japanese, operating from bases in Indochina, would land an invasion force in Thailand and northern Malaya in the event of war and move rapidly south down the peninsula's system of well-made roads. This sensational information cut no ice with the powers that be who clung to the belief that a combination of the monsoon and the impenetrable jungle would rule out any such invasion. Hayley Bell fell even further from favour when it was discovered that his small force of intelligence gatherers was using methods not included in any Sandhurst manual to uncover spies and agents provocateurs and, where necessary, impose summary justice. Faithfully echoing Chamberlain's appeasement of Hitler, the colonial rulers of the East promptly ostracised Hayley Bell and his minions.

Nevertheless, this little group of irregulars remained active and Ivan Lyon was one of its most vigorous members. He spent weeks trying to track down a Japanese transmitter which was sending signals from the heart of Singapore, but although he amassed a great deal of information which led to police raids on several premises, the rogue radio operator remained at large.

Even in those early stages of Japanese militarism, Lyon had one eye on the future. One of his preparations for the war to come was to familiarise himself with the seas and straits in the Singapore region.

Clive Lyon says:

He did a lot of lone trips in a yacht which he shared with another officer called Francis Moir-Byres from a very old Aberdeenshire family. He and my father were great friends and they shared this three ton, ocean-going yacht, *Vinette*. My father wrote for a yachting magazine before the war and seemed to get more than his fair share of the use of that boat. There was no problem about getting extra leave from his commanding officer if he were doing something valid. This is when he improved his knowledge of Malay and became fluent.

The British Navy had enforced Pax Britannica in civilised parts of the globe for the past hundred years but held little sway over the Straits of Malacca where Sumatran pirates and assorted cutthroats still raided shipping and seized hostages. This was where Ivan headed in *Vinette*. He sailed down the Riau Archipelago to Sumatra and learned the vagaries of the currents and rip-tides that flowed around the clusters of islands, meeting the headmen of Malay villages on the way and establishing contacts for the future.

He also sailed north to remote areas of Malaya and Thailand, moored his yacht and struck into the heavily timbered interior to check on likely routes that Japanese invaders would take in the event of war. He filed a comprehensive report to Hayley Bell which confirmed many of his boss's suspicions about Japanese intentions. On one of Lyon's expeditions he met John Dalley, head of the police force in the eastern Malay state of Trengganu, who had the revolutionary idea of recruiting Chinese workers, mostly Communists, as jungle fighters against the Japanese. Lyon listened to the plan and stored it away for future reference.

It was at this time—around August 1938—that Ivan fell in love with Gabrielle Bouvier, the beautiful daughter of the French governor of the prison island of Poulo Condore in adjacent French Indochina. Gabrielle had already married, divorced, and given birth to a baby, Christienne, all before she turned nineteen.

Ivan had heard about the chestnut-haired, blue-eyed beauty in his travels and contrived to meet her by sailing to Poulo Condore in *Vinette* and paying a call on her father, Commandant Georges Bouvier. Although he was employed on the legal side of the French Colonial Service, Commandant Bouvier had also served with distinction in World War I, winning the *Légion d'Honneur*. He was only too happy to invite the dashing, young, French-speaking son of a British general to dinner.

At first Gabrielle was wary of Ivan's fierce Gaelic romanticism and the fact that he imbibed a little too freely at the dinner table. There was also the question of the huge tiger tattoo. 'My mother loathed it,' says Clive Lyon. But over the next few months the ardent young suitor gradually overcame Gabrielle's reluctance to give married life a second chance. She accepted his proposal and they were married in Saigon on 27 July 1939, just three months before the outbreak of World War II in Europe. There was a further ceremony in Singapore and the newlyweds moved into a married-quarters bungalow with palm trees at the back in Orchard Road.

Gabrielle had left her daughter with her parents in their island prison home and, after the fall of France in June 1940, she took a job as secretary to the head of the Singapore section of the Free French organisation. She interpreted for Special Branch detectives when they arrested Commandant Maurice Lenormand, the chief Vichy agent in the region, and questioned him in Singapore before he was sentenced to death for treason. Other Vichy agents were simply shot without the formality of a trial.

Meanwhile, Hayley Bell's unorthodox methods had upset just about everybody in authority in Singapore. Although he reported

*Gabrielle*

directly to his boss, Colonel Sir Vernon Kell, head of MI5 in London, copies of his reports which contradicted the official policy of non-provocation of the Japanese Government were issued to the Governor of Singapore, Sir Shenton Thomas, and the new general officer commanding Malaya, Major General Lionel Bond. Both men were outraged at the explosive contents and called for Hayley Bell's head. He was recalled to England in May 1939 and his counterespionage organisation disbanded just as the time of greatest need was approaching.

AN ADMINISTRATOR with no military experience, Sir Shenton Thomas was the colony's nominal commander-in-chief. He had been affronted by Hayley Bell's insistence that the Japanese would strike at Thailand and Malaya from bases in Indochina. Thomas had been assured that any invader would be wiped out by RAF squadrons operating from secret airfields which had been carved out of the Malayan jungle. While it was true that several such airfields existed, Sir Shenton had overlooked the fact that the only available aircraft were four squadrons of Blenheim bombers, two squadrons of RAAF Hudson light bombers and four squadrons of American-built Brewster Buffalo fighters. There were also two squadrons of obsolescent Vildebeest biplanes, which were still in service as dive-bombers, and a flight of three Catalina flying boats. These were no match for the modern Japanese Air Force. Blooded in the war against China, Japanese pilots were equipped with fast, light and easily manoeuvrable Mitsubishi A6M Zero fighters or the big Mitsubishi G4M 'Betty' bombers.

Sir Shenton Thomas and the British Ambassador in Bangkok, Sir Josiah Crosby, were doing everything in their power to maintain the status quo when the trembling, avuncular figure of sixty-two-year-old Air Chief Marshal Sir Robert Brooke-Popham arrived to set the seal on Singapore's fate. Brooke-Popham remained Commander-in-Chief Far East from the end of 1940 until he was ordered home in December 1941 when it became apparent to Churchill that a major catastrophe was taking place.

But while all three branches of the British services found excuses to avoid taking the necessary defensive measures, the spies were secretly hard at work. The ante in the Great Game had been raised in May that year when Lieutenant Colonel Alan Warren of the Royal Marines opened Oriental Mission, the Singapore office of the SOE. Warren was attached to Military Intelligence and was charged with carrying out sabotage, subversion and black propaganda in enemy or enemy-controlled territories. He offered Ivan Lyon the chance to join him in these enterprises and Ivan jumped at it.

At the end of July 1941, Ivan and Gabrielle had just celebrated their second wedding anniversary and Gabrielle was expecting their first child when the Japanese occupied French Indochina as a prelude to overrunning Thailand and attacking Malaya, just as Hayley Bell had predicted. In retaliation, Roosevelt imposed severe economic sanctions on Japan, which, when supported by Britain and Holland, cut off nearly all her supplies of raw materials including, crucially, oil. As nine-tenths of Japan's oil was imported, she was forced to turn to her vast reserves of petroleum and

29

derivatives, which had been stockpiled over many years in case of emergencies.

With the prospect of her factories (not to mention her war machine) grinding to a halt, Japan's militant leaders were faced with a stark choice: abandon their territorial ambitions in Asia, or go to war and capture the oilfields of the Dutch East Indies. In August 1941, with Hirohito's approval, they opted for war. The decision placed a huge burden on the shoulders of Nippon's armed forces, but the High Command believed that the fanatical faith of their young soldiers, sailors and airmen in their emperor's infallibility might just enable them to pull it off.

As commander-in-chief of Japan's armed forces, Hirohito sanctioned the subjugation of French Indochina as part of the wider plan to strike against Malaya and the Dutch East Indies. He also gave his approval to a plan for a sneak attack on America's Pacific Fleet at Pearl Harbor. Giving the lie to the notion that his title of commander-in-chief was merely an honorific, he moved military headquarters into the imperial palace itself and, as the time for action drew near, insisted on being kept informed of every important diplomatic and military move.

Everything depended on the element of surprise. Tricks to gain an advantage over an opponent were highly regarded in the samurai warrior code of *bushido* which had been practised by the noble Zen warriors who supported the lords of the shogunate in medieval times. But there was nothing noble about the conduct of the conquering Japanese army in China, where drug-crazed troops massacred an estimated 250000 people in Nanking. The Japanese soldier was a figure of fear throughout Asia.

*Important to mark*

When the arch-nationalist Tojo, former head of the *Kempei Tai*
secret police in Manchuria, became Prime Minister of Japan in
October 1941, he adapted the martial mysticism and harsh discipline
of *bushido* into a soldier code which committed the soldier to
winning, regardless of personal cost. Young soldiers going into
battle were urged to fight fearlessly 'so as not to shame the spirits
of the departed'. The accent was shifted from the chivalry of old,
with its veneration of age and its respect for women, to personal
sacrifice. The Japanese soldier would rather die in battle than live
with the shame of surrender and, as the defenders of Malaya,
Singapore and the Philippines discovered, he loathed anyone who
didn't share that view.

This was the enemy that Ivan Lyon and his comrades were
preparing to meet but they were having difficulty convincing the
authorities that they should be prepared at all. The new general
officer commanding Malaya, Lieutenant General Arthur Percival,
opined that 'defences are bad for morale—for both troops and
civilians'. He also felt that some of Warren and Lyon's activities
were definitely not cricket and put an immediate stop to them.

The two men plus John Dalley, the police chief from Trengganu,
had been operating at 101 Special Training School, set up by SOE
in a two-storey bungalow with spacious grounds at Tanjong Balai
in August 1941. The school's commandant was Jim Gavin, an officer
in the Royal Engineers, and his second-in-command was Freddie
Spencer Chapman, a Seaforth Highlander who had once taught
the future Duke of Edinburgh at Gordonstoun. Spencer Chapman
had been assigned to 101 Special Training School from Australia,

31

where he had founded a similar training camp for independent companies, or commandos, on rugged Wilson's Promontory.

The group were training 'stay-behind' parties of British, Malay, Chinese and Indian guerrilla fighters to harass the Japanese. Malaya Command, however, considered this kind of thinking to be 'defeatist' because it presupposed that a Japanese invasion would be successful. The scheme was abruptly curtailed on Percival's orders.

Ivan was overjoyed when Gabrielle presented him with a son, Clive, born in Singapore on 12 September 1941 but, although he had a family to protect, his work was becoming ever more dangerous and he was frequently away on missions, secretly planting dumps of arms and explosives in Malaya despite the official embargo on such activities. Nor was Gabrielle a 'stay at home wife' and mother. She was still in the thick of the action with the Free French in their battle against Vichy, while her father, Commandant Bouvier, supplied Ivan with valuable intelligence data from behind enemy lines.

Clive Lyon says:

He was passing information about the movement of Japanese troops down to Singapore for my father's use. It was useful but dangerous for him. He got into big trouble. The Vichy caught up with what he was doing and they treated both my grandparents as traitors. My grandfather was badly beaten up and eventually died of his treatment. He was awarded the posthumous Cross of Liberation by de Gaulle, a very high honour. My grandmother was more or less killed by the Vichy. She died

Gabrielle's parents helped Ivan

of appalling injuries in hospital—my mother would never talk about it.

Britain, preoccupied with surviving the war against Hitler, continued to misread the threat to her eastern dominions. At the end of September 1941, Sir Robert Brooke-Popham estimated that it was 'highly improbable Japan can be contemplating war in the south for some months'. He went further in the middle of October when he told the Australian Government's Advisory War Council in Melbourne during a visit that Japan would not be able to undertake a large-scale attack on Malaya for the next three months.

This view was reinforced by Churchill who telegraphed the new Australian Prime Minister John Curtin that, in his opinion, Japan would not go to war 'unless and until Russia was decisively broken'. As Stalin was prepared to sacrifice millions of his subjects' lives to save Mother Russia, this was deemed to be some way off. As a deterrent, however, Churchill ordered Britain's newest battleship HMS *Prince of Wales* with the veteran battle cruiser HMS *Repulse*, the modern aircraft carrier HMS *Indomitable* and four destroyers to take up station in Singapore.

The *Prince of Wales* was commanded by Admiral T.S.V. 'Tom Thumb' Phillips, who had spent the previous three years in a desk job as Vice Chief of Naval Staff. As his nickname suggested, Phillips was short of stature—he was only five feet two inches tall—but reputed to have a towering intellect. Tragically, he had no experience at all of an air attack on a task force at sea and dismissed as poppycock the idea that aircraft posed a serious threat to a properly armed battleship. An exasperated colleague had once stormed at

no experience

him: 'One day, Tom, you will be standing on a box on your bridge, and your ship will be smashed to pieces by bombers and torpedo-aircraft.' Phillips remained unconvinced. He was so entrenched in his opinions that another admiral, Somerville, referred to him as 'the Pocket Napoleon'.

Once the Far Eastern Fleet—named Force Z—reached Colombo, Phillips flew ahead to Singapore, arriving on 30 November, to consult with Brooke-Popham, even though he was aware that the old man was to be replaced within a couple of weeks in yet another switch of commanders.

Still, there was something to celebrate at last and the whole of Singapore turned out on 2 December to welcome the *Prince of Wales* as she entered Keppel Harbour, the city's port on the southern side of Singapore Island. With her ship's complement lined up on deck in dazzling white and the band playing stirring anthems, it seemed as though King George VI had spared his greatest Christmas present for his Far Eastern subjects. The next day the headlines hailed HMS *Unsinkable*, the glamour ship of the Royal Navy that was going to save Singapore from the Japanese aggressor. *Repulse*, the old campaigner, hardly rated a mention.

Phillips knew by now that he was going to have to make do without *Indomitable*. The carrier had run aground leaving harbour in the West Indies and had limped to an American naval shipyard for repairs. On board were the forty-five aircraft, including nine Hurricane fighters, which were intended to act as air cover for Force Z.

On 5 December, three days after Phillips entertained local dignitaries to cocktails in his flagship, he boarded a Catalina flying boat and set off across the South China Sea to discuss the deteriorating military situation with the commander of America's Asiatic Fleet, Admiral Thomas C. Hart. The two men met at Cavite Naval Base, near Manila, and spoke for most of that afternoon. 'I had pictured a big, husky, personable, magnetic sort,' Hart wrote in his diary. 'He's a bare 5' 2" and decidedly the intellectual type.'

The following day Hart introduced Phillips to America's most decorated soldier, General Douglas MacArthur. MacArthur had been spending his retirement as a highly paid military adviser to the Philippines President, Manuel Quezon, when he was recalled to active service as Supreme Commander of United States Army Forces in the Far East on 26 July 1941. Although he informed Washington that the Philippines could be held against a Japanese attack for up to six months, he personally doubted there would be an invasion—not while he was around anyway.

According to Hart, MacArthur gave Phillips 'his usual wordy spiel' about Japan's lack of willingness to fight before the British admiral caught his plane back to Singapore. It was 6 December 1941 and the world was about to change.

# CHAPTER 3
# HIROHITO'S GUESTS

WINSTON CHURCHILL learned of Japan's sneak attack on the American Pacific Fleet at Pearl Harbor from his butler, Sawyers, while he was entertaining Roosevelt's special envoy Averell Harriman and the American ambassador, John G. Winant, to dinner at Chequers. The butler heard about the calamity on the BBC and informed his master. Roosevelt confirmed the news a short time later on the hotline from Washington. 'It's quite true,' he said. 'They have attacked us at Pearl Harbor. We're all in the same boat now.'

The first Japanese bombs exploded at Pearl Harbor at 7.55 a.m. Hawaiian time on 7 December 1941, a Sunday described by Roosevelt as 'a day that will live in infamy'. Manila was nineteen hours ahead of Hawaii on the western side of the international dateline and MacArthur was asleep in the penthouse suite of the Manila Hotel when the phone rang around 4 a.m. on 8 December.

The caller was his Chief of Staff, Brigadier General Richard K. Sutherland, breaking the news of the Japanese attack.

Seventy minutes before Pearl Harbor, troops from General Yamashita's 25th Army had poured ashore at Kota Bharu on the north-east coast of Malaya and a few minutes later they formed beachheads in southern Thailand, yet nothing was done to warn the Americans that a Japanese attack could be expected, either in the Philippines or further east in America's island possessions.

The Japanese landings had been foreseen by British intercept operators working at the Kranji listening post in Singapore. They had been monitoring Japanese naval signals so thoroughly for the previous two months that they knew the names of every ship in the Japanese invasion fleet that had amassed in the Gulf of Thailand. A further message from the Japanese ambassador in Bangkok to Tokyo revealed one of the ships' destination as Kota Bharu. That, too, was dismissed by Malaya Command as 'defeatist'.

Brooke-Popham had been forced to act, however, when he was informed on 6 December that a massive Japanese convoy of transports, escorted by warships, was heading in the direction of the Isthmus of Kra, the narrow neck of land above the Thai–Malay border. He alerted Admiral Hart, who was in conference with Admiral Phillips in Manila, then waited to see whether the Japanese ships maintained their aggressive course or whether it was a bluff to force the British to react and thereby start the war that Malaya Command was so anxious to avoid.

The Japanese convoy had been spotted by three Hudson bombers of the Royal Australian Air Force flying reconnaissance missions from Kota Bharu. Brooke-Popham wasn't convinced that an invasion was imminent but put British forces in Malaya in a state of readiness to execute Operation Matador, Britain's plan for a pre-emptive strike that would destroy the Japanese as they were going ashore.

After spending a night keyed up to attack the enemy, the troops were stood down the following day when General Percival informed Brooke-Popham that it was already too late to forestall the Japanese landings. Instead of attacking the enemy, the troops were ordered into defensive positions and Matador, Britain's one chance of stopping the Japanese, was cancelled. The effect on troop morale was shattering.

There was only one telephone link between Kota Bharu and Brooke-Popham's War Room and he received the grim news in the early hours of 8 December that the Japanese invasion had started at twenty-five minutes past midnight. Resistance had been ineffectual. The Thai army did nothing to prevent the main landings at Singora and Patani, which would have been in British hands had Matador gone ahead.

Australian Hudsons bombed enemy landing craft and transports off Kota Bharu and actually prevented about half the invasion force from getting ashore there. The Japanese still landed 5500 troops, however, who fought so fiercely that they overran defensive positions manned by units of the 8th Indian Brigade. Japanese aircraft also bombed the airfield at Kota Bharu and gained air superiority on the very first day of the campaign. They never lost it. The Vildebeests were almost wiped out while trying to bomb Japanese troopships.

Over in Manila, MacArthur dithered. Instead of taking immediate action to bomb Japanese forces in the northern stronghold of Formosa, he waited to see what would happen. It was a fatal mistake. At 12.35 p.m. local time on 8 December, Japanese aircraft attacked the Philippines and MacArthur's command virtually collapsed when the US bombing force at Clark Field, north of Manila, was caught on the ground. Eighteen out of thirty-five B-17 Flying Fortresses were lost in the Japanese attack, as well as fifty-three fighters and twenty-five other aircraft, at a cost of only seven enemy aircraft.

Two days later, on 10 December, Japanese aircraft sank the *Prince of Wales* and the *Repulse* off the coast of Kuantan, Malaya, after Admiral Phillips had taken them north to intercept Japanese troopships. The British warships had no air cover but, even so, the eighty-five Japanese bombers—thirty-four high level bombers and fifty-one torpedo bombers of the Naval Air Arm based near Saigon—had attacked without fighter escort and provided ideal targets for the British gunners manning the ships' multiple pom-poms, or 'Chicago pianos' as they called them. 'The unswerving approach of the compact formation of Japanese aircraft at a constant speed and height was a gunner's dream,' commented the official history of Britain's war with Japan.

Tom Phillips, however, botched a golden opportunity. At 10.05 that morning he heard that one of his destroyers, limping back to Singapore with engine trouble, was being attacked by Japanese bombers and at 10.20 he knew he was being shadowed by a Japanese spotter plane. But instead of radioing for fighter protection, which was available just seventy-six minutes flying time away in Singapore, he engaged in cumbersome fleet manoeuvres by flag. He never got a second chance. The Japanese attacked at 11.00 a.m. but for some reason Phillips did not give the order to fire until ten minutes later. Although the gunners filled the sky with a shattering barrage of glowing tracer shells, they succeeded in shooting down only eight enemy bombers and that was a generous count.

Both capital ships were hit by torpedoes and bombs and went to the bottom with the loss of eight hundred and forty-five lives, the *Repulse* at 12.30 p.m. and the *Prince of Wales* fifty minutes later. In the words of one survivor, the Royal Navy's glamour ship was like 'a mortally wounded tiger trying to beat off the *coup de grâce*'. Tom Phillips did not attempt to leave the bridge. He asked for his best hat, put it on his head and went down with his ship.

Churchill received the news when his bedside telephone rang. 'I was thankful to be alone,' he later wrote. 'In all the war I never received a more direct shock.'

Had the Singapore fighter planes, piloted by members of the RAAF, arrived on the scene at the height of battle, they could well have saved both ships, or at the very least have made a fight of it. As it was, having been alerted by the captain of the *Repulse* at 12.04 p.m., they arrived overhead just in time to see the *Prince of Wales* go down. The loss of face involved in such a one-sided victory was enormous. Japan's prestige soared around the world when the news was broadcast and the ease with which both ships had been sunk bolstered a belief in Japan's 'invincibility'. In Berlin, Hitler was cock-a-hoop when he broke the news to his generals.

SINGAPORE, however, remained unmoved. After dinner, Europeans still strolled along the Esplanade, where Chinese fishing boats

*cricket*

bobbed at anchor, and danced to the strains of the Dan Hopkins Band in Raffles Hotel. The sound of bat on ball echoed from the hallowed turf of the Singapore Cricket Club and the bridge games continued.

Governor Thomas, a former schoolteacher, enforced strict censorship on what the population was allowed to know about the progress of the war and any bad news was either omitted from the *Straits Times* and radio broadcasts altogether, or downplayed. When Singapore was bombed for the first time, with the loss of sixty Chinese lives, Thomas refused to order a blackout because it might cause panic. Moreover, he suppressed the information that civilians could avail themselves of free passage from the colony in ships sailing to India, Ceylon and Australia. As no one knew about this offer, hundreds of ships left Singapore with empty berths until the last dire days of the campaign.

After just three days of war, Japan was master of the South China Sea and the Pacific Ocean, and the British Army and its Commonwealth Allies were in full retreat down the Malayan Peninsula towards the supposedly impregnable fortress of Singapore.

With Churchill demanding action, Malaya Command swung behind John Dalley's idea of training a guerrilla force of Chinese Communists to fight the Japanese. Shenton Thomas held a meeting with Chinese leaders on Christmas Day 1941 which formalised the creation of the Dalforce Irregulars. Recruits would be put through an intensive two-week course in weapons and explosives at 101 Special Training School, then smuggled into jungle hide-outs. Ivan Lyon and John Dalley worked with other SOE operatives, notably

*un Rao LIM BO SENG* 41

Englishmen John Davis and Richard Broome, shuttling between Johore and Singapore to set up secret supply dumps and to assist the newly graduated Chinese guerrillas in slipping past the advancing Japanese.

Disguised as a Tamil, Freddie Spencer Chapman, the instructor at 101 Special Training School, led one operational party behind enemy lines and created mayhem. Over the ensuing months, his team were credited with wrecking seven trains, blowing up fifteen bridges, destroying forty motor vehicles and killing hundreds of Japanese troops.

But no amount of sabotage could stem the Japanese advance. With an Arisaka rifle slung over his shoulders, a ration of fish and rice balls in his pack and rubber-soled boots on his feet, the Japanese infantryman mounted a bicycle and pedalled furiously southward, while artillery and tanks followed along the paved roads, mending blown-up bridges as they went. In front of them swept a human tide of soldiers and civilians, all desperate to escape captivity and most of them heading for Singapore.

The Australian 8th Division, virtually the only trained jungle fighters among the Allied armies, had been stationed in Johore, immediately to the north of Singapore, and did not come in contact with the enemy until after the Battle of Slim River on 6/7 January 1942. By then it was too late. The enemy's momentum had brought them to within two hundred kilometres of Singapore and despite their commander Major General Gordon Bennett's boast that 'one AIF man is equal to ten Japs', the enemy continued to push forward.

The Australian 2/30th Battalion staged a copybook ambush on the main road at Gemas on 14 January in which hundreds of

Japanese were killed and there were other isolated victories. But there was no escaping the fact that Allied commanders were making colossal blunders in the field, that many of their troops were frightened and exhausted, and that the battle-hardened Japanese were superior in almost every department. Despite popular myth, the big guns on Singapore *could* fire inland but they had mainly armour-piercing shells for sinking ships, rather than explosive shells to stop infantry. The Allies also did not have a single tank to put into the field. With every passing hour, Britain's most prized possession in the Far East came closer to disaster.

AUSTRALIA'S representative to London was the former Prime Minister, Sir Earle Page, Bob Page's uncle. He was not privy to the deliberations of the British chiefs of staff and nor was he a member of the British Defence Committee but that did not prevent him from getting his hands on a copy of an explosive, top-secret memorandum written by Churchill on 21 January 1942 to his chiefs of staff following a prediction from General Wavell, Supreme Allied Commander in South-East Asia, that the battle for Johore was almost certainly lost and that it was unlikely Singapore could be held for very long.

In his memo, Churchill told his military supremos that, in view of Wavell's 'very bad telegram', the Defence Committee would consider the whole position of defence in Malaya and Singapore. Churchill wrote:

If General Wavell is doubtful whether more than a few weeks' delay can be obtained, the question arises whether we should

43

not at once blow the docks and batteries and workshops to pieces and concentrate everything on the defence of Burma and keeping open the Burma Road [into China].

Obviously the decision depends upon how long the defence of Singapore Island can be maintained. If it is only for a few weeks, it is certainly not worth losing all our reinforcements and aircraft...the fall of Singapore, accompanied as it will be by the fall of Corregidor, will be a tremendous shock to India, which only the arrival of powerful forces and successful action on the Burma front can sustain.

Page immediately telegraphed the contents of Churchill's memo to Canberra and on 24 January Churchill received an angry cable from Curtin expressing Australia's horror at what was being proposed.

The Prime Minister wrote:

Page has reported that the Defence Committee has been considering the evacuation of Malaya and Singapore. After all the assurances we have been given the evacuation of Singapore would be regarded here and elsewhere as an inexcusable betrayal. We understood that it was to be made impregnable, and in any event it was capable of holding out for a prolonged period until the arrival of the main fleet. Even in an emergency, diversion of reinforcements should be to the Dutch East Indies and not Burma. Anything else would be deeply resented, and might force the Dutch East Indies to make a separate peace. On the faith of the proposed flow of reinforcements, we have

*For Dalforce build up*
*Expectation of*
*aims went — Empress*
*Ane*

acted and carried out our part of the bargain. We expect you not to frustrate the whole purpose by evacuation.

Talk of 'inexcusable betrayal' deeply wounded Churchill and he never forgave Curtin but, fearing a propaganda backlash in the United States to what would be perceived as a British 'scuttle' from Singapore, he did nothing to stop British reinforcements, notably the 18th Division and fifty-one Hurricane fighters packed in crates, from reaching Singapore. Many of the Hurricanes were shot down within days of going into action and the remainder were withdrawn to Java. As for the recently arrived troops, unacclimatised and untrained in close combat, they simply swelled the numbers facing captivity when the Allied armies withdrew to Singapore Island and blew up the causeway on 27 January.

There was a serious setback for Dalforce on 5 February when the *Empress of Asia* was bombed as she approached Keppel Harbour and her cargo of small arms, which was intended for the Chinese irregulars, was lost at sea. Two thousand Chinese men, who had been trained to take the line beside the Australian 8th Division, were pitched into the Battle of Singapore with ancient, breech-loading rifles and just five rounds of ammunition each. Every one of them was killed in action.

As the Japanese stranglehold tightened on the doomed island, one of Alan Warren's priorities was to assist the safe passage of refugees to friendly countries. He ordered Ivan Lyon to establish supply bases along an escape route from Singapore to Dutch-held Sumatra. Ivan's superior officer was H.A. 'Jock' Campbell, manager

*Lyon → Sumatra*

*Did Ivan know about Dalforce before he went?*
*No.*

45

of a large rubber plantation, who had re-enlisted as a major in his old regiment, the King's Own Scottish Borderers.

In early February 1942 the two Scots cruised the Riau Archipelago in the small coastal trader *Hong Chuan*, with Ivan using his Malay and liberal amounts of cash to bribe the headmen of small island communities into helping refugees from Malaya and Singapore. Gabrielle Lyon and Clive departed for Australia by ship in early February, arriving in Perth a few days later. Ivan was greatly relieved that they had reached safety when he returned to Singapore and witnessed the shambles that was unfolding. The Gordons had been in the thick of the action and were braced for the final battle after the Japanese swarmed across the 'moat' and created a bridgehead on Singapore Island on 9 February.

But any suggestion that Ivan Lyon might rejoin his old regiment was overruled by Colonel Warren, who ordered him back on to the Sumatran escape route. 'The route led up the Indragiri River, one of the main rivers in Sumatra,' says Clive Lyon. 'The idea was that people fleeing Singapore would be met at the mouth of the Indragiri and be ferried two hundred and forty kilometres upriver, using supplies of food and medicines laid down by my father. When they reached the port of Rengat, they would be conducted through the mountains to the west coast port of Padang. There they would take their chances about getting to India or Ceylon. My father was responsible for saving the lives of many hundreds of people.'

It was at this time that Ivan Lyon first laid eyes on the *Kofuku Maru*, a Singapore-based, motorised Japanese fishing boat which an Australian, Bill Reynolds, was using to save hundreds of refugees in round trips between Keppel Harbour and Sumatra.

'He bumped into Bill Reynolds—literally—when their two boats collided on the Indragiri and they became friends,' says Clive Lyon. 'Then events took over. Colonel Warren ordered my father and a few people whom he thought were key personnel to the war effort to sail to India in a native *prahu* which he had commandeered. Alan Warren stayed behind and was captured. My father got to India and met up with Bill Reynolds, who had sailed all the way in the *Kofuku Maru*. They decided that, if they stayed alive, they would do something with that boat.' As it happened, the *Kofuku Maru* would play a central role in the drama of Ivan Lyon's war.

The Gibraltar of the Orient went down to just three Japanese divisions on 15 February 1942 in what Churchill called 'the greatest disaster and capitulation in British history'. With Major Cyril Wild carrying the white flag of surrender, General Percival arrived at Japanese HQ in the Ford motor works on Bukit Timah—the Hill of Tin—and handed over the Union Jack to Yamashita. When Wild realised the surrender was being filmed by Japanese cameramen, he threw the white flag down in disgust.

Singapore was renamed Shonan (Sunny South) and the clocks were put forward ninety minutes to correspond with Tokyo time. One million Chinese, Malay and European civilians and 125 000 Allied troops, including 14 972 Australians, mainly members of the 8th Division, found themselves 'guests' of the Emperor Hirohito.

GOOD

SHOWA TENNO Hirohito, to give him his Japanese designation, was born in Tokyo in 1901 and had reigned over the Japanese people since the death of his father in 1926. His father, Yoshihito, suffered from meningitis and had been too sick to rule effectively.

He was also too weak to protect his son from the machinations of court reactionaries who treasured the memory of Yoshihito's father, the Meiji emperor, whose 'restoration' in 1868 had laid the foundations of Japan's emergence as a modern nation capable of competing with the West. Surrounded by expansion-minded courtiers, Hirohito was raised to believe that respect and conquest amounted to the same thing.

After the war, it was claimed that the emperor had favoured peaceful means to achieve Japan's aims. Yet the emperor, now forty years old and no longer a malleable youngster, made no attempt to prevent the Pacific War which was being waged by the Japanese general staff in his name. Indeed, instead of using his powers to block the militarists he reacted enthusiastically to their grand strategy and he took an abiding interest in Japan's military progress. It would be naïve to suggest that he would have done otherwise.

Hirohito's influence in motivating Japan's armed forces was incalculable. The state religion, Shinto, preached that the emperor was a deity and Japanese troops were indoctrinated with the belief that they were on a divine mission, ordained by him, to liberate their Asian brothers and sisters from white tyranny. According to a political pamphlet handed to every Japanese soldier on his way to war:

> The aim of the present war is the realisation, first in the Far East, of His Majesty's august will and ideal that the people's of the world should each be granted possession of their rightful homelands. To this end, the countries of the Far East must plan a great coalition of East Asia. Through the combined strength

JAP empire

of such a coalition we shall liberate East Asia from white invasion and oppression.

Thus, through force of arms, Hirohito found in February 1942 that his empire stretched from the Arctic Circle to the equator. Furthermore, his divine status would shortly be invoked to justify the inhuman treatment of millions of his enslaved peoples. Far from freedom, the Greater East Asia Co-prosperity Sphere, as Japan's armed expansion was known, brought its nominal beneficiaries nothing but economic chaos, hunger, devastation, torture and political suppression.

Japan's conquests were unprecedented. Allied generals were forced to concede that the Japanese campaigns of December 1941 through to the early months of 1942 had produced some of the most devastating victories in military history. With battles still raging in China only eleven Japanese divisions had been devoted to the southward expansion, but Japan had deployed these limited forces against successive targets with such bewildering speed and to such stunning effect that British, Dutch and American prestige in Asia sank to a low point from which it never recovered.

Britain's military disasters in Malaya, Singapore, Hong Kong and Burma also damaged her reputation with the Americans in the South-West Pacific. When MacArthur was ordered by Roosevelt on 9 March to evacuate Corrigidor and set up headquarters in Australia, his ego suffered such a blow that he was not about to go easy on his British allies. His staff, the fourteen members of the Bataan Gang whom he took to Australia with him, were dismissive of Britain's South-East Asia Command, claiming that the initials

49

SEAC stood for 'Save England's Asiatic Colonies'. It did not bode well for future co-operation.

IVAN LYON arrived like a breath of fresh air at SOE headquarters in India. As a fully-fledged member of Oriental Mission, he was readily accepted by the members of India Mission. The head of Force 136, as it was known, was Colin Mackenzie, a Cambridge honours graduate who had lost a leg in World War I but whose mental agility more than compensated for that handicap.

Mackenzie had joined J. & P. Coats, the Glasgow cotton firm, and it was largely due to a fellow director and personal friend, Lord Linlithgow, the Viceroy of India, that Mackenzie had been appointed to run Force 136. Its headquarters were at Meerut, sixty kilometres from Delhi, although it later moved to Kandy, Ceylon, to be alongside Lord Mountbatten's South-East Asia Command headquarters.

By the time Mackenzie heard about Lyon's apparently insane plan for a raid on Singapore shipping, using Bill Reynolds' clapped-out Japanese fishing boat to slip through the Japanese blockade, it had gathered some impressive new detail. Bill Reynolds had given the *Kofuku Maru* a name more suited to its purpose: the *Krait*, after a deadly black and gold Malay snake. Pronounced 'Crite', the vessel would deliver a poisonous sting to the enemy in its home port. Ivan Lyon had also come up with a name for the mission: Jaywick, derived from Jay Wick, a powerful deodoriser which removed noxious smells from Singapore homes. Mackenzie decided that it would be far more practical for such a raid to be carried out from Australia, where a new commando organisation was being set up.

One of Lyon's old sailing friends—and, incidentally, a cousin of the luckless Cyril Wild—was Bernard Fergusson, the future Lord Ballantrae, Governor-General of New Zealand, who was working on Wavell's planning staff in Delhi prior to taking over as a commander of the legendary Chindits. Wavell had returned to India following the collapse of his joint Allied command in Java and Fergusson arranged for Lyon to meet him.

Wavell, who had lost his left eye from a shell splinter in World War I, was having a terrible war. Defeated by Rommel in the Middle East, he had been ordered by Churchill to change jobs with Auchinleck and become commander-in-chief in India. His forces had suffered one defeat after another in Malaya, Singapore and Burma and there was even a chance he would still lose India. As an omen to the fall of Singapore, he had fallen over a sea wall on his last trip to the besieged island and had been badly shaken.

Delighted to be able to do something positive after endless setbacks, Wavell wrote the young officer a letter of introduction and wished him well. Lyon set off for Australia, arriving in Perth on 6 July 1942. His wife and son had set sail in the *Nankin* from the same port a few weeks earlier to join him in India. He never saw them again.

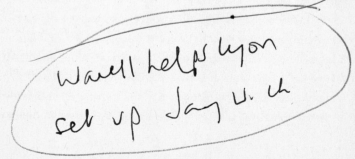

Wavell helps Lyon set up Jaywick

# CHAPTER 4
# THE YOUNG MASTER

HE IS vivid in memory to all who met him. Robert Charles Page was a classically handsome young man, an athlete, a brilliant medical student with a rollicking sense of humour. But being a Page he also possessed an instinct for national service. It was part of the Page family's *modus vivendi*.

James Page, Bob's great-grandfather, came to Australia in 1855 from Bromley, Kent, where he had been born in 1814. After attending London University College he became headmaster of Lambeth School and while still a young man was chosen to assist the colony of New South Wales when its Board of National Education decided to assimilate the New South Wales system with that of the Irish National system then in vogue in England.

Soon after his arrival he opened the first national school north of the Hunter River at Grafton. He contributed leading articles to the *Clarence and Richmond Examiner*, helped found the Grafton hospital, began building co-operatives in the district, and finally became town clerk and accountant of the Grafton branch of the New South Wales Savings Bank until his death in 1878. His portrait still hangs in the Grafton Council chambers.

His son Charles started a coach-building business which became very successful and he was the mayor who introduced the famous avenue of jacarandas down Grafton's main street. Of Charles and Anne Page's eight sons and three daughters, the two men who would help to form Bob Page's character were his father Harold and his uncle Sir Earle Page who became Leader of the Country Party in the Federal Parliament, Treasurer, Health Minister and Prime Minister (albeit briefly). Earle Page had served in World War I as senior medical officer on the HMAS *Ballarat* and as a surgeon to Australian troops in Egypt and France. In Parliament his career was as turbulent as his causes were various. He was a leader in the fight for a national health insurance scheme in the 1930s and he struggled in vain to have a new state carved out of northern New South Wales. Every week some new enthusiasm overtook him and he would buttonhole his parliamentary colleagues, pressing his case with such rapid-fire wordage—punctuated every few moments with 'You see, you see'—that he often left them bemused and breathless as he moved on to his next target.

He developed a passionate hatred for the rising star of the conservative forces, Robert Menzies, whose political 'treachery' he believed had contributed to the death of his friend, Prime Minister Joe Lyons. In perhaps the most notorious speech ever delivered in the Australian Parliament, Sir Earle excoriated Menzies, accusing him of cowardice by scheming to avoid service in World War I. So blistering was the attack that for three decades afterwards the Hansard record was censored and only a severely bowdlerised version released publicly. Even now there are strong doubts that an unexpurgated version has finally seen the light.

In 1941 Sir Earle was appointed by the Australian Government to be its representative on the British War Cabinet in London— it is no coincidence that by then Menzies had become prime minister. On his return to Australia in 1942 he became a member of Curtin's Advisory War Council and remained in that post until the end of the war.

Sir Earle's brother Harold, Bob's father, was a genuine hero of the Great War. He served at Gallipoli and in France, rising from the ranks to acting lieutenant colonel. He won the DSO and the Military Cross and was four times mentioned in dispatches. He was wounded three times in action and on the last occasion in a battle across the trenches was almost given up for dead. However, he recovered completely.

The *Clarence and Richmond Examiner* kept the big Page clan in touch with Harold's exploits. In 1918 he wrote home and the paper printed a cheery excerpt:

You would smile to see some of the diggers, as the Australian Tommies call themselves. Most of the villagers near the front line have been evacuated very quickly and quite a lot of clothing has been left behind.

You can see our chaps wearing frock coats, stiff collars and ties etc. But the funniest of all things was when we had the stunt the other night and several were wounded. When they got back to the clearing station they were undressed to be got ready for bed. You can imagine the nurses' consternation when they found the men wearing camisoles and chemises for undershirts and ladies' knickers as underpants.

They evidently found the clean clothes in their billet and put them on to have the pleasure of clean clothes as their own stuff gets frightfully dirty.

Harold returned to the cheers of his townsfolk and the Page family which by now exceeded one hundred souls in the Grafton area alone. In 1919 he married Anne Miller Brewster of 'Scoon' in nearby South Lismore. By now the *Examiner* had become a daily and it told its readers of the big crowd that was 'evidence of the great popularity of the bride, who was one of Lismore's sweetest singers, and her soldier bridegroom—one of Lismore's gallant Anzacs'.

Harold had attended Sydney University before the war, majoring in geography, French, Latin, arithmetic, algebra and geometry. He tried to put his learning to use in the Electoral Department of the Public Service in Sydney but couldn't settle. His real skill was as a leader of men so in July 1921 he, his wife and their tiny son Robert Charles left Lismore on a fine Saturday morning for Brisbane and then upon the SS *Mataram* for Rabaul to take up the position of Commissioner of Native Police in the former German New Guinea Territory.

Life in the territory was primitive and tough. Two years after her arrival Anne came back to Lismore for an extended holiday with her parents in 'Scoon'. But she returned to her growing family and it was not until 1933 that she, Harold and their four children returned in the *Nankin* for 'a 12-month furlough in Sydney while they establish their children at school and enjoy a holiday'.

Young Bob, now thirteen, would enrol in Sydney Boys High School, one of the GPS (Great Public Schools) fraternity but without the exorbitant fee structure of some. By now his father was rising in the Australian colonial service. At the outbreak of war he would have become, as government secretary and deputy administrator, the real power in the territory.

Australia had sent the 2/22nd Battalion AIF to Rabaul to guard its forward airfields, even though the chiefs of staff knew this token force stood no chance of withstanding the Japanese. Many civilians, including Anne Page and the children, were repatriated. Rabaul fell on 23 January 1942 when an entire Japanese division swept ashore and, after encountering some plucky resistance from the Australian fighters, massacred most of the garrison.

Deputy Administrator Page went straight to Japanese headquarters to confront them and demand civil behaviour toward the native population.

'Only a Page would have done that,' said Roma. 'That was just the way they operated.'

The Japanese may have been momentarily taken aback but they soon recovered and rounded up the Australian colonial administration, planters, businessmen, professionals and missionaries and slapped them into makeshift prisons.

In Australia, Bob was in his second year of medical studies at Sydney University and a member of the university regiment. He abandoned his studies and joined the AIF and soon after was posted to Darwin with the rank of lieutenant.

When he made known his desire to return to Rabaul to help rescue his father, the authorities acted. As it happened, Captain Sam Carey who had worked as an oil geologist in New Guinea was hatching just such a scheme. Carey was ostensibly on the General Staff compiling topographical intelligence on New Guinea. In fact, he was secretly liaison officer between Z Special Unit commandos under the commander-in-chief of New Guinea operations, Lieutenant-General Sir Edmund Herring, and the commander-in-chief of all Australian land forces, General Sir Thomas Blamey.

Carey proposed a strike on shipping in Rabaul Harbour by a handful of men dropped from a submarine twenty kilometres offshore. They would paddle their folboats into the harbour, attach limpet mines to ships, then retire to Vulcan Island which had risen inside the harbour during a massive 1937 eruption. There they would hide until the Japanese panic had died down and they could again rendezvous with the submarine. And there just might be the chance for Bob Page to learn the whereabouts of his father and even to break him out of prison.

Gordon Thomas, pre-war editor of the *Rabaul Times*, witnessed the humiliation of the men who had helped develop Rabaul into a thriving business town and community. As Government Secretary, Harold Page was made to carry cargo from the ships to stores on the shore and was frequently kicked and beaten, as were most prisoners. Captain David Hutchinson-Smith, who was imprisoned in Rabaul, said: 'The Japanese never lost an opportunity to ridicule and humiliate prisoners, particularly officers.'

At the end of May 1942 the Japanese Army handed the prison camp over to the navy and on 22 June 1942 Japanese marines and guards roused the camp and organised internees into parties of fifty. Half-starved and ill, 849 Australian military prisoners and about 200 civilians were marched from the compound at 9 a.m. to board the 7267 ton steamer *Montevideo Maru* for Japan.

In the early hours of 1 July 1942 the *Montevideo Maru* was torpedoed by the American submarine *Sturgeon*, commanded by Lieutenant Commander William 'Bull' Wright, off the coast of Luzon in the Philippines, taking everyone aboard to their death. The news was not officially released until 23 November 1945. Throughout all his behind-the-lines exploits, Bob Page believed his father was still a prisoner of the Japanese.

WHEN WAR broke out, Roma Prowse was eighteen and living at Hill Station, the beautiful showplace sheep and cattle property on the fringe of the national capital. She had moved there with her parents and three brothers in the early 1930s. Her people were from the land—the rich, rolling downs of Bowral in the New South Wales Southern Highlands—and her father came to the infant capital in 1926 and began a newsagency which prospered. This allowed him to buy Hill Station, build its productive capacity and gradually move his base of operations back to the land.

Roma had a job at the Commonwealth Scientific and Industrial Research Organisation (CSIRO) assisting Dr Betty Allen who was auditing its research effort. In December 1942 there was a letter from her cousin, Lieutenant Ken Prowse, who was coming south on leave from Darwin. He was bringing a mate. 'You'll like him,' he said.

'It really was love at first sight,' Roma said. 'In three days Bob and I knew we were going to be married.'

Bob did not return to Darwin. His next stop was the special forces training camp on Wilson's Promontory, the most southerly tip of the continent. It was there that he signed up for Z Special Unit. Sam Carey's plan for Rabaul Harbour had acquired a codename—Operation Scorpion—and in January 1943 General Blamey gave him a letter authorising the highest priority in putting the mission together.

Bob grabbed a few days leave, headed for Canberra and there he and Roma announced their engagement on 28 February. Then he was gone.

By the end of March Sam Carey had assembled the nine men he needed for Scorpion in a training camp outside Cairns. First they worked on their physical fitness, then on swimming, sailing and paddling the one- and two-man folboats. All took the course in 'limpets', both the magnetised variety for steel-hulled ships and a special type with a steel spike for wooden hulls. In each instance on the outside of the casing there were two holes—one for the 'use and time pencil', the other for the handling stick used to position the mine two metres below the waterline.

By mid-June they were ready for a practice run using dummy limpets on some real shipping. Cheekily, Carey chose the most heavily guarded forward base on the Australian coastline: Townsville Harbour.

On night one, the ten men and their gear reached Magnetic Island, twenty kilometres across the bay from Townsville, where they stowed their canoes and stores and rested. The next night was cloudless and a waxing moon illuminated a phosphorescent trail as the five crews headed for the minefields protecting the harbour. If they were spotted they would undoubtedly be taken for Japanese and the mines detonated from a control point on the southern breakwater. With Carey leading, they rounded the breakwater silently just after midnight.

The wharf was noisily active as ships were unloaded and all eyes were focused on the stevedoring. One folboat crew was able to limpet two destroyers and the cargo vessel *Katoomba*; Carey and his offsider dealt with a Dutch ship and two Liberty ships. When Bob Page tried to attack the *Akaba* there was a barge moored alongside and it was an awkward task to attach the pattern of three limpets at sufficient depth. Finally it was done and they drifted up harbour to another team, Downey and Grimson. They had already done two ships but as they approached a third a sailor on board spotted them.

'What are you doing?' he asked.

'Just paddling 'round,' Grimson replied.

'Ah. Good night, mate.'

And he trundled off. Downey and Grimson secured the limpets and joined the others near Ross Creek, dismantled their folboats and headed into Townsville for an early breakfast.

At 10 a.m. panic broke out across the harbour when Page's improvised wiring on the *Akaba* was revealed by the falling tide. Soon other merchant ships discovered similar sinister attachments and the navy stopped all ship movements and sent emergency signals to southern headquarters seeking advice. Townsville was suddenly ablaze with rumour of sabotage and Japanese attacks.

Then a senior American intelligence officer, Colonel Alison W. Ind put two and two together and sent word to find Captain Carey.

At 3 p.m. he was woken from his sleep and arrested. Hauled before an angry port authority and enraged merchant ships' captains he defended his actions and offered to remove the limpets. They would have none of it. He was to be prosecuted to the full extent of the law. Only when he produced General Blamey's letter did the shouting subside.

The navy commanders had been enjoying the discomfiture of the harbour security authorities and the cargo captains. They had been trying to get security to bring its performance up to navy standards for months. This simply proved their point. They ceased to be amused, however, when Carey revealed that two of their own destroyers had been limpeted.

Bob Page and his teammates were quietly pleased. Next stop was Rabaul. At last he'd have the chance to strike back at the forces that held his father and threatened his country.

It was not to be. The Americans were to have taken the Australian commandos by submarine to the target area. But then they lost a submarine to a Japanese destroyer in the waters off Rabaul and suddenly it was too difficult. In any case, MacArthur's island-hopping plan was being developed and Rabaul was one of the strongholds to be bypassed.

The young man was devastated. But not for long. Ivan Lyon was just around the corner.

'Bob Page was the link man between the Australian majority and my father and Davidson,' says Clive Lyon. 'He was an amazing and inspiring man. He pulled them together. Gosh, what a team they were.'

# CHAPTER 5
# ULTRA'S LETHAL SECRETS

AS A STUDENT of military history, Douglas MacArthur knew that intelligence held the key to victory. The subject was dear to his heart; he lectured his cadets on it during his term as superintendent of West Point from 1919 to 1922. He gave it high priority as US Army Chief of Staff from 1930 to 1935. And he applied it as much to the clash of nations as to the daring, behind-the-lines forays so beloved of Ivan Lyon and his ilk.

The Lion of Luzon, as MacArthur was styled in the American press, had turned sixty-two on 26 January—Australia Day—1942. He was a curious combination of vanity and valour, a mother's boy who had been firmly tied to the apron strings of the formidable Mary Pinckney 'Pinky' Hardy. She never let him forget that his father, Captain Arthur MacArthur Jr, had won the Congressional Medal of Honor in the Civil War. Pinky exhorted Douglas to 'grow up to be a great man like your father', then made it plain to him that she would forever be disappointed in him no matter how much he achieved.

When Douglas was a cadet at West Point, Pinky took up residence off-campus and saw to it that he topped every year. Her interference sabotaged his first marriage to a vivacious divorcee and, when the marriage broke down, he went home to mother while secretly keeping a young Filipina mistress named Dimples in a Washington hotel. Mother and son stayed together until her death in 1935 when he was fifty-five years old.

With this background it was hardly surprising that MacArthur attracted misfits who became devoted to him and whom he could treat with a patrician fondness of his own.

In the summer of 1942, with the US Navy grabbing the lion's share of the glory, MacArthur was prepared to use any method at his disposal to relaunch his faltering career.

One of the most valued members of the Bataan Gang was his signals intelligence officer, Colonel Spencer B. Akin, a Mississippian who had been the military head of the Signal Intelligence Service, America's code-breaking organisation, when it cracked the Japanese diplomatic machine cipher, Purple, on 20 September 1940.

Akin had been close to MacArthur in Manila at the outbreak of the Pacific War, had shared the rigours of Corregidor with him and had been evacuated to Australia by torpedo boat and B-17 bomber, along with MacArthur's wife Jean, his son Arthur, and other hand-picked staffers including Richard Sutherland and Charles Willoughby. Wherever MacArthur roamed, from the time he arrived in Melbourne on 21 March 1942 until the end of the war, Akin stuck to him like a shadow.

In Melbourne, MacArthur established himself and his family in a suite on the sixth floor of the Menzies Hotel and set up head-quarters in an office building a few blocks away at 401 Collins Street. He promoted Akin to brigadier general and made him head of a new joint American–Australian signals intelligence outfit called Central Bureau, which came into being on 15 April with the purpose of intercepting and decoding Japanese military signals. Akin had unrestricted access to MacArthur to present him with the latest intelligence data as it came to hand.

The Bataan Gang was led by General Richard Sutherland, the Yale-educated son of a West Virginian senator. When Sutherland started drinking too much and became argumentative, even with his boss, MacArthur told him: 'The trouble with you, Dick, I am afraid, is you are a natural-born autocrat.'

Privately, MacArthur summed up his chief of staff as 'a brilliant officer whose own ego is ruining him. He bottlenecks all action over his own desk. The staff is scared to death of him and they all hate him.' Yet MacArthur retained him as chief of staff despite the serious damage he was doing.

One of Sutherland's problems was that, although he had a wife and children in the United States, he had acquired a mistress among the Toorak set in Elaine Bessemer-Clark, a married woman of thirty-two and the mother of a three-year-old son. With her hair dyed blonde and bathed in Chanel No. 5, slim, smart and sophisti-cated Mrs Bessemer-Clark was hired as a receptionist at General Headquarters in Collins Street to be near her lover. She was also commissioned as a captain in the American Women's Army Corps, much to the disgust of American service personnel who knew that her only qualifications were sexual.

'Elaine Bessemer-Clark was a floozy blonde,' said one of the men who knew her at GHQ. 'She wore so much perfume you could smell it eight floors up.' MacArthur did not intervene in his chief of staff's love life. Sergeant Bill Bentson, who worked at GHQ throughout the war, said: 'MacArthur knew what was going on, but he never did anything about it.'

The other key figure in the Bataan Gang, as far as British and Australian service chiefs were concerned, was MacArthur's intelligence chief, Brigadier General Charles Willoughby. Three months after arriving in Melbourne, MacArthur established the Allied Intelligence Bureau (AIB) as an umbrella organisation to control all American, Australian, British and Dutch special operations. He placed it under Willoughby's direction.

Prussian-born, boorish and single-minded, Willoughby was devoted to MacArthur for saving his skin by getting him out of Corregidor. Viewing the world through a pince-nez which dangled from his neck on a black silk cord, Willoughby had a reputation for having the most perfect hindsight of any officer in the US Army.

Sutherland despised him but knew he was a protected species because MacArthur needed the facts and figures supplied by the intelligence chief's network of interceptors, coast-watchers, fifth columnists and agents throughout South-East Asia, even if his interpretation of their data was liable to be wildly inaccurate. General Robert Eichelberger, commander of the 32nd Division in the Battle of Buna in which Willoughby catastrophically underestimated Japanese strength, sourly noted that he was 'always positive in his views and usually wrong'.

At the beginning, Willoughby had access to all signals intelligence that passed through Akin's Central Bureau but it was fairly low-grade stuff and MacArthur acted on very little of it during his early months in Australia. The main source of high-grade intelligence in 1942–43 came from his great rival, the United States Navy, through intercepts of the Japanese naval code JN25, which the Americans had broken themselves shortly after Pearl Harbor. But from 1944 onwards, MacArthur came to rely ever more heavily on the material known as Ultra, the crown jewels of the secrets world.

Drawn from the phrase 'Ultra-secret', this was the name given in the Pacific War to signals intelligence (sigint) summaries derived from decoded Japanese army, navy and air force radio messages. In Europe, it had originally referred to sigint summaries emanating from the German Enigma machine cipher and other German and Italian codes. As in the European theatre, where Alan Turing and the code-breakers at Britain's Bletchley Park had cracked the Enigma cipher, myth and fable surrounded the operations of the Japanese Ultra team in Australia. And, as at Bletchley, it certainly had its share of brilliant minds—from the prickly Commander Eric Nave of the RAN's cryptographic unit to the eccentric Scot, Hugh Foss, with his straggly red beard, kilt and sandals, to the urbane American co-ordinator, Colonel Abraham Sinkov.

Sinkov had led a delegation to London when the Americans had brokered an alliance with Britain in January 1941 to share technical details of their work on Japanese crypto systems but not the contents of actual intercepts. One of the 'presents' that the American visitors had handed over to the startled British staff at Bletchley Park was a functioning Purple code-breaking machine, which had been constructed by another member of the team, Lieutenant Leo Rosen.

Nave and Foss were responsible for breaking most of the Japanese naval codes and ciphers in the pre-war years. The difficulty of the task was of a different order from the German operation. The Japanese written language was based on *kanji*—pictorial characters originally borrowed from the Chinese—and about seventy phonetic symbols called *kana*. To adapt the Morse code, a system of transliteration known as *romanji* was developed in which the *kana* syllables were spelt out in Roman letters.

Happily, Nave's Royal Navy operators intercepted a practice message in which the Japanese operator had obligingly run through the entire Japanese Morse code symbol by symbol. Then, when the Emperor Yoshihito died at the end of 1926, the official report of his death and the succession of his son Hirohito to the Chrysanthemum Throne were relayed word for word to every Japanese diplomatic, naval and military outpost around the world.

It was a simple task to follow it through the various codes, breaking each in turn. However, in the secret world nothing stays the same for long and in 1939 Japan adopted a totally new coding system known as super-enciphered codes, including the main Japanese Navy code, JN25. It first appeared in June 1939 and Bletchley Park had broken it within weeks.

Then in the northern summer of 1942 they had another triumph in breaking the Japanese military attaché code. But most of the enemy's plans remained hidden behind coding systems that would prove far more difficult to crack.

CENTRAL BUREAU'S first home for its combined force of Australian and American code-breakers was 'Cranleigh', a spacious, ivy-clad residence in South Yarra, and it moved to a rambling Queensland timbered house at 21 Henry Street, Ascot, when MacArthur shifted GHQ north to Brisbane in July 1942. By then Central Bureau comprised US and Australian Army signal units, together with an RAAF unit. Veteran intercept operators of the Australian Special Wireless Group, who had worked against Rommel in North Africa, and members of a British signal attachment evacuated from Singapore were also part of the Australian Army contingent. On the American side, Akin was in overall charge, with direct and unfettered access to MacArthur, though Abe Sinkov was in charge of the high grade code-breaking section.

For MacArthur and the other American commanders, the best intelligence results derived from a combination of the cryptographers' work in Central Bureau, the Fleet Radio Unit Melbourne (FRUMEL), and out in the field, where the retrieval of codebooks was a top priority. FRUMEL was an exclusively naval operation and its personnel were wary of the oriental court surrounding MacArthur.

Indeed, the so-called Senior Service from Britain, Australia and even the United States itself made common cause in Melbourne, where they processed their own intelligence sources and dealt directly with Washington and London.

Part of the problem can be sheeted home to a single individual: Charles Willoughby, a figure of appalling destructive power in the Allied war effort. He might have enjoyed MacArthur's confidence but to those who knew him best he was a schemer, a bully, a liar, a toady, and a shameless cheat. Willoughby covered his tracks at the end of the war by the simple, if illegal, act of destroying all documents he could find that might have revealed his shortcomings or cast anything but the most favourable light on his vainglorious master.

Akin distrusted Willoughby and Central Bureau habitually bypassed him by sending their daily siftings of Japanese radio traffic to Akin's office. He alone determined which items were significant enough to warrant MacArthur's attention. Much to Willoughby's chagrin, this process continued throughout the war. As late as October 1944 a War Department representative reported to Washington that Willoughby received only delayed information copies of Ultra. In short, the head of the Supreme Commander's intelligence material exercised no control over the organisation which supplied it.

Outside Central Bureau, the situation was even more fractious. Captain Rudi Fabian, who helped initiate FRUMEL as the US Navy's principal listening post, still cannot conceal his bitterness. After yet another bureaucratic confrontation with Central Bureau in late 1942, he says, 'We just went our separate ways.'

When MacArthur learned communications had broken down, he demanded that the FRUMEL chief, Vice Admiral Herbert F. Leary, commander of the Allied Naval Forces, South-West Pacific Area, hand over their information. Fabian says:

I felt that certain restrictions were necessary to ensure security. At my suggestion, Admiral Leary issued the following requirements:

(1) Fabian or one of his unit's representatives will report to MacArthur's headquarters each day at 1400 hours. The FRUMEL representative will never be kept waiting in MacArthur's outer office.

(2) No one will be authorised to make copies of any material provided by FRUMEL.

(3) During the briefing of FRUMEL material, only MacArthur and his Chief of Staff, General Sutherland, will be present. Everyone else, including MacArthur's chief of intelligence, General Charles Willoughby, will be excluded from these briefings.

It almost beggars belief that one intelligence arm refused point blank to communicate with the head of another. But the Australian Navy's official historian, Joe Straczik says: 'We provided intelligence to the US military; Central Bureau were army and air force; they worked for MacArthur. There was a big difference.'

In such poisonous air, some group was certain to suffer. Almost inevitably, the men in the field—and those behind the lines—bore the brunt of it.

IN THE FIELD, the Australians were scoring some notable successes. Geoffrey Ballard, an Australian officer in Central Bureau tells of the capture of a new codebook from a Japanese bomber that crashed just west of his radio intercept camp in the bush near Darwin in

1942. 'Since we were instructed to send the book to [Brisbane] the next morning, we spent the night hand-copying as much of it as we could,' he says. 'We were really encouraged by how much of the code we had recovered by ourselves.'

Decrypts of Japanese naval messages were used to dictate American actions in the Battle of the Coral Sea in May 1942 which prevented the sea-borne invasion of Port Moresby and the subsequent invasion of Australia. They had also given the American Pacific Fleet an invaluable advantage in the Battle of Midway in June, the last chance Admiral Yamamoto, architect of Pearl Harbor, would have to destroy America's aircraft carriers.

Then in April 1943 a joint Australian–American effort in Central Bureau cracked the Japanese army marine transport code, giving the Allies access to all their plans to deploy army personnel within the Pacific theatre. As Ballard says, 'The Japanese detailed plans, their unit names and strengths, their air strength and serviceability status, the composition and routes of their convoys, their intentions and appreciations were as readily available to us as to their own forces; and generally as quickly.'

General George C. Kenney, who had taken over as MacArthur's air force commander in July 1942, made full use of decrypts to launch a number of victorious tactical raids on Japanese convoys. But on 1 January 1944 the Japanese changed their mainline codes and the Allies temporarily lost their advantage. This was followed by the most spectacular breakthrough of the Pacific War.

It happened when the Australian 9th Division was in hot pursuit of retreating units of the Japanese 20th Division in the Sio area of New Guinea. The Japanese were carrying their entire cryptographic

71

library in a steel trunk and were faced with the prospect of manhandling it over the mountains toward Madang. This, they decided, was simply beyond them. But then they were in a quandary: they couldn't lose face by admitting the physical struggle was too great; and they couldn't burn the codebooks because conditions were too wet and Allied aircraft might detect columns of smoke. So they buried the trunk near a creek bed, having first ripped off the covers to 'prove' to the Tokyo High Command that the books had been destroyed.

A few days later an Australian engineer who was sweeping the area for mines discovered the trunk. It was 19 January. The capture included, among other things, the codebook itself. The material was immediately flown to Brisbane where American cryptanalysts Charles Girhard and Hugh Erskine could scarcely believe their luck.

Sixty years later Girhard recalled the find: 'There was so much mildew on the material that each page had to be dried in the large commercial cooking ovens in our kitchen. But our cleaning efforts were definitely worthwhile. From the time of capture of the Sio material until the end of the war, we read approximately two thousand messages a day!'

And the beauty of it was that the Japanese High Command never suspected what was going on because they had 'proof' that the codebooks had been destroyed.

While there was formal cooperation on the surface, however, such was the dissension between the various Allied sigint units that they might well have been fighting different wars. In many respects they were.

ONE OF THE biggest problems was how to use Ultra material without jeopardising the Pacific War's greatest secret—that the Allies were reading Japan's telegraphic mail. In the run-up to the Battle of the Coral Sea, the *Washington Post* published a story that a big naval battle was about to take place in the South-West Pacific. The main suspect was MacArthur, whose personal publicist, Colonel LeGrande A. Diller, formerly of Bataan, had only one mission in life: to see that his boss was given credit for every main event in the Pacific War.

As MacArthur's role in the Battle of the Coral Sea was negligible, it was plausible that Diller leaked the news to a reporter who, even so, could be relied on to present the Supreme Commander in a favourable light. Certainly, General George C. Marshall, head of the American Joint Chiefs of Staff in Washington, had reason to believe this was the case because he accused MacArthur of engineering the leaks and observed that the Japanese 'would be justified in believing their codes had been broken'.

MacArthur was furious. He denied that his headquarters was responsible and pointed the finger at the Australian Government, where Curtin, a former journalist, was known to take certain trusted reporters into his confidence. MacArthur stormed: 'It is utterly impossible for me under the authority I possess to impose total censorship in this foreign country.' He then demanded such authority from Curtin and it was granted by the Advisory War Council. From mid-May 1942, the only authorised source of frontline war news in the South-West Pacific was MacArthur's headquarters or, more specifically, his mouthpiece 'Killer' Diller.

The problem arose again the following year when both Central Bureau and FRUMEL, as well as the intercept station at Hawaii, picked up signals transmitted in JN25 and other, lower-level codes to Japanese bases that General Yamamoto would be making an inspection tour in the Solomon Islands. On 18 April his bomber would take off from the giant Japanese base at Rabaul and could be intercepted over Bougainville, just beyond the eastern tip of New Guinea.

Sixteen Lightning fighters of 339th Squadron USAAF were scrambled to intercept him. While twelve of the American fighters dealt with Yamamoto's Zero escort, four American crack-shot pilots dispatched the mastermind of Pearl Harbor. His Betty bomber was seen crashing through the jungle canopy in flames and Yamamoto was later found dead in the wreckage, still clutching his ceremonial sword.

It was a huge risk for the American Air Force to have taken and one that may well have led to the scrapping of JN25 but the determination to avenge Pearl Harbor had overruled that consideration. Fearing that JN25 had been breached, Japan ordered an inquiry which fortunately concluded that the disaster had resulted from the use of a low-level code by a junior army officer.

But if the US Navy was surprised by the decision to risk compromising the breakthrough with such a flamboyant gesture, their British Allies were simply appalled. And they made their feelings plain to anyone who would listen, including both Churchill and Roosevelt. From that moment a new appreciation of the need for complete secrecy in all dealings with Ultra material entered the scene.

Ironically, a most-secret signal was sent by MacArthur himself which could have given the game away:

The utmost secrecy is to be used in dealing with Ultra information. Attention is called to the fact that if from any document that might fall into the hands of the enemy or from any message that the enemy might intercept, from any words that might be revealed by a prisoner of war, or from any ill-considered action based upon it, the enemy were to suspect the existence of the Ultra source, that source would probably forever be lost to our cause.

This loss would vitally affect operations on all fronts, not only the particular front on which the source had been compromised. Commanding officers of those commands authorised to receive Ultra material are to be instructed that Ultra messages are for them, their personal representative and their senior intelligence staff officer only and are not to be seen by, read to, or discussed with, any other person. Ultra messages are to be destroyed by fire immediately action has been taken on them. No records of Intelligence based on Ultra information may be kept, except at the HQ of the commander-in-chief.

If any action is to be taken based upon Ultra information, the local commander is to ensure that such action cannot be traced back by the enemy to the reception of Ultra intelligence alone. A momentary tactical advantage is not sufficient ground for taking any risk of compromising the source.

No action may be taken against specific sea or land targets revealed by Ultra unless appropriate air or land reconnaissance

has also been undertaken. Names of enemy ships revealed by
Ultra source may never be quoted.

The precautions were sensible. But they were the start of a
process that raised the fear of compromising Ultra to almost
hysterical levels. Even among the naval men, there was a growing
sense of distrust.

Captain Fabian and his second in charge, 'Honest John'
Lietwiler, shared a tiny office in one of the 'Monterey' apartments
in Melbourne and one of them was on duty at any hour of the day
or night. By early 1944, the smouldering paranoia among the secret
services was becoming incandescent. On 19 February there was a
'flap' about the improper classification of an Ultra cable from
Central Bureau to London. The Australian commanding officer in
Central Bureau, Colonel 'Mic' Stanford wrote to 'Ral' Little, the
top signals officer in Melbourne: 'London have just signalled asking
me to investigate your MC.602 of February 8th. They state that
this signal contained Ultra intelligence but that was sent Most
Secret I(E) only. You will remember that the only cipher systems
appropriate for the passage of Ultra material are Bones Typex
settings or one-time pads.'

Little replied: 'I have already advised them that we know we
are naughty boys and will not do it again.'

Several days later Sutherland issued orders governing a new TOP
SECRET classification:

A new Combined Security Classification Agreement has been
issued to United States and British Armed Services and will be

the guide for classification on and after 15 March 1944, at which time the TOP SECRET classification becomes effective.

All staff sections, General Headquarters, and each subordinate headquarters of this command will require one or more officers to be designated as TOP SECRET CONTROL OFFICERS. All TOP SECRET matters for the section of headquarters will be transmitted to them for delivery to the proper person and will be opened only by the addressee of a designated TOP SECRET CONTROL OFFICER.

All TOP SECRET documents will be inclosed [*sic*] in duplicate sealed envelopes for transmission, the inner envelope being marked TOP SECRET. In case of extreme importance the inner envelope may be addressed to a particular addressee by name or office. All TOP SECRET documents will be transmitted by especially designated couriers, who shall, in all cases, where it is practicable, be officers of the Armed Services.

The desperate need to protect Ultra had an inevitable consequence in that the paranoia about secrecy spread like a stain throughout the Allied units. The need to know gradually became more tightly defined.

By mid-1944 the resources of the Allied sigint operation were at full stretch. In Brisbane, the Americans had established a middle-sized township of huts and tents on Eagle Farm racecourse. The controllers had taken over half a dozen traditional Queensland homes with their wide verandas shaded by purple and crimson bougainvillea. Most notable was the house at 21 Henry Street, where the top cryptanalysts worked ceaselessly on the thousands of Japanese signals received daily from listening posts in Outback Australia, New Guinea and the Islands of the South Pacific.

As MacArthur looked ever further north towards Manila, Spencer Akin's old outfit, the Signal Intelligence Service (SIS), was activated in Brisbane as a component of the US Armed Forces in the Far East (USAFFE). 'This is a goal which we have long desired to attain,' Abe Sinkov said when the news was announced. 'It is hoped we will now be able to solve several types of problems whose control has previously been outside our hands. It is going to lead to greater unity, to better *esprit de corps* and a clearer appreciation of the function of the unit as a whole.' Within a matter of months, Sinkov was running the SIS show and, rather than being more accountable to Washington, MacArthur had even greater control over the gathering and dissemination of high-quality Japanese signals intelligence in the South-West Pacific.

In Melbourne, naval types from the FRUMEL team made their breakthroughs from interceptions by ships at sea and their own listening posts to the north and west, while in New Delhi, Colombo, London, Ottawa, Washington and Wellington some of the best brains in the world bore down on the information to make sense of it, to uncover the enemy's plans and anticipate his devices.

But the system could only work at the optimum while the raw blood of data that fed the heart of the great creature of war could be turned back to the limbs to deal violent blows against the enemy. When panic and paranoia blocked those arteries, the men at the extremities were suddenly in peril.

# CHAPTER 6
# JAYWICK: STRIKING BACK

THE SPECIAL Operations Executive had reached Australia in the bustling form of Colonel Egerton G. Mott, a Force 136 man who had flown to Java with General Wavell shortly before the fall of Singapore. When the Japanese overran Java, Mott set sail for Australia in a fishing boat. He was picked up by an Australian corvette and, after stepping ashore at Fremantle on 10 March 1942, signalled his whereabouts to London. He was instructed to make his way to Melbourne and establish SOE's first Australian mission.

Mott's arrival in the Victorian capital coincided with that of General MacArthur and the Bataan Gang from the Philippines but John Curtin made time to receive the Englishman and treated him courteously, even though he was exchanging furious words with Churchill over the defence of Australia following the fall of Singapore. With the approval of the new commander of Allied Land Forces South-West Pacific Area, General Thomas Blamey,

Mott set up the first SOE mission in 'Airlie', a mansion at 260 Domain Road, South Yarra.

This outfit was first known in Australia as the Inter-Allied Services Department (ISD) and was placed under Australian operational control but, as it had been agreed that it could use its own ciphers for direct communication with London, it was referred to inside SOE as Force 137.

Its independence was short-lived. On 6 July 1942—the day Ivan Lyon arrived in Australia with the Jaywick plan in his head—ISD and all its sections, including Z Special Unit, the name for Anglo-Australian operations, came under MacArthur's command.

MacArthur was in the process of packing up and moving his headquarters to Brisbane and Ivan Lyon found it difficult to get a good hearing from the Americans. Charles Willoughby was heading north with his master but Egerton Mott arranged for Lyon to meet him. As Singapore didn't figure in MacArthur's grand strategy, Willoughby had no interest in it, nor in Lyon's seemingly crazy plan to blow up Japanese shipping there.

The Australian Army was more receptive. The idea, from Jaywick, of using a Japanese fishing boat to slip through enemy lines appealed to them but they thought that Singapore was too far away and that Timor would be a better target. Ivan Lyon knew that the big game was in Singapore and he wasn't interested in wasting his idea on a smaller target.

Through family contacts, Lyon was staying in some splendour at Government House, Melbourne, as a guest of the Victorian Governor, Sir Winston Duggan. He enlisted Duggan's support and also approached the Governor-General, Lord Gowrie, who responded enthusiastically. Gowrie arranged for Lyon to meet Commander R.B.M. Long, Director of Naval Intelligence, Royal Australian Navy, on 17 July. Long sent him to Admiral Royle, head of the Australian Naval Board, with a recommendation for support and the board duly gave its approval. General Blamey was also persuaded to lend the support of the Australian Army.

The first controller of the AIB whose task was to co-ordinate the intelligence effort was an Australian, Colonel C.G. Roberts, a dull man who appeared to think and work in slow motion. His lassitude drove Mott and his Australian colleagues to distraction and, although they could go over his head, the man above him was the obstructive Willoughby. After that, representations had to be made to MacArthur, which meant going through Sutherland, who despised Special Operations only marginally less than he despised Willoughby.

And where did this mistrust come from? Despite his utterances, MacArthur was implacably opposed to any intelligence agency operating in his theatre unless he had complete control over it. America's own Office of Strategic Services, modelled on the SOE and headed by MacArthur's World War I buddy William 'Wild Bill' Donovan, was banned from the South-West Pacific Area by MacArthur despite personal pleas from Donovan to be allowed to operate there.

There was also the question of money. AIB's financial control was in the hands of Colonel Alison W. Ind, the American officer who had berated Sam Carey over the Scorpion raid on Townsville Harbour. It was largely his decision whether funds would be made available to carry out any particular project. Here, Lyon held a

KILL THE TIGER

trump card. The cost of Jaywick—an estimated £11 000—had been underwritten by SOE in London, almost a quater of which had been sent on already to Melbourne.

JOCK CAMPBELL arrived in Australia in August 1942 to act as administrative officer for Jaywick. He was accompanied by Ron Morris, a former Welsh miner who had been Lyon's batman in Singapore. Morris had taken part in some of Lyon's Sumatran adventures and had answered his call for volunteers. Neither man, however, was suitable as a second-in-command. The name of Donald Davidson, a lieutenant in the Royal Navy Reserve, was raised with Lyon at Government House and his face lit up when he heard it. He already knew Don Davidson, an adventurer after his own heart.

That Davidson was a maverick, and an interesting one at that, became apparent to anyone reading his service file. He had worked as a jackaroo on a Queensland sheep station before abandoning the Outback in favour of a job with the Bombay Burmah Trading Company, which needed an able-bodied man to supervise its timber-getting activities in the teak forests of Thailand.

While this was impressive outdoors stuff, there was a much quieter side to Davidson's character. He was something of a naturalist and studied bird and insect life in painstaking detail through a monocle. He had amassed a butterfly collection during his six years in the Thai forests which was so exquisite that it was later acquired by a London museum. That minute attention to detail appealed to Lyon because observation and map-making would be an integral part of the Jaywick mission.

There was one other attribute which made Davidson the perfect candidate as 2IC: he was a master canoeist. (He took up the sport when he began working with the forestry department in Burma.) Enormously powerful, Davidson had paddled the entire length of the Chindwin River in a one-man canoe. He returned to civilisation just long enough to get married when Nancy, an old girlfriend, arrived at his jungle retreat and resumed their relationship. Nancy went back to Australia and gave birth to a daughter, coincidentally on the same day that Ivan Lyon's son was born in Singapore.

After the Pacific War broke out in December 1941, Davidson was commissioned in the Burma Frontier Force but, a sailor at heart, had resigned and been recommissioned in the Royal Naval Volunteer Reserve in Singapore. There, he met Ivan Lyon but they went in opposite directions when the Japanese closed in. While Lyon headed for Sumatra and India, Davidson made it to Sandakan, Borneo, and thence to Australia, arriving in March 1942. He was feeling sidelined in routine work at the Navy Office when Ivan Lyon walked back into his life and asked him to train a group of commandos for an unspecified mission.

With the agreement of the Royal Australian Navy, Davidson looked for volunteers at Flinders Naval Depot and put a group through six weeks preliminary training at the Army's Physical and Recreational Training School at Frankston on Port Phillip. Eleven of the original eighteen were then chosen to go to Camp X, which

Lyon had set up above a cliff in Broken Bay, north of Sydney. Here, the men were worked mercilessly for eighteen hours a day, learning to handle rubber-covered folboats in all weather and to attach limpet mines to the hulls of ships, while Davidson assessed their suitability for the mission. To see how they coped under extreme conditions, there was no leave, no beer and no cigarettes for three months.

The *Kofuku Maru*, now bearing its new name, *Krait*, arrived in Australia as deck cargo in November 1942. She was powered by a Deutz four-cylinder engine but it blew up when Bill Reynolds, who had arrived to take on the all-important role of skipper, was transporting the team of fledgling commandos up the Queensland coast to another training camp near Cairns. As no other suitable craft was available, Lyon was forced to disband the team and put Operation Jaywick on the backburner.

Colonel Mott returned to England in April 1943 and Jaywick might have remained a dream except that big changes were afoot in the world of dirty tricks which enabled Lyon to resurrect it. ISD was changed to Special Operations Australia (SOA), which used the cover name Services Reconnaissance Department (SRD). It was placed under the command of Colonel P.J.F. Chapman-Walker, a London solicitor.

Psychologically, Lyon knew that the time was right for a commando attack to press home the advantages gained through orthodox warfare. He argued that Jaywick would let the Japanese High Command know that nowhere was safe, not even Singapore, which they regarded as the main strategic centre for control over the southern region for which they had gone to war. Some of Lyon's enthusiasm rubbed off on Chapman-Walker who agreed that the mission should be carried out. Jaywick was back in business.

A replacement engine for *Krait*, a Gardiner Diesel 6L3 of 103 horsepower, was found and flown to Cairns. The little fishing boat, sixty tons, seventy feet long with an eleven foot beam, a top speed of six-and-a-half knots and a range of thirteen thousand kilometres, was soon undergoing sea trials off the coast of Cairns. As an additional defence against air and sea attack, heavy armour plating was fastened to her sides and deck.

There would be six canoeists: three officers and three men, with two reservists. The party included five of the original team but Bill Reynolds was no longer available as skipper and was replaced by Lieutenant Ted Carse of the Royal Australian Navy Volunteer Reserve. Almost at the last minute one of the most promising men, Captain Gort Chester, was assigned to another mission which was heading for Borneo and when his replacement reported for duty it turned out to be Lieutenant Robert Page of the AIF, a member of the now notorious Scorpion team.

*Krait* sank ever deeper into the water as supplies were taken on board: food and water for four months, medical supplies, cigarettes and tobacco, £200 worth of golden Dutch guilders, forty-five limpet mines and 70 kilograms of plastic explosive, two Lewis guns, two Bren guns, eight Sten guns, eight Owen guns, fourteen Smith and Wesson revolvers, two hundred hand grenades, knives and jungle parangs, paddles and the folboats themselves, dismantled and stored in bags.

Fully loaded with men and equipment, HMAS *Krait* chugged out of Cairns into the Coral Sea on the morning of 8 August 1943 and headed for the tip of Cape York Peninsula. Ivan Lyon, promoted to major, was in command of the mission, with Lieutenant Donald Davidson as his second-in-command. The other commando members of the Jaywick team were: Lieutenant Robert C. Page (AIF), SRD, of Potts Point, Sydney, born Sydney on 21 July 1920; Able Seamen W.G. 'Poppa' Falls, SRD, dairy farmer, born Aberdeen, Scotland, on 5 January 1920; A.W. Jones, SRD, grocer's assistant, Perth, born Guildford, WA, on 24 February 1922; and A.W.G. Huston, SRD, of Brisbane, born Brisbane on 25 December 1923.

The *Krait* was captained by Lieutenant H.E. 'Ted' Carse (RANVR), SRD, foreman, of Sydney, born Rutherglen, Victoria, on 28 May 1901. The crew were: Leading Stoker J.P. 'Paddy' McDowell, SRD, born Belfast on 23 September 1900; Leading Telegraphist H.S. Young, SRD, of Sydney, born Western Australia on 11 April 1921; Leading Seaman K.P. Cain, SRD, of Brisbane, born Brisbane on 13 August 1915; Corporal R.G. Morris (RAMC), SRD, Welsh-born coalminer; and Corporal A.A. Crilley (AIF), SRD, labourer, of West Ipswich, Queensland, born Fauldhouse, Scotland, on 23 October 1913.

The two reserves were F.W.L. Marsh, SRD, apprentice, born Brisbane on 20 January 1924; and Able Seaman M. Berryman, SRD, sharebroker's clerk, of Adelaide, born Adelaide on 9 November 1923.

Everything went well; even the weather was fine. *Krait* sailed around Cape York into Torres Strait, crossed the Gulf of Carpentaria and came down the coast of Western Australia to Potshot, the United States Naval Base at Exmouth Gulf. While she was restocked and refuelled for the long voyage to Singapore, Lyon discussed the mission with Potshot's American commander, Admiral Christie. The Jaywick mission was leaving base on 1 September when the *Krait* jinx struck again. Just one hundred metres from the dock, her tail shaft broke and Lyon's team of expertly trained commandos was left drifting helplessly. But the accident couldn't have happened at a better spot. *Krait* was towed into dry dock where mechanics and engineers worked nonstop to weld the shaft back together.

After that anti-climax, *Krait* set off again at 1400 hours on 2 September without further mishap. As the early tropical night closed in on the tiny craft, she was clear of the gulf and steering a course which would take her about eighty kilometres west of a direct line between Exmouth and the twin volcanoes that marked the entrance to Lombok Strait. A fresh southerly breeze produced an unpleasant sea on the port quarter. It was the first opportunity for the party to gauge *Krait*'s seaworthiness and she did not perform well. Even when the heavy deck armour was removed and slung overboard, she still rolled precariously and was sluggish in her recovery. On one occasion she lay over until one of the men standing beside the wheelhouse found himself waist-deep in water. The following morning, however, the swell had subsided and *Krait* had found her sea legs. She never behaved so badly again.

Lyon briefed his men on their mission and they were astounded to learn that their target was Singapore, not Surabaya as they had been led to believe. Once they reached enemy-controlled waters, the Blue Ensign would be lowered, the Japanese flag would be hoisted, uniforms would be stowed below and they would disguise themselves as Malay fishermen in sarongs. Their bodies would be stained nut-brown with spirit-based make-up and whenever other craft were visible, or if aircraft were approaching, all but three would go below deck. The three were Lyon, Carse and Jones, who were either olive-skinned or had already been burned a darker brown by the Australian sun.

The *Krait* would sail through the Lombok Strait into the Java Sea and head for a suitable forward base on an island off Singapore, where three folboats would be launched to attack Japanese shipping. Lyon and Huston would man one of the folboats, Davidson and Falls another and Page and Jones the third. If anything happened to one of the commandos on the way to the forward base, the reserves Berryman and Marsh would take their place.

The first part of the plan worked smoothly. The Japanese flag— 'the poached egg'—was flown from the stern, the men changed into sarongs and plastered their bodies with brown dye. Ted Carse hoped that *Krait* would slip through Lombok Strait between the islands of Lombok and Bali under cover of darkness, with the seasonal haze that swirled above the waters making her difficult for patrol boats to spot. Approaching Lombok Island, however, it was evident that the fine, dry weather had cleared any haze from the area and Lyon decided that there was little point in trying to hide. He elected to go through the strait nonstop and take his chances with patrol boats and air reconnaissance. It didn't work out that way.

No sooner had *Krait* reached Nusa Basar Island at the entrance to the strait on 8 September than she hit a powerful tidal stream flowing due south. It stopped the little boat in her tracks. With her engine revving wildly, she struggled to prevent herself from being swept backwards. It was only when the tide started to turn that she began to make a little progress. Still, it took four hours to pass the six-kilometre coastline of Nusa Basar.

Night had fallen and the raiders were disconcerted to see that the island, scantily inhabited in Dutch times, was now a centre of military activity, with camp fires burning and lights blazing from one end to the other. However, they passed along the shoreline unchallenged. During the night, the tide started running north and *Krait*'s speed picked up to around ten knots, which brought her to the strait's northern entrance at dawn.

Ground haze was spotted on the Lombok coast, where some sailing craft were milling about, but there was no sign of a patrol boat. Using the haze, the *Krait* slipped unseen into the Java Sea and, rounding the Kangean Islands, headed for the Karimata Strait south of Borneo. On the way she was inspected by two Japanese aircraft but passed muster as a genuine Japanese fishing craft. Carse wrote in the ship's log: 'Our lookouts are particularly keen and so far have always sighted any objects long before we could possibly be seen by them.'

Sailing north through the Lingga Archipelago, *Krait* made for Pompong Island, one of the main stepping stones on the Jaywick trail. In the hands of her engineer, Paddy McDowell, *Krait*'s new engine was performing well. 'He has worked day and night training crew and operatives to help him in his duties and to be able to operate the engine should anything happen to him,' Carse wrote in his log. 'In fact he looks after the engine better and treats it more carefully than a mother would a baby.'

Nearing the equator, the deck was too hot for bare feet but *Krait* was so low in the water that, even in calm sea, her waist was continually awash. She arrived at Pompong Island in the early afternoon of 16 September and, although the company spent a night here, it was decided that, rather than *Krait* hiding out there as had originally been planned, it would be safer to rely on her disguise and keep moving. Provided she avoided all contact with Malays and never appeared twice in the same locality on the same day, she could poke around the islands unmolested while the commandos carried out their raid.

After dark that day, it became clear from enemy activity that they had entered a hostile area. Searchlights were probing the waters from Champa Island, twenty kilometres south-west of Pompong, and the number of float planes taking off and landing showed that the formerly undefended Lingga Group now contained a base for amphibious aircraft. Carse noted: 'Each day as the sun goes down I mutter a heart-felt "Thank God!"'

*Krait*'s mast was lowered to decrease the vessel's visibility but while the crew were stowing the rigging some Malay fishermen in a canoe were seen approaching. *Krait* got under way with indecent haste and headed north.

*Krait* dropped off the sabotage team at Panjang Island in the Riau Archipelago, about sixty kilometres from Singapore, on 18 September. The countdown to Jaywick had begun.

# CHAPTER 7
# THE BIG BANG

UNDER THE Jaywick plan, the six commandos were to be picked up between the hours of dusk and dawn on the night of 1 October at Pompong Island, some one hundred kilometres distant from Singapore. That gave them twelve days to get to Singapore, sink as much shipping as they could, and rendezvous with *Krait*. As the little ship disappeared over the horizon to potter about the north coast of Borneo, Lyon's team hauled their kit into the undergrowth at the top of the beach, found a sheltered spot and bedded down for the night.

In the morning, two members of the group carried out a more extensive reconnaissance which revealed that there was a village about four hundred metres away on the other side of the island but there was no sign of a track linking it with their camp. Lyon decided to stay put and, as a family of sea otters was playing in the rock pools, he named the spot Bay of Otters.

Leaving one man as sentry, Lyon ordered the others to move the stores back about twenty metres into the jungle and set up camp beside a waterhole. Food reserves for the return journey were then hidden halfway up a cliff-face. On returning to camp they found that their tracks leading off the beach had been obliterated by an army of obliging hermit crabs.

Small junks and fishing craft plied past the Jaywick base but there was no danger and the commandos ignored them. They had arrived a day ahead of schedule and rested all through the nineteenth, then checked their equipment before turning in. Departure at dusk on 20 September was delayed by the passing of a seventy-foot patrol launch a mile to seaward of the bay. They had already heard the noise of her exhaust the previous day so they were not unduly worried.

For the trip into Singapore Harbour, each man wore a black, two-piece suit of waterproofed silk, two pairs of black cotton socks and black sandshoes with reinforced soles, and was armed with a .38 revolver and one hundred rounds of ammunition. On his belt he carried a knife, compass and first-aid kit. Lyon also gave every man a cyanide capsule in case of capture. Each folboat carried 300 kilograms of equipment, including magnetic limpet mines, and food and water for a week.

When the two-man crew slipped aboard, the canoes were low in the water and sluggish to handle but they set off in close arrowhead formation, with Lyon and Huston in no. 1 canoe, Davidson and Falls in no. 2, and Page and Jones in no. 3. Davidson navigated.

At their first lying-up spot, tiny Bulat Island some twenty kilometres away, they left their canoes on the beach and went to sleep. In the morning they were awoken by the sound of a motorised sampan approaching. According to Davidson the sampan stopped within two hundred metres of the party 'and drifted inshore almost on top of us, while its crew held a protracted breakfast meeting. The canoes were plainly visible from offshore. An hour later the motor boat departed without so much as having glanced at our island.'

Setting off again there was a near disaster when all three canoes were caught in a rip-tide and Lyon and Davidson's canoes collided with a sickening thud. Lyon's canoe was damaged and thereafter veered to the left, making it hard work to control.

After midnight on 22 September they pulled into Bulan Island, a sandfly-infested swamp separated by just three hundred metres of water from a busy kampong on the island of Boyan. The party spent the day watching the village's maritime comings and goings from their uncomfortable vantage point.

The following evening the three canoes reached Dongas Island, which Lyon had decided to make his forward observation post. They were just twelve kilometres from Singapore and its lights were clearly visible in the night sky.

SINCE THE Japanese invasion eighteen months ago, security on the former Crown Colony had been so tight that almost no intelligence had reached Australia to describe conditions there. The Jaywick team had no way of knowing that Allied prisoners were in a concentration camp established by the Japanese in Towner Road on the outskirts of Singapore City. The POWs could also see the lights. Even more tantalising, they could catch the tinny fairground sounds of the Great World amusement park, where off-duty Japanese servicemen enjoyed themselves with Chinese, Malay and Eurasian girls. The giant Ferris wheel still turned and everything blazed with light.

Dongas Island was uninhabited and covered in jungle, with a swamp on the south side. Arriving at midnight on 22 September, the Jaywick team negotiated a narrow inlet in the swamp with a sandy cove at its head. A sandbar ran back into the swamp, providing concealment and some comfort. In daylight, reconnaissance revealed that the high ground on the north side of the island provided an excellent location for an observation post and that drinking water could be fetched from an old well.

Through a powerful telescope, the Jaywick team could see the Roads, Examination Anchorage outside Keppel Harbour and the harbour itself. They seemed close enough to touch. Ivan Lyon recorded in his journal:

There was no change to be seen in the general outline of the city. A row of five to seven tall wireless masts have been constructed on the site of the former Paya Lebar station and there is a single mast on the roof of the Cathay building. On the southernmost point of St John's Island there is now a small signal station. At Sambu, three miles from our OP, all visible oil tanks were still as left by the Dutch. There was tremendous activity on the western side of the island; the hammering of plates and drone of engines by day and night suggested either ship repairing or building. In the harbour and roads of Singapore there was considerable movement of shipping. At no time during the five days of observation was there less than 100 000 tons at the same time.

Lyon had no way of knowing that, out of sight in the harbour, half-starved Allied prisoners were doing backbreaking labour at the docks, loading scrap metal, copra and rubber into freighters for the journey to Japanese factories.

When night fell the commandos maintained their watch until 2300 hours which showed that no blackout was in force in Singapore and, apart from some searchlights, there seemed to be no special wartime precautions. Car headlights could be seen moving along Beach Road. Further observation the following day, the 24th, showed a great deal of movement in the harbour and the Roads, and the freedom of movement enjoyed by medium-draft vessels showed that minefields had not been laid.

Lyon decided to wait until a large tonnage had built up in one place, then carry out the attack. By late afternoon that day a concentration of shipping totalling 65 000 tons had assembled in the Roads area opposite the Dongas Island vantage point. While it was feared that unfavourable tides would make an attack extremely difficult, it was too good an opportunity to miss.

At 2000 hours that night the canoes left Dongas and proceeded towards the target area. There was no sign of patrols or any other enemy activity until a searchlight, probably located on top of the Cathay building, picked up the canoes in its beam. The men froze, pointing the canoes front-on to the shore to present the least visible profile. The light remained stationary for about thirty seconds, then moved on. The watchers hadn't spotted the Jaywick men and there was no alarm.

That near miss was followed by a serious setback. As they approached the Roads, the current increased in strength until the canoes were making no progress whatsoever. After struggling in the swirling waters until 0100 hours, Lyon abandoned the attack.

Canoes no. 2 and no. 3 reached Dongas without mishap before daylight but canoe no. 1, the damaged folboat containing Lyon and Huston, was caught in the current and swept eastwards. They reached land just as day was breaking. To avoid detection, the two men were forced to hide among boulders in a swamp. It rained consistently and they spent a tense and uncomfortable day before being reunited with their comrades that night.

Throughout 25 September bad weather and strong tides continued to make Dongas an unsuitable base for attack and Davidson suggested that they should move immediately to a more favourable hide-out. That night they paddled west past Sambu Island, site of a huge oil depot just eight kilometres south of Singapore, to Subar, a small, bracken-covered outcrop overlooking Examination Anchorage in the roadstead.

It was now 26 September and unless Jaywick attacked that night they would not be able to make it to Pompong Island in time for their rendezvous with *Krait* on the night of 1 October. The men could see a total of nine ships at anchor off Singapore and Lyon formulated his plan of attack. This called for the party to be split up, with Davidson and Falls attacking Keppel Harbour, Lyon and Huston taking Examination Anchorage, while Page and Jones tackled shipping off the Pulau Bukum wharves. Davidson, the strongest canoeist, would attempt to reach Pompong first and hold *Krait* until the others arrived.

Surprisingly, Davidson and Falls found no ships in Keppel Harbour and made for the Roads where Davidson chose three large cargo vessels, the first 5-6000 tons and heavily laden; the second a 5-6000 ton vessel later identified as the *Taisyo Maru*; and the third a 5-6000 ton unladen vessel. 'We attacked in each case on the port side as it was away from Singapore lights,' he said. 'Fortunately, our work was dead silent without any hitches or clanging. We had been timing ourselves by the quarter-hourly chimes of the clock in the direction of Saint Andrew's Cathedral. Our time to approach, limpet and get away averaged twenty minutes per ship.'

On completion, Davidson and Falls headed for the Riau Straits and were about twenty kilometres from Singapore when they heard an explosion. 'Our speed increased phenomenally but no excitement occurred in Singapore,' Davidson said.

Lyon and Huston had reached their target area at 2230 hours to find all shipping at Examination Anchorage, except tankers, completely blacked out and almost impossible to see. Running out of time, Lyon decided to attack a tanker, two of which were identifiable from their red riding lights. Approaching directly from astern, he placed two limpets abreast the engine room of a 10 000 ton tanker, later identified as *Sinkoku Maru*, and another limpet on the propeller shaft.

Lyon said in his journal: 'Halfway through the work Huston drew my attention to a man who was watching us intently from a porthole ten feet above. He continued to gaze until just before we left the ship, when he withdrew his head and lighted his bedside lamp.' The seaman did not raise the alarm and Lyon and Huston paddled the twenty kilometres to Dongas, making it at 0515 hours while it was still dark.

Meanwhile, Page and Jones had reached their target area at 2200 hours to find that the wharves were well lit and that a sentry was stationed near a large tanker. After examining the entire length of the wharves for an hour, Page attacked a freighter of the *Tone Maru* class from the stern. The tide had turned at 2300 hours and he and Jones were carried to their next ship, a modern freighter later identified as the *Nasusan Maru*, where they placed their charges. Further along the line they chose an old freighter, identified later as either the *Yamataga Maru* or the *Nagano Maru*, as their third target. Page and Jones returned to Dongas in good time, beating Lyon and Huston by half an hour.

Lyon immediately set up an observation post to monitor the results of the raid. Between 0515 and 0550 on the 27th they counted seven distinct explosions, incontrovertible proof that Jaywick had been a huge success. Four of these explosions had come from the direction of Examination Anchorage and Pulau Bukum, while the other three had come from the Roads area. As the rising sun lit up the scene, the damage at Examination Anchorage and adjoining Pulau Bukum could be clearly seen. One of the ships attacked by Page and Jones had sunk by the stern and her bow was protruding from the water, while *Sinkoku Maru*, the tanker that Lyon and Huston had mined, was blazing fiercely. A pall of thick black smoke from burning oil covered the area, obliterating much of the view.

Fifteen minutes after the first explosion, ship sirens started to blare and fifteen minutes later the lights on Singapore and Pulau

Sambu were blacked out. Some ships upped anchor and cruised aimlessly about, risking collision in the confusion. Stretching metaphors, Colonel Jack Finlay, General Staff Officer (Operations), claimed in his official report on the raid that 'bedlam reigned with a vengeance'. Certainly Japanese patrol boats started searching along the coast of Batam Island to the east while spotter aircraft crisscrossed the sky looking for suspicious craft.

Lyon, Page, Huston and Jones stayed out of sight on Dongas Island all day on the 27th, then set off at dusk and reached a small island where they rested in what turned out to be a Chinese graveyard. Davidson had taken a longer route to Panjang Island but had reached it without incident and he and Falls rested at the Bay of Otters on 29 September. Before they took off for Pompong Island, Davidson left a note in a prearranged spot for Lyon to reassure him that he would hold the *Krait* for as long as it took the others to get there.

The next night a storm 'like the wrath of God gathered from all the cardinal points' broke above Davidson and Falls, with

a screaming wind lashing the calm sea into a maelstrom of breaking waves and thrashing spray. The thunder and lightning were magnificent, the lightning left one blinded for nearly a minute. Then came the rain. The only thing possible and safe was to keep the canoe headed into the sea and wind. With eyes tight shut and steering by the feel of the wind on our faces we rode out nearly two hours of this. When the wind dropped, we had cause to thank heaven for the rain. In five minutes, the sea was flat. The canoe behaved admirably.

After resting, Davidson and Falls set off on the last lap to Pompong. At dusk on 1 October 'we moved to Fisherman's Bay for our rendezvous with the *Krait*, which appeared at 0015.' In four nights of paddling, he and Falls had covered more than one hundred kilometres. They had had little sleep for thirteen days and were alternately hot and sweaty, or cold and damp.

Canoes 1 and 3 reached the Bay of Otters, Panjang, in the middle of that violent electrical storm in the early hours of the 30th. Lyon found Davidson's message and ordered the men to lay up for a day to avoid further bad weather. The two canoes then set off an hour apart on the final, blistering, fifty-kilometre leg to Pompong, part of it in daylight. They arrived together at 0300 hours on 2 October and, completely fatigued, fell asleep on the beach, awaking to see *Krait* about a kilometre offshore heading for the Temiang Strait. They were on the wrong beach.

There was no panic. Searching the island, the men found traces of a newly vacated camp site and ascertained that Davidson had made the rendezvous and that *Krait* would return within forty-eight hours. Just in case, they prepared for a long wait. Page started to build a hut, while Lyon contacted some friendly Malays who promised to provide supplies of fish and vegetables to the party. If necessary, Lyon intended to seize a Malay vessel and sail to India on the change of the monsoon. Knowing he had done it once before, Page, Huston and Jones believed him.

But at 2200 hours on 3 October they were overjoyed when *Krait* suddenly appeared in the bay. Carse, who had been drinking heavily while waiting for the rendezvous, had lost his nerve and Davidson had held his .38 on him, threatening to shoot, unless he came back for the others. It was the nastiest moment of the whole trip.

Apart from receiving a few minutes of unwanted attention from a Japanese destroyer in the Lombok Strait, the homeward journey was uneventful. The Japanese ensign was hauled down at 7 p.m. on 12 October. Carse recorded in his log: 'From now on we once again become an efficient fighting force and instead of skulking by the by-ways and corners of the sea can now travel the main shipping lanes. It's a grand feeling to be free again on no-man's sea.'

*Krait* arrived back at Potshot at dawn on 19 October after forty-eight days away from base, having covered some 8000 kilometres (5000 miles) on the round trip. Admiral Christie listened in admiration as Lyon and Page described the mission and its explosive climax.

Lyon and Page were flown to Melbourne for debriefing at SRD headquarters after which they were reunited with the rest of the Jaywick team in Brisbane. It was impressed on every man that it was imperative for the success of future missions that Jaywick remained top secret. On 11 November—Armistice Day—a party was held in their honour at 'Miegunyah', Brisbane, and they were photographed together. Although there had been rousing toasts and hearty speeches, the team photograph reflects nothing but the team's gritty determination. Only Jock Campbell, resplendent in tartan cap and trews, shows the ghost of a smile, while Ivan Lyon, Don Davidson, Bob Page and Ted Carse stare stony-faced at the camera and the rest of the men, in the uniforms of their particular service, stand stiffly to attention. It is a portrait of pride rather than jubilation.

Jaywick's achievement can be gauged by one simple statistic: its tally of seven ships was more than twice as many Japanese ships sunk by British land-based aircraft in the entire war—just three. It was also the only completely successful operation mounted by SRD during the entire war.

According to Colonel Jack Finlay's report to the Australian Director of Military Intelligence, Brigadier John Rogers, and copied to the War Office, London, the raiders inflicted losses totalling 46 000 tons of shipping.

Finlay wrote:

A number of captured Jap documents and radio broadcasts show that this attack had a very considerable effect on the harbour defence precautions throughout the South China Seas, and even as far as Manila. A general warning was issued against potential strikes of this nature, and all harbour defences specially guarded. The correct method of attack was never appreciated, and was regarded by the Jap authorities as due to local Chinese guerrilla activities from within Singapore itself.

One of the captured Japanese documents read:

Singapore shipping espionage is carried out by natives under European instructions. An enemy espionage affair developed early in the morning of 27 September 1943 at Singapore and was commanded by Europeans hiding in the neighbourhood of Pulai in Johore. It was carried out by Malayan criminals through a Malayan village chief, and the party was composed of ten or more persons, all of whom are Malayans. As a result of the raid, six ships of 2-5000 tons (three tankers among them) were sunk by bombs due to a clever plan.

Even though the reporting officer recorded the number of ships lost as six rather than seven, the document contains a surprising admission of security failure.

Curtin recommended Ivan Lyon for the highest valour award in the British Empire—the Victoria Cross—for the Jaywick raid but, we can reveal, the old boy network in London turned it down. Clive Lyon says:

I'd long known that my father had been recommended for the Victoria Cross because I have a marvellous letter which was written by Lord Selborne. My grandfather had put an advertise-ment in the *Times* asking for information about my father because for a long time he was missing, believed killed in action.

Selborne wrote a very nice letter saying that he'd met my father only once at Baker Street, but he'd formed a very high impression of him. He said to my grandfather, 'Your son, in my opinion, fully deserved the award of the Victoria Cross and indeed I put him up for it'. I always thought for years that something must have gone wrong at the Australian end, that maybe he'd put people's back up and it had got squashed there.

But when Clive Lyon visited Australia in 1997 he was shown a letter that Curtin had written to the acting governor-general of the time, Lord Gowrie having departed from the post.

103

TOP SECRET

14 September 1944

My Dear Acting Governor-General,

With reference to the communication of Lord Gowrie on 22 May 1944 advising that the bestowal of the Distinguished Service Order on Major Ivan Lyon, the Military Cross on Lieutenant R.C. Page and the Military Medal on Corporals A. Crilley and R.G. Morris have been approved, it will no doubt have come to Your Excellency's knowledge that for certain reasons the promulgation of these awards was suspended pending further investigations.

In the light of information which has since been made available concerning the operation in which these four persons were engaged, it would appear that recognition of a higher standard would be justified in the first two cases, namely Lyon and Page, and I should be obliged if Your Excellency would kindly seek His Majesty's consent for the cancellation of the Distinguished Service Order and Military Cross approved in these cases.

I consider that the services rendered by Major Lyon would be more appropriately recognised by the bestowal on him of the Victoria Cross for great valour and devotion to duty in most hazardous undertakings and that the Distinguished Service Order would be more fitting in Lieutenant Page's case for gallantry, skill and devotion to duty in most hazardous under-takings and I recommend accordingly.

An additional reason for the proposed change in Page's case is that the services rendered by him were similar and equivalent to those rendered by Lieutenant D.K.N. Davidson RNVR, who has already received the Distinguished Service Order on the recommendations of the United Kingdom authorities.

John Curtin

The letter was forwarded to London. Bob Page was awarded the DSO but Ivan Lyon's VC was turned down by a committee of naval and military personnel. The reply telegram, received from the Secretary of State for Dominion Affairs, London, was addressed to the governor-general. Dated 28 October 1944, it was received in Canberra 30 October 1944:

No. 12 Secret Honours

Your telegram 24th October. The case of Lyon has been most carefully considered in view of the authorities here including Admiralty who were consulted as the expedition was undertaken at sea. His action although an extremely gallant one did not quite reach the very high standard of outstanding gallantry required for the award of the Victoria Cross. It is accordingly proposed to submit his name to the King for the Distinguished Service Order. The recommendation that the award of MC to Page be augmented to DSO will also be submitted to His Majesty. It is hoped that action will in the circumstances be agreeable to your Prime Minister.

Clive Lyon says: 'The Prime Minister put him up for the Victoria Cross and, in my opinion, that was a very great honour.'

# CHAPTER 8
# MACARTHUR'S PROMISE

JAPAN'S HOPES of winning the war had disappeared with its defeat in the Battle of Midway in June 1942 after Yamamoto bungled his big chance to destroy the American carriers. Two-thirds of the Imperial Japanese Navy's carrier strike force had gone to the bottom of the ocean and the same proportion of trained flight crew were wiped out in that heroic battle with Admiral Chester W. Nimitz's Pacific Fleet at the midpoint of the North Pacific.

From that moment on, Emperor Hirohito, the Imperial General Staff and the country's militarist rulers under Premier Tojo knew that the United States would rapidly outstrip Japanese war production and inflict ever greater defeats on their army, navy and air force. In autumn 1942 only three American aircraft carriers were still in action; a year later there were fifty. The number of aircraft coming off the production lines ran into the thousands.

But the Japanese leaders had no intention of surrendering. To admit defeat would not only be a national disgrace, it would also leave them and other Japanese warmongers, such as the big industrial combines that were still churning out the components of Japan's war machine, open to criminal charges.

As the conquerors of South-East Asia grew more desperate to hold on to their occupied territories, they sank to new depths of barbarity. Thousands of British and Australian prisoners of war had been transported from Singapore to work as slave labourers on the Death Railway between Thailand and Burma. Little bamboo crosses testified that thousands of them were already buried in jungle cemeteries and many more would die in the ensuing months.

In Singapore, prisoners who were too sick to work at the docks or digging fortifications were confined in the vast Changi concentration camp, formerly a peacetime army barracks consisting of spacious blocks for the troops, a separate officers' quarters and rows of neat little houses for married couples. The Changi regime was merciless. Anyone disobeying orders was punished, anyone caught smuggling food in from a nearby *kampong* was beaten and, in some cases, executed.

The attack on Singapore Harbour by the Jaywick team and the loss of shipping was an enormous blow to Japanese prestige and they reacted aggressively. Ivan Lyon and the Jaywick commandos were still paddling back to meet the *Krait* when a man-hunt was unleashed by the *Kempei Tai* to find those responsible. After scouring the environs of Singapore Harbour and finding no trace of an Allied commando party, they concluded that the raid was the work of fifth columnists who had already perpetrated a series of far less spectacular acts of sabotage, such as burning down warehouses and cutting telegraph lines. A branch of the *Kempei Tai*, under Lieutenant Sumida, had been charged with finding the culprits.

When the harbour exploded in flames in the early morning of 27 September, the investigations into the fifth columnists' earlier acts of sabotage were well advanced. European suspects were identified in Changi Jail, which housed civilian internees, and others were found among the Chinese and Malay communities in Singapore City. Goaded by his superiors, Sumida plunged into his gory work without restraint. The result was the 'Double Tenth Massacre', which began on 10 October, the tenth day of the tenth month, and lasted for months. Suspects were rounded up from their homes and places of work, or in the case of internees, their prison cells, and taken to the *Kempei Tai* interrogation chambers at Outram Road Jail. There they were subjected to torture, starvation and other brutalities to make them confess to acts of sabotage and treason. Even the bishop of Singapore was dragged in as a suspect.

The Japanese criminal justice system stipulated that a prisoner had to confess to a crime before he or she could be charged with it. Therefore, the interrogator was permitted to use any amount of force, intimidation or coercion to extract a confession. As none of the suspects had even heard of Jaywick, let alone been part of it, any confessions they made were meaningless. This further enraged the Japanese. Many hundreds of Chinese and Malays, and more than twenty Europeans, died under torture or were executed for a crime they could not possibly have committed. Many others were sentenced to long terms of imprisonment on fabricated evidence.

Lieutenant Sumida was mystified. Despite great suffering, not one of his victims had told him anything about the raid itself, how it had been organised or where the explosives had been obtained.

THE GREAT FEAR of every Japanese soldier and administrator in the Occupied Territories was that he would be cut off from the sacred Home Islands, the archipelago formed by the tears of a goddess. Stretching 3800 kilometres from the subtropical waters of Okinawa to the frozen north of Hokkaido, Japan's island economy was particularly vulnerable to blockade. It was therefore imperative that the Imperial Japanese forces kept her defensive perimeter intact.

As supply lines for the import of oil, coal and raw materials stretched in an improbable arc from Attu in the north Pacific via the Marshall and Gilbert Islands down to the Central Solomons and New Guinea, then through the East Indies to Singapore and Malaya and across the Bay of Bengal to Burma, this was a super-human task. The Combined Fleet was based at Truk, a central position from which it could move to plug any gaps, and there were huge air bases at Rabaul, Saipan and Formosa.

Since June 1943 American strategists had pursued a two-pronged offensive to recapture the Philippines, smash through the Central Pacific defences and invade Japan. MacArthur's forces, supported by Admiral William F. 'Bull' Halsey's Third Fleet, eighteen hundred aircraft and seven divisions, were advancing on Rabaul, while Admiral Nimitz's Pacific Fleet fanned across the Central Pacific towards Saipan and Formosa.

Nimitz was Admiral Ernest J. King's man and one of Mac-Arthur's *bête noires*. He had been appointed to command the US Pacific Fleet shortly after Pearl Harbor and one of his first actions had been to unleash a submarine offensive against Japanese merchant shipping in the South China Sea which was having a devastating effect on the Japanese economy.

MacArthur was also making good progress. With the US Seventh Fleet, one thousand aircraft and fifteen divisions of Australian and American troops at his disposal, he finally had the firepower he had been demanding ever since he had arrived in Australia. In September 1943 three of his Australian divisions captured Lae and Salamaua, the important strategic bases on New Guinea's north coast which protected Rabaul.

George Kenney, whose Fifth Air Force flew men and guns to the frontlines in Lae and neighbouring Nadzab, said:

> At the last minute the Australian gunners who were to man the battery of twenty-five pounders decided to jump with their guns. None of them had ever worn a parachute before but they were so anxious to go that we showed them how to pull the ripcord and let them jump. Even this part of the show went off without a hitch and the guns were ready for action within an hour after they landed. General MacArthur swore that it was the most perfect example of discipline and training he had ever seen.

MacArthur hadn't, in fact, seen any of the action but was monitoring it closely from reports reaching his headquarters at

Government House, Port Moresby. His star was in the ascendant again and he strolled around dressed much of the time in white silk pyjamas and a Japanese silk dressing-gown with a large black dragon embroidered on the back.

The Australians won another notable victory to seize the port of Finschhafen on the Huon Peninsula, which opened up the western approach to New Britain. Rabaul, Japan's most powerful base in the South-West Pacific, was suddenly vulnerable. In December US Marines stormed ashore and gradually increased their grip on New Britain and the surrounding islands until 140 000 Japanese were cut off and effectively out of the war.

MacArthur was back in uniform on 29 February 1944 at the US landing at Los Negros in the Admiralty Islands, just north of New Guinea. Wearing nothing more substantial on his head than his field marshal's cap, which had been flown to New York to be rebraided, he stepped ashore in a dress rehearsal for his triumphant return to the Philippines.

Back in Brisbane he was in an effervescent mood. Grabbing the Admiralties meant that he now had an advanced naval base to continue his drive westward along the northern coast of New Guinea. He had prevented his mission to liberate Luzon from being lost in Nimitz's leapfrogging offensive across the Central Pacific to Formosa. The door to the Philippines was finally ajar.

MacArthur, however, left nothing to chance. When Curtin hosted a state dinner in Canberra on 17 March to celebrate the second anniversary of MacArthur's arrival in Australia, he responded:

The last two years have been momentous ones for Australia. You have faced the greatest peril in your history. With your very life at stake, you have met and overcome the challenge. It was here the tide of war turned in the Pacific and the mighty wave of invasion rolled back. Two years ago when I landed on your soil I said to the people of the Philippines whence I came, 'I shall return.' Tonight I repeat those words. I *shall* return.

IVAN LYON was in England acquainting himself with the capabilities of the Sleeping Beauty for Operation Hornbill when Major General Sir Colin McVean Gubbins, head of SOE, set off from Baker Street to inject some British phlegm into the Australian operation. Born in Japan to a Scottish mother and English father in 1896, Gubbins had inherited enough of his consular father's nous to adopt a softly-softly approach. He knew that SOE's remit did not amount to much with the Americans in the South-West Pacific.

Indeed, the head of Special Operations Australia, Lieutenant Colonel John Chapman-Walker, had to negotiate a minefield involving British, Australian, American and Dutch military aspirations and political sensitivities. It was a clumsy set-up.

Inside the South-West Pacific area, Chapman-Walker was answerable to General MacArthur for operations by members of the Services Reconnaissance Department, both the SOA's *nom de guerre* and its strike force, but he was responsible to Blamey for administrative matters. Within South-East Asia Command, Chapman-Walker was responsible to Mountbatten, yet he could not undertake any special operations without the approval of Baker Street.

SOE paid the wages and allowances of all British officers, office expenses and expenses for civilian staff. The Australian Government met the pay and allowances of all Australian personnel, provided army stores and picked up the bill for special equipment. AIB paid special expenses for projects within MacArthur's command area, such as gold and sterling for agents to distribute in enemy territories and the pay and allowances of Asiatic personnel. With so many masters and so much red tape to contend with, it is miraculous that SOA managed to function at all.

On his arrival at SOA headquarters in Melbourne on 3 April 1944 Gubbins ascertained that Chapman-Walker needed all the help he could get. He went into a huddle with General Blamey, who was leaving with Curtin in two days time for England, via the United States, to attend a meeting of Commonwealth prime ministers in London. Gubbins impressed upon Blamey the importance that Whitehall attached to his support for Chapman-Walker's special operations. Gubbins then flew to Brisbane to see MacArthur, Sutherland and Willoughby.

The first thing that caught his attention was that the city's main hotel, Lennon's, had been taken over by the supreme commander and members of his staff for accommodation and that a great deal of loose behaviour was taking place as the Americans availed themselves of the services of willing Australian women. 'The Australians resent being unable to use their Grand Babylonian Hotel, which is the centre of life in Brisbane,' he noted in his official report.

He knew that MacArthur had met Ivan Lyon soon after he had returned from Operation Jaywick and had promised his help and his submarines for future SOA missions. He also knew that MacArthur appeared to have reneged on that promise by refusing to provide a submarine to make a reconnaissance of the Natuna Islands, which was the first step in Operation Hornbill. This decision had been conveyed to South-East Asia Command (SEAC) on 20 March 1944 and was delaying the whole operation to set up SOA operations on the Borneo coast and in the South China Sea. Gubbins had promised Chapman-Walker that he would do his utmost to make MacArthur reconsider.

This was uppermost on his mind when he was ushered into MacArthur's office—Room 809—in the AMP building on the corner of Queen and Edward Streets, Brisbane, on 6 April 1944. The two men shook hands. In light khaki uniform with no medals on his chest, MacArthur towered over the British general. The meeting began cordially with MacArthur telling Gubbins about his interview with Ivan Lyon and how tremendously impressed he had been with the courage and efficiency with which Jaywick had been conducted.

Gubbins responded that SOA was eager to press ahead with other operations of a similar nature but that a shortage of submarine transport 'was proving a stranglehold on almost everything that SOA want to do'. MacArthur agreed. Once again he declared that he himself was greatly in favour of special operations and that SOA could be assured of his support. He had found it impossible, however, to convert Admiral King to his view and to persuade him to provide extra submarines.

This was disheartening news for Gubbins. King, chief of naval operations since March 1942 and a member of the US Joint Chiefs of Staff, was an implacable opponent of British influence in South-East Asia. He had fought to build up the US Navy's role against Japan at the expense of MacArthur's command and to keep the Royal Navy out of the Pacific altogether. In fact Ernie King was an irascible oddball: his own daughter described him as 'the most even-tempered man in the Navy—he's always in a rage'.

Then MacArthur switched tack and said he was hoping for an additional six to nine British submarines by September. That being the case, Gubbins raised the question of Hornbill. 'I explained the objects of the scheme,' Gubbins says, 'for *extended* Jaywick operations in SEAC's theatre and also in his own.' MacArthur then became more cagey. He repeated that there was a shortage of submarines and pointed out that such an operation would divert them from their primary role—the sinking of Japanese shipping, a strategy which was proving extraordinarily successful. 'I pressed him hard on this matter as it is so vital to SOA,' says Gubbins, 'and he agreed that he would reconsider the matter.'

Feeling he had scored a concession, Gubbins thanked Mac-Arthur and told him that Chapman-Walker would put the matter officially to Sutherland and Willoughby. But if Gubbins thought he could leave gracefully on that note, he was mistaken. MacArthur launched into a harangue about the war, mainly on the role of Russia, stating that he was nervous about the position that the Soviets would hold after the war. He hoped that the British were not going to throw everything into the invasion of Europe while Russia stood back and waited to see them bleed for a year or so before going all out to win the war quickly.

'I did not interrupt,' says Gubbins, 'but joined in the discussion when I could get a word in.'

Gubbins returned to Baker Street and reported to Lord Selborne on his Australian mission. He did not paint a very attractive picture, especially on the vital issue of Britain's place in South-East Asia:

> The whole military situation in Australia is very involved and there are a maze of crosscurrents which are very difficult to chart and to navigate unless one proceeds with the greatest precaution and with a good background of understanding. General Blamey's position is difficult and he is frequently sidetracked in the exercise of his command, orders being given direct from General MacArthur's GHQ to military formations and even occasionally to Australian forces. Thus in practice the Americans have complete command and control, and are in no way diffident of showing that that is the position.

Gubbins noted that GHQ considered the South-West Pacific Area campaign to be a purely American affair 'and that applies particularly to Sutherland and Willoughby'. MacArthur, he thought, took a wider view but it was difficult to get personal access to him 'with so many Cyclops and Cerberus on guard'. He added: 'I am quite sure that many matters, more particularly those concerning SOA, are dealt with by Sutherland in MacArthur's name without any reference to him whatsoever.'

Gubbins said that Chapman-Walker made many trips to Brisbane to consult Willoughby in his capacity as head of the Allied Intelligence Bureau and while Willoughby's position meant he was obliged to listen, he used what Gubbins described as 'unfair means' to dismiss Chapman-Walker's requests.

Chapman-Walker also had to go through Colonel Roberts, the AIB controller whom Gubbins found to be 'a remarkably stupid and unimaginative officer [who] works very slowly indeed'. He added: 'Thus SOA has not only to fight its battle with GHQ but has to put up with certain stupidities on the part of Australian staff officers as well.'

Chapman-Walker's deputy, Lieutenant Colonel A.G. Oldham, also received a bad report. 'He is, I am afraid, a small man and under no possible circumstances could act as substitute for Chapman-Walker,' said Gubbins. 'He is fussy and no leader. He can just about compete with getting personnel and stores out of the Australian Army.'

Nor was SOA's representative at the sharp end in Brisbane, Major Pegg of the Australian Army, considered 'up to the job'. 'It is most important to get a good man into the Brisbane office at once,' said Gubbins. 'I suggested Bunny Phillips but I am afraid his known connection with SEAC renders him impossible.'

Phillips's 'known connection with SEAC' was that he was the lover of Dickie Mountbatten's wife, Edwina. Dickie and Edwina were husband and wife in name only and Dickie heartily approved of the relationship. He had even invited 'The Rabbit', as he called Phillips, to his headquarters because he enjoyed his company.

Gubbins concluded that Chapman-Walker would have to 'keep pegging away at GHQ like the importunate widow until he gets a fair chance to show the capabilities of SOA'. He urged that Churchill should impress upon Curtin and Blamey while they were in London 'the importance of the contribution which SOA can make towards maintaining the Australian part in the Pacific War'. He added:

> I am sure that Blamey particularly will appreciate this point. It is essential for the Empire's prestige that Australia should play a wide part and should have a properly developed weapon in SOA which can influence events after the war far more widely than its small expense would seem to suggest.
>
> One has to admit that GHQ generally are not inclined to give SOA a fair run, partly through inherent jealousy and partly because their sledge-hammer methods of making war suggest to them that more delicate methods are unnecessary. Fundamentally, it is only Blamey who can change that picture. There is one point to remember—anything that is told to Mr Curtin, he will tell to General MacArthur.

Lord Selborne was well aware of that implication. He was a crafty politician himself: when Churchill had placed him in charge of SOE, he found that much of the policy was made by Gladwyn Jebb, formerly of the Foreign Office, whom Churchill referred to as 'gibbering-jabbering Jebb'. Selborne did not want a Foreign Office mandarin working on SOE matters, so he told Jebb he would prefer a businessman. When he mentioned Charles Hambro, Jebb was incensed and left in a huff. Hambro had been Jebb's old fagmaster at Eton.

Curtin, however, came from entirely different stock and played by different rules. He had been born at Creswick, Victoria, in 1885 as the son of an Irish police constable who turned his hand to managing pubs when he couldn't support his family on police wages. Curtin had moved to Perth in 1917 and, after winning the marginal Federal seat of Fremantle for the Labor Party in 1928, had worked his way into the party's hierarchy until he became leader in 1935. He had become prime minister on 7 October 1941, just two months before the outbreak of the Pacific War.

A New Year article written by Curtin to the Australian people at the end of 1941 showed where his loyalties lay:

> The Australian Government regards the Pacific struggle as primarily one in which the United States and Australia must have the fullest say in the direction of the democracies' fighting plan. Without any inhibitions of any kind, I make it quite clear that Australia looks to America, free of any pangs as to our traditional links or kinship with the United Kingdom.

There had never been anything like this pro-American challenge to British authority in the young country's history. Selborne knew that he would have to play his cards carefully to keep Australia in line for the end-of-war scramble for power in South-East Asia.

But MacArthur was already one jump ahead of him. On 22 April he performed the biggest leapfrog of the war so far by hopping over heavily fortified Japanese bases on the north coast of New Guinea and landing in Hollandia, former capital of Dutch New Guinea. Lightly defended Hollandia was 800 kilometres (500 miles) west of the most forward Allied base and the daring move caught the Japanese completely by surprise.

Quite rightly, MacArthur had named his manoeuvre 'Operation Reckless' and it succeeded brilliantly.

# CHAPTER 9
# RIMAU: THE PLAN

JAYWICK, AS WE have seen, had set the air on fire at SRD head-quarters in Melbourne and the top brass were shouting for an encore. 'There was tremendous enthusiasm,' says Clive Lyon. 'Jaywick was such a success that everybody wanted more of the same thing.' But while the Australian operatives pawed the ground for another crack at the enemy, much grander forces were at work at the top levels of British society.

In Westminster, Whitehall and Buckingham Palace itself, there was a sudden realisation that Special Operations Australia was the key to the return of imperial Britain to the former colonies of South-East Asia. Royal and vice-regal circles were particularly engaged. Ivan Lyon was feted by Governor-General Lord Gowrie on his return from Jaywick. Roma Page remembers the afternoon Bob went to Admiralty House, the Governor-General's Sydney residence, at Gowrie's invitation. 'Bob told me he was terribly interested,' she said. 'He got on the floor with Lord Gowrie and the map and explained everything—where they'd been, what they'd done.' Gowrie reported directly to the Palace.

Mountbatten, Supreme Allied Commander of South-East Asia, was also keen to continue the success of Operation Jaywick and happily put to work all resources in his area of influence. Mountbatten's grandiose title was, however, somewhat misleading. Theoretically, Mountbatten was responsible for all operations by sea, land and air in India, Burma, Ceylon, Thailand, Sumatra and Malaya but he was hampered by having very few mainline forces at his command. Like MacArthur, he was self-aggrandising. Whereas MacArthur's ambitions swung towards the American presidency, Mountbatten had dynastic pretensions concerning the British monarchy.

His nephew Philip Mountbatten, a lieutenant in the Royal Navy, was in regular correspondence with Princess Elizabeth, heiress to the British throne, and Mountbatten had every hope that he might marry her. The House of Mountbatten would then replace the House of Windsor. Seizing on the propaganda value as well as the military worth of a decisive blow against the Japanese, he had given Operation Hornbill the green light.

Operation Hornbill was a major operation centred on the Natuna Islands between Borneo and the South-East Asian mainland. Allied forces, including native Malays but with Americans deliberately excluded, would secretly occupy the small archipelago one thousand kilometres behind the enemy lines. Operating a fleet of three motorised junks custom-made in Melbourne and dubbed 'Country Craft', they would make raids on Japanese naval assets in French Indochina and on the shipyards of Malaya and Singapore. The colonial nature of the exercise was underlined by the presence of twelve Free French commandos in the early plans.

Far from resting on his laurels, all of Lyon's attention was directed towards Hornbill. It was a massive undertaking. Literally hundreds of Intelligence flights would pave the way for detailed planning. Spies in Saigon and Singapore, escaped Allied prisoners, and the few Japanese POWs would be milked for the latest information. It would all be assembled in a massive effort of documentation which today remains redolent of the dash and flair that inspired it.

Phase 1 is to establish the base at Great Natuna. The party will sail in mid-July 1944. They will forward their report to Australia by the return journey of the submarine but will themselves remain at the base until relieved by the main party.

The operational party in HMS *Porpoise* will consist of thirty-five men who will sail from Exmouth Gulf about 1 September, ETA Natuna about mid-September. A team of three Country Craft operating under the orders of D/Navy and commanded by a Senior Naval Officer [Davidson] will sail from Western Australia at such time to reach the Natunas seven days after the main party. Each Country Craft will carry approx. ten tons of stores.

The Senior Naval Officer will be based on the Natunas. He will command all non-operational personnel and will be responsible to OC Hornbill [Colonel Lyon] for the administration of the base and for the carrying out of operational requirements as agreed upon by [Lyon]. His role will be the provision and co-ordination of transport for the operatives, liaison with the submarine and the maintenance of signals communications through SOA or RAN channels.

This was Davidson's job and, as can be seen, there was then (and there remained) a clear and specific role for radio communications.

The first of many operations designated for the Hornbill force was:

Target A—Singapore Naval Base and Seletar [Air] Base, Singapore.

Target B—Singapore Roads and Keppel Harbour.

Target C—Saigon Port.

For A and B, reconnaissance groups working from the Natunas by Country Craft and folboats would carry out a detailed survey of the approaches to the targets during the first fortnight of October. The attack, scheduled for early November, would be undertaken in a small fleet of one-man Sleeping Beauties. The SBs were but one of the attractions of the operation for Mountbatten who loved new gadgets. Ivan Lyon could immediately see the advantage of SBs over folboats which exposed their crew to discovery from sea and shoreline. There were disadvantages in handling and transportation that would become apparent in the days ahead, but the SBs were intrinsic to the attack plans for targets

A and B on Singapore Island. The Saigon raid would employ folboats alone.

And that was just the beginning. From his redoubt on Great Natuna, Lyon would be like some pirate king, striking unexpectedly with a variety of forces—the innocent-looking junks sidling up to a dockyard with their Malay crew on deck and commandos down below setting the mechanical timers for limpets to explode long after they had gone; the sleek and silent Sleeping Beauties gliding beneath the surface to enemy warships at anchor; the folboats cutting through the phosphorescent water on yet another night mission of destruction.

Sixty officers and men were selected for training in a camp attached to Potshot at Exmouth Gulf. Further south, another training area was established in Careening Bay on Garden Island in Cockburn Sound for instruction and practice on the Sleeping Beauties. This base was just off the coast of Fremantle where the staff of the United States Naval Commander-in-Chief of the South-West Pacific had been in residence since March 1942.

Apart from some wild wallabies, the only other inhabitants of Garden Island were the units manning a coastal defence battery and one consisting of women operating searchlights from a hill overlooking the base. The base was well-equipped with workshops, mess huts and a shower block, and there was a wharf with a small crane to launch the Sleeping Beauties when they arrived.

The RAAF provided radio equipment for the Country Craft and airborne freight and personnel facilities for getting the whole party assembled at their points of departure in Western Australia. A complicated transportation regime saw them assembled from across Australia and around the world as Major Walter Chapman joined them from London.

The administrative headquarters was in Perth, while the Country Craft were being built in the Melbourne dockyards. The Australian Army, through Z Special Unit, had turned over five 66 foot seine net trawlers and provided engines and equipment for them to be fitted out in the guise of junks. The latter provided the first glitch in Lyon's meticulous plan when industrial action halted production.

Ironically, the problem was one of secrecy—not too little but too much. So circumspect had the Australian Government been in its management of war news that neither then, nor for decades afterward, did the population understand the reality of the Japanese threat. The forty-five bombing raids on Darwin, the twenty-two merchant vessels sunk by Japanese submarines off the Australian coast and the touch-and-go nature of the battle for New Guinea had all been kept from the Australian public by the censors.

The presence of more than half a million Americans passing through the nation's ports on their way to the frontlines many thousands of kilometres to the north gave the impression that the danger was neither real nor immediate. So the waterside and dockyard workers made untenable demands and laid down tools when their conditions seemed endangered. This industrial action, combined with material shortages, interrupted work on the Country Craft. Other problems would follow but at this juncture the spotlight swung to the Mother Country.

CURTIN CAME face to face with Britain's determination to recoup her empire during his visit to London for the prime ministers' conference. He travelled to England via the United States, stopping off in Washington in April 1944 for talks with Roosevelt who had expressed concern about the first stirrings of Australian nationalism.

While the war with Japan was still at its height, the far-seeing Curtin and his Minister for External Affairs, Dr H.V. Evatt, wanted to convene a conference of powers with territorial interests in the South and South-West Pacific. The President told Curtin that he felt such a regional conference would be premature until an international security system had been put into place once the war had been won.

Curtin made no binding promises, then travelled to London with General Blamey and Sir Frederick Shedden. The main item on the agenda, as far as the Australians were concerned, was a clear definition of just how British forces would be deployed in the liberation of South-East Asia and the South-West Pacific. How many British troops would be stationed in Australia? Would British ships operate under American commanders in a combined fleet? Would Britain confine her activities to Burma and Malaya—the 'Bay of Bengal' policy—or would she seek a wider role in the Pacific?

If Curtin expected to get answers to these questions, he was to be disappointed when he attended the first session of the conference with Churchill at 10 Downing Street on 1 May 1944. There were speeches of welcome, photographs in the garden and a convivial glass of sherry.

After lunch, Churchill addressed the prime ministers for ninety minutes on his European strategy but failed miserably to galvanise them. 'Dull, lifeless and missing the main points,' Brooke, Chief of the Imperial General Staff, noted in his diary. 'He looked very old and tired, and in my opinion is failing fast.' It was not an auspicious start.

Curtin knew how much animosity existed between him and Churchill over the fall of Singapore and the subsequent return of the Australian 7th Division from the Middle East to defend Australia, rather than Burma, as Churchill had wished. But he had little concept of just how much of a division existed between Churchill, a political genius but a woeful amateur strategist, and his chiefs of staff. They had to resist his wilder excesses on an almost daily basis for most of the war. Fortunately, the British public never found out about his meddlesome, truculent behaviour or the blow to morale would have been devastating.

The following day, 2 May, Curtin attended a War Cabinet meeting and on 4 May, Lord Bruce, the Australian High Commissioner, held a lunch in his honour at Claridge's. Meanwhile Blamey had failed to rise to the occasion. He attended a meeting of the British chiefs of staff on 5 May which discussed the vital subject of future operations from Australia and the size of the Australian contribution but he was in poor shape and made a bad impression. 'Blamey is not an impressive specimen,' Brooke, a fastidious ornithologist in his spare time, wrote in his diary. 'He looks entirely drink sodden and somewhat repulsive.'

This view was confirmed later that day when the Australian contingent threw a sherry party for their imperial brethren. There seemed to be liquor everywhere, although Curtin, a recovering alcoholic, adhered to a painful abstinence. Following further dinners at Greenwich and 10 Downing Street, however, the Australian

Prime Minister at last came into his own at a lunch at the Mansion House on 10 May after receiving the Freedom of the City of London. He caught the mood perfectly and made an excellent speech on ways to achieve greater empire consultation.

But Blamey blotted his copybook again when he arrived for a meeting with the chiefs of staff to continue discussions on future Anglo-Australian operations. 'Blamey looked as if he had the most frightful "hangover" from a debauched night,' noted Field Marshal Brooke. 'His eyes were swimming in alcohol!'

Nevertheless, the meeting made considerable progress and ended with a forecast of the total British, Australian and New Zealand forces which could be made available for operations in South-East Asia. It was now clear to all that the United States was intent on monopolising the battle honours in the Pacific but Churchill was determined, as Brooke put it, that Britain would not be tied to America's apron strings. The scene shifted to lunch with the Australian Club at the Dorchester where Churchill, Curtin, Bruce and the Duke of Gloucester, the King's bibulous brother and incoming Governor-General of Australia, all made speeches.

Somewhere in the middle of the wining, dining, handshaking and speech-making, Lord Bruce found time to compose a coherent report of Britain's objectives with regard to Special Operations Australia and telegraph it to Canberra. Bruce summarised the British position succinctly:

In view of the general trend of Far Eastern strategy, great importance is attached here to an Australian–British organis-ation like Special Operations Australia doing this work.

The real crux of the matter, however, is the political aspect. Whatever may be the final outcome of present discussions on Far Eastern strategy, there is no doubt that the main weight of attack on Japan will be delivered by commands which are overwhelmingly American.

In these circumstances, it is felt here to be of the utmost importance to preserve and, if possible, develop an organisation which will increase the representation of the point of view and the interests of the British Commonwealth in this area. If [Lord Mountbatten's] South-East Asia Command continues to have an offensive role at all in the war against Japan, SOA working from Australia as a base can render the greatest assistance to Mountbatten in the area east of the Malay Peninsula and increase and speed up the Commonwealth contribution to a convergence of all forces on the China coast for the final blow against Japan.

If on the other hand the SEAC is virtually eliminated from the main campaign against Japan, it obviously becomes more than ever important to make the most of such relatively slight British Commonwealth representation as will remain. This applies particularly to the China Sea and the China coast areas where the nature of SOA–SOE activities and the contacts likely to be involved may make possible the exercise of a degree of influence out of all proportion to the magnitude of the operations undertaken.

Despite Bruce's assertions, Curtin dug his heels in at the next strategy meeting with Churchill and declined to allow British troops to operate from Australian soil at all in case it created conflict with the Americans. General Brooke noted: 'The meeting started badly as Curtin who is entirely in MacArthur's pocket was afraid we were trying to oust MacArthur!' Assured that this wasn't the case, Curtin agreed that Darwin and Fremantle should be developed by Britain for future operations and that British staff officers should be accepted to work alongside Australian general staff. There was little option, really. Blamey, who was also present at the meeting, had already been dumped by MacArthur as commander of Allied Land Forces and the role of Australian troops in MacArthur's grand strategy was far from satisfactory.

THE PRACTICAL response to Britain's imperial ambitions had been Operation Hornbill but it was not going well, either in England or Australia. When Ivan Lyon left London at the beginning of May, Walter Chapman had stayed behind with the express purpose of designing special J containers, as they were called, to store the Sleeping Beauties in HMS *Porpoise* once they and the containers had been brought to Fremantle in separate cargo ships.

Neither the Sleeping Beauties nor the containers had arrived, yet on 3 June a message went out under Lyon's signature, giving every indication that the plan was on track. The message stated that on 1 September, the operational party would sail by submarine for a base in the China Sea. It would carry fifteen Sleeping Beauties in pressure containers and enough stores to last a full nine months. In addition, three Country Craft would each carry ten tons of stores and the submarine would return with a second supply. A 'misdirection' plan had been developed including the spreading of false rumours about the operation and cover stories had been created in case personnel were captured. The communications plan would be based on radios in the Country Craft and the first phase of the operation would run from 15 September to 29 December.

On 23 June a memo was circulated through the top echelons of Services Reconnaissance Department confirming Lyon's plan in all its essentials. But it turned out to be a false hope. MacArthur failed to deliver an American submarine for the reconnaissance of the Natunas and industrial disputes delayed the production of the Country Craft still further. Lyon was informed that there had been a dramatic change of plan. Hornbill, as such, was dead.

He must have been disappointed but he was not discouraged. On 17 July a new plan was flashed around SRD. Lyon drafted it himself in the spare surroundings of his Perth HQ. Hornbill had been 'modified'; it still carried the original codename, but without the Country Craft there would be no need for the big base on Great Natuna which could so easily attract the attention of the Japanese. Now it was a matter of getting there before the monsoon season, striking with maximum impact and getting away before the Japanese knew what had struck them.

The Frenchmen were discarded, along with the small Malay contingent. Indeed, the whole operation would concentrate on the southern base of the Japanese war machine, Singapore Harbour.

HMS *Porpoise* will embark at Fremantle twenty operatives and their stores which include ten Sleeping Beauties and ten folboats and proceed via Lombok Passage to a point which will be known as Base A. This base will be on Pulau Merapas on the eastern flank of the Riau Archipelago. *Porpoise* will deposit food and stores for twenty men for two months. This will be the rendezvous to which the operatives will return on completion of their attack.

HMS *Porpoise* will then proceed to the vicinity of Pedjantan Island where she will intercept and capture a large junk, disposing of the crew. In the lee of this island HMS *Porpoise* will transfer operational stores and operatives to the junk, then HMS *Porpoise* will return to Australia.

The junk with the Sleeping Beauties and folboats and explosives will proceed to Keppel Harbour, Singapore, and carry out their attack. On completion of the strike the Sleeping Beauties will be scuttled and the operatives return to rendezvous at Base A by folboat. HMS *Porpoise* will proceed to Base A and pick up operatives and return to Australia for Christmas.

Home for Christmas. Lyon could not have resisted a grim smile. It was the perennial promise of every army commander: 'Fear not, the boys will be home for Christmas.'

The reduction of the operation to a single strike was a kick in the guts to the mission leader. Lyon relished mightily the prospect of wreaking havoc on the Japanese from his redoubt on Great Natuna. But that was postponed, not cancelled. 'However,' he wrote, 'should HMS *Porpoise* be made available sufficiently early it is proposed that she proceed to reconnoitre the Natunas as originally planned, leaving thereon approx. twenty-five tons of fuel for Country Craft [when finally completed]. SRD place tremendous importance on the establishment of the Natunas base as it is from there that they intend to carry out a series of further operations.'

Lyon was no longer the pirate king-in-waiting but a new persona was in some ways even more congenial. Henceforth he would take on the role of a hungry tiger, venturing from his lair to savage the intruder then slipping away to blend in with the tropical surroundings. The enemy would be thrown into confusion, never knowing if they were being betrayed by those they had 'liberated' or if some Allied air raiders had broken through their defences.

The operation needed a change of name to reflect its new dynamic. In the warmth of his unadorned office in Perth, we may suppose, he paused in his writing and rubbed a hand across his chest beneath the open-necked shirt of his uniform. He flexed his muscles and the tattooed tiger snarled silently in the afternoon light. 'Rimau,' he wrote. 'Operation Rimau.'

# CHAPTER 10
# DOUBLE JEOPARDY

ALL AUSTRALIA cheered when it was reported that Tojo, the most hated of the Japanese war lords, had resigned in July 1944 after the fall of Saipan had brought Tokyo into range of American bombers. The first huge gap had appeared in Japan's defensive arc when her fleet had been defeated by Vice Admiral Raymond A. Spruance's Fifth Fleet in a blistering battle for the Marianas on 19–20 June 1944. Three Japanese aircraft carriers were sunk and the Japanese fleet air arm was virtually annihilated. Officially, it was designated as the Battle of the Philippine Sea, but to its American participants it was known as 'the Great Marianas Turkey Shoot'.

With so many developments taking place in the Pacific theatre there was a new air of urgency about Operation Rimau and, from mid-July, things started to move quickly. The training was sorting the men from the boys. From the sixty initial recruits, Ivan Lyon wanted a party of thirty-two swimmer–canoeists who would be known as Group X.

It was an extraordinarily tough regime. Donald Davidson and Bob Page were the only certainties for the mission. Roma Page said when Bob returned to their Melbourne flat on a brief leave his hands were covered in calluses. 'I didn't ask,' she said. 'I thought perhaps he might have been fencing or chopping wood. I learned later they had been paddling for miles and miles.'

After Operation Jaywick she had married her soldier in Canberra at St Andrew's Presbyterian Church in a simple family ceremony. 'We went to Bowral for our honeymoon,' she said. 'It was only three days, then he was recalled to Brisbane.'

That was when the Jaywick heroes were summoned to Mac-Arthur and they all had their photographs taken. 'Ivan and Donald were there. When they heard we were married they said to Bob, "Oh, go and have three weeks' leave".'

It was December 1943 and the newlyweds stayed at the family property, Hill Station, on the outskirts of the Australian capital. The sheep station needed work. All three of Roma's brothers were in the army and her father joined up to do his bit in the Transport Corps. Roma was living in the big homestead with her mother when Bob came to stay.

'He loved it,' she said. 'He rode and worked around the property. It was very difficult to go anywhere—there was no petrol. We couldn't fly anywhere—there was only the train—so there were not many places we could go. But really, we didn't want to go anywhere. We were just happy to be together.'

Later, when Operation Rimau was on, Roma moved to Melbourne and on Bob's final leave they were staying with the Davidsons. 'It was a lovely old place called 'Paisley' in Domain Road, South Yarra,' she said. 'It was a huge old place and it had been made into apartments.'

They rubbed along well with the older couple. Nancy Davidson was a bit of an odd fish. 'She wore slacks all the time and when she was invited to Government House she *really* didn't have anything to wear,' Roma said. 'There was an older woman in the apartments and she and I had to dress her up. It was the only time I saw her in a dress.'

But Donald and Bob were so fit they were dangerous. 'They would try out all kinds of surprise attacks on one another,' she said. 'They were always tackling and tumbling about the place.'

As well as Lyon, Davidson and Page, three other members of Operation Jaywick were chosen for Operation Rimau: Able Seamen Wally 'Poppa' Falls, 'Happy' Huston and 'Boofhead' Marsh, a man of few words.

Lieutenant Walter J. Carey would come aboard as a second 'Conducting Officer', the same role as Walter Chapman. Carey's brother Sam had a strong connection with Bob Page: it was he who had organised the aborted Operation Scorpion raid on Rabaul. As far as Page knew, his father Harold was still a captive of the Japanese.

Lieutenant J.F. Lind-Holmes, DSO, arrived at the Careening Bay camp from Melbourne on 13 July to help Davidson knock the men into shape. Three Sleeping Beauties had been removed from their British cargo ship when she docked in Fremantle but Sub

Lieutenant Riggs, who had accompanied the SBs from England, had to continue on to Melbourne where the other twelve SBs would be unloaded in line with the ship's manifest. Lind-Holmes said:

Training did not actually start until Saturday, 19 July. At first sight this may appear to be rather a long period. However, it should be appreciated that there was nothing but a very vague plan as to how the camp should be laid out.

The maintenance personnel were there and [some of] the SBs were there, but meanwhile Ellis, our stores officer, and I had to obtain everything from spanners to lathes, sulphuric acid to heavy charging plants, and all the tools, machine tools, cranes, trucks and paraphernalia which go to produce a maintenance base. During this period we received tremendous co-operation from the army and the navy.

When training started my immediate policy was, as so many excellent personnel had been supplied, we should cut down as soon as possible and thus avoid training an unnecessarily large number. Consequently, by 24 July, eight men had been discharged on medical grounds and five others were returned for other reasons.

Meanwhile, training proceeded rapidly and satisfactorily. The operatives were given a lecture on shallow water diving and equipment maintenance and were then given about four hours diving. This was followed by lectures on the Sleeping Beauties, SB static diving, and day diving. The classes had been divided up into three groups of fifteen and each class was brought on as fast as the material could be maintained. Thus, by 13 August, 'A' Class was diving SBs at night, 'B' Class was diving SBs by day; and 'C' Class was doing static dives alongside the jetty. As soon as night diving started, further weeding out became possible, and a small trickle of bodies returned to Melbourne.

When Riggs arrived from Melbourne, Lind-Holmes turned over the 'polishing up' of the more promising divers to him. 'My own method had been fairly brutal and callous in order to break the spirits of the unsuitable,' he said. 'A number of night exercises were then carried out. It soon became apparent that the handling and behaviour of the SBs in a group was similar to the handling of a group of folboats so this part was cut out of the training. Meanwhile, we concentrated entirely on the handling of the SBs in the last stage of an attack on ships or jetties.'

HMS *Porpoise* arrived from Ceylon on 15 August and Lyon called a series of conferences to decide the best method of loading the stores and submersibles. The key figure was the moustachioed Walter Chapman who appeared to epitomise the type of superior English officer Australians despised. Some wag dubbed him the 'Pommy Pongo Plumber'—for English Army engineer—and the name stuck.

Chapman was being blamed because the J containers had not yet arrived to house the Sleeping Beauties. Time was of the essence, with the monsoon season providing a September deadline for the launching of Rimau. The only saving grace was that Lind-Holmes and Riggs had a little extra time to sharpen the operatives' skills with combat exercises.

Lind-Holmes said:

Day and night attacks were carried out on HMAS *Adelaide* on 17 August. This showed us that the best method of attack is from either the bow or the stern. To place a 'set' of three limpets, it was decided that the compass should be removed from the SBs and a flat limpet stowage provided instead. This permitted us to attach six limpets to the upper deck and protect them with a streamlined fairing and canvas cover.

By Thursday 24 August, the class was virtually trained. Our training differed considerably from that suggested by London in that I advanced the class into night diving as rapidly as possible. The reason is quite obvious—any fool can drive a car by day but it needs a great deal more skill to drive in the dark without headlights.

The class was then given a few days' leave while Lyon awaited the arrival of the J containers. They finally reached Fremantle on 30 August and were at Careening Bay twenty-four hours later. Despite the urgency, the containers had been placed on a slow merchant ship from Colombo to Australia and the captain had insisted on taking them to Melbourne in strict accordance with the ship's manifest rather than off-loading them in Perth.

Chapman-Walker ordered Commander Geoffrey Branson, head of SRD's naval department, over to Fremantle to assist with the fitting of the containers. Branson, who had retired from the Royal Navy in 1930 to go into business in Australia, had favourably impressed Sir Colin Gubbins during his trip to Australia. In his report to Selborne, Gubbins described him as 'a man of great personality and drive—a good officer'.

Another SOE officer who met Branson in Melbourne in June 1944 was even more glowing in his assessment of the man's character. Branson, he said, was:

> an excellent type and a good disciplinarian and leader who made something of a reputation under difficult circumstances at Milne Bay when Australian forces had driven off Japanese invaders. He is extremely frank in his dealings, a tendency which he may perhaps overdo. His frankness however is in general a desirable quality. He takes a realistic view and is unlikely to be led astray by wild views. He speaks with authority on naval matters and gives the impression of having a good grasp of his profession. The Mission is very lucky to have a man of his force and drive who will be invaluable as the Mission's Naval commitments increase.

After such fulsome testimony, it is difficult to comprehend that Branson single-handedly almost sank Operation Rimau before it had even set sail from Fremantle, but that is exactly what happened. And the fact that it happened at all must cast doubt on Gubbins's judgment and on that of Chapman-Walker. Either Branson was a clever actor who managed to conceal his true nature, or his superior officers were poor judges of character.

Shortly after he had arrived at Careening Bay, Branson wrote a highly inflammatory report to Chapman-Walker on the question of the J containers. The matter had been discussed at several conferences since Lyon had returned from England and, according to Branson, Lyon had given an assurance that Major Chapman had remained behind in England to complete the necessary arrangements. In his report to Chapman-Walker, Branson said:

I took Major Chapman on board *Porpoise* and conferred with the Commanding Officer Lieutenant Commander Marsham and Commander Helbert, Staff Officer (Operations) to Captain Fourth Submarine Flotilla. It was immediately apparent that Major Chapman's design for the so-called "J" containers was totally impracticable for the following reasons: (i) they were too long and too high to eject over the stern without fouling the roof of the mine gallery as they canted up; (ii) the suggestion that rails be extended over the stern of the submarine was not feasible owing to the lack of any suitable underwater surfaces for attaching supports; (iii) Major Chapman's alternative of cutting away the roof of the mine gallery over the last 13 ft was quite unacceptable to the Commanding Officer of the submarine and also Commander Helbert.

The submarine officers expressed very considerable surprise and dissatisfaction that such elementary planning had been neglected. I entirely agree with them and consider that both Lyon and Chapman, and London office, were grossly negligent in leaving matters of this sort to be settled on arrival of the submarine in Australia.

In addition, it has now been discovered that the length of the mine gallery [on the submarine's hull] is only sufficient to take fourteen, not fifteen "J" containers. I fail to understand why Major Chapman did not carry out the necessary measurements.

This had meant further delay while a new plan was devised and carried out. 'As a result, Lieutenant Commander Marsham and Commander Helbert are extremely perturbed as to the short time available for carrying out loading and disembarkation exercises.'

In making his comments, Branson was relying on Chapman's drawings for the containers and a wooden mock-up because his report is dated 21 August and the completed articles didn't arrive in Western Australia until the end of the month. There is nothing in the SOA files to indicate what action, if any, Chapman-Walker took when he received Branson's complaints but it seems probable that he did nothing, because Walter Chapman was not asked to respond to Branson's allegations until seven months later in March 1945. Then, he indignantly pointed out that he had had very little time to measure the submarine in Glasgow before she set sail for the Far East and that he had always known some adjustments would have to be made once the containers reached Australia.

But even though Chapman hadn't seen Branson's report in August 1944, it should have been patently obvious that the clash of personalities between the two men was damaging preparations for the highly sensitive operation. Branson and Chapman were barely on speaking terms and Marsham had ceased talking to Branson altogether after he had walked up to him on the dock and announced that he knew he was heading for Singapore.

Marsham, whose nerves were on edge from battle fatigue, was so affronted that another officer should break security in this

manner that he alerted the commanding officer of the Eighth
Submarine Flotilla, Captain L.M. Shadwell. The fact that Branson
even knew the destination of Operation Rimau casts doubt on
Chapman-Walker's security arrangements.

When Ivan Lyon was told about the breach, however, he wasn't
overly perturbed. Branson, after all, was SRD and he had been
talking to an officer involved in an SRD mission. Lyon pressed
ahead with making the final selection of the operational team.
Fifteen men made it from Group X:

Major Reginald M. Ingleton, twenty-five (Royal Marines)

Lieutenant Bruno P. Reymond, thirty-one (RANR)

Lieutenant H. Robert Ross, twenty-seven (British Army)

Lieutenant Albert L. 'Blondie' Sargent, twenty-five (AIF)

Warrant Officer Alfred Warren, thirty-two (AIF)

Warrant Officer Jeffrey Willersdorf, twenty-two (AIF)

Sergeant Colin B. Cameron, twenty-one (AIF)

Sergeant David P. Gooley, twenty-seven (AIF)

Corporal Archibald G. 'Pat' Campbell, twenty-six (AIF)

Corporal Colin M. Craft, twenty-one (AIF)

Corporal Roland B. Fletcher, twenty-nine (AIF)

Corporal Clair M. Stewart, thirty-five (AIF)

Lance Corporal John T. Hardy, twenty-three (AIF)

Lance Corporal Hugo J. Pace, twenty-five (AIF)

Private Douglas R. Warne, twenty-four (AIF)

They joined the Jaywick veterans Davidson, Page, Falls, Huston
and Marsh and the SB expert Riggs.

As a group, they were rambunctious, full of daring and aggression, trained to kill at close quarters and skilled in all the other arts of survival in war, from Morse code to navigation to living from the land and sea. Their equipment included the usual tinned rations and portable stoves, medical packs and saltwater conversion shakers. But as well, each man had a .38 revolver in a holster, an ammunition pouch with five hundred rounds, a black beret, two jungle green shirts, two pairs of trousers, two pairs each of underpants, singlets and socks, a pair of jungle boots, a black polo neck sweater, a green mosquito veil, an American jungle hammock, a sheet of green calico, a packet of razor blades, a shaving set, a toothbrush, a shaving brush, a cake of salt water soap, shaving cream, toothpaste, a comb, an enamel mug, a set of cutlery, a billycan, two water bottles, a clasp knife with lanyard, a leather belt, a compass, a torch, four spare batteries, two pack straps, a sweat towel, a waterproof watch, a notebook and pencil, a box of waterproof matches, a water sterilising outfit, clothes washing soap, a field service dressing, two tubes of skin dye, a pair of sunglasses, a twelve foot length of parachute cord, a cigarette lighter, an emergency map, a tin of emergency rations, a fishing kit, a rubber water container, $27.50 in 10c pieces, a paddle, two tins of tobacco and twenty cigarettes.

They were also given the latest war news in the region and once they were under way Ivan Lyon, Donald Davidson and Bob Page would brief them in detail on the task ahead. Then, as each member of the Rimau team, as well as Chapman and Carey, was issued with cyanide pills in black, Bakelite capsules by Dr Balforth of the Royal

Marines, each would be forced individually to confront Operation Rimau, and the possibility of violent death.

The hulking Major Ingleton, for example, would keep himself to himself as he had done throughout the training course.

Lieutenant Albert 'Blondie' Sargent would be sustained by memories of his family in country Victoria. He had joined the AIF in 1941 and gone abroad as Sergeant Sargent to fight in the Syrian campaign where he was promoted in the field, no doubt to the relief of all concerned.

Indeed, Syd Wright, Secretary of his local RSL Branch in Boomahnoomoonah, via Tungamah, wrote to him from their Perchelba sub-branch to congratulate him when the promotion came through. 'We hope for a speedy conclusion of the war and we will be very glad to welcome you back to this district,' he said.

Blondie had gone on to fight in New Guinea in late 1943 and during a leave earlier in 1944 he'd married his girlfriend Norma. They had been together briefly and now God knew when he'd see her again.

Pat Campbell, the Queenslander, didn't know it yet but his brother would in time become governor of the Sunshine State.

Bruno Reymond, part-Maori, had been born in the Gilbert Islands; as Rimau unfolded he would draw on all his experience of a childhood sailing in the Pacific.

Jeff Willersdorf, the young Melbourne butcher, had looked death in the face the previous year in his parachute course. Whatever awaited him, it couldn't be much more scary than jumping out of an aeroplane. Two days earlier he'd been promoted to acting warrant officer. Confirmation would come through army channels on 18 January 1945.

Hugo Pace, who had been born in Port Said, Egypt, and whose mother had returned there in January 1944, was also a parachutist. But Hugo had seen it all—from the Middle East where he'd been wounded in action and evacuated back to Australia; then in New Guinea where he'd contracted malaria before taking a Japanese bullet in the arm and thigh in January 1943. The former clerk who had enlisted in Rockhampton, Queensland, was now an acting corporal. He too would have his new rank confirmed in January 1945.

Colin Cameron, who had given his occupation as electrical powerhouse assistant when he'd enlisted aged only eighteen in December 1940 in Wedderburn, Victoria, had not previously ventured from Australian shores. His only wounds had been in accidents in road convoys in the backblocks of his native state where, on two occasions, he had suffered minor concussions. He had risen to the rank of sergeant and his father, Ken, was proud of him. He hated the fact that he couldn't tell his dad about his latest exploit.

Clair Mack Stewart would think of his wife Juanita waiting back in Mosman Park, Western Australia. He'd worked on the railways before he joined up in August 1941 and this was also his first time out of Australia. But he had prepared for it—first at the radio school at Bonegilla, Victoria, and then at the parachute school. The previous month he had come down with a bout of gastroenteritis and had been admitted to hospital in Port Augusta, but after eight days he'd been released as fit.

**Above:** Training in the folboats used in Operation Jaywick.

bove: Members of Operation Jaywick on board the *Krait*.

Australian War Memorial Negative Number 067336

**Above:** Members of Operation Jaywick after the successful completion of mission, photographed in Brisbane, 1943.
Front (L-R): Ted Carse, Donald Davidson, Ivan Lyon, Jock Campbell, Page.
Centre (L-R): Andrew Crilley, Cobber Cain, Paddy McDowell, Horrie You Poppa Falls, Taffy Morris.
Back (L-R): Moss Berryman, Boofhead Marsh, Joe Jones, and Ha Huston.

Australian War Memorial Negative Number 045424

**Right:** Page, Lyon and Davidson, to the right, celebrate the successful completion of Operation Jaywick.

Australian War Memorial Negative Number 045423

**ove:** SRD operatives preparing for 'Sleeping Beauty' training at Careening
y, Western Australia.

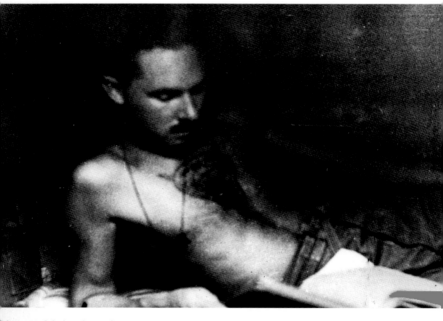

**Above:** Major Ivan Lyon on board the *Krait*. Lyon's tiger tattoo is visible on chest.

Australian War Memorial Negative Number 045422

**Left:** Major Ivan Lyon and his wife Gabrielle Singapore.
Photo courtesy of Clive Lyon

**Right:** Robert and Roma Page on their wedding day.
Photo courtesy of Roma Page.

**Above:** The *Mustika*

**Above:** The *Mustika* boarding party.

**Above:** General Douglas MacArthur with Prime Minister John Curtin.

Australian War Memorial Negative Number 139812

**Above:** Outram Road Prison, front entrance.

**Above:** Outram Road Prison, aerial view.

Colin Montagu Craft, the young school teacher, was one of the most highly trained men in the team. Almost from the time he had joined up in Perth in April 1941 he had specialised in the signals division. He had completed courses in New South Wales and the elite school at Bonegilla before joining Z Special Unit in December 1943. Since then he had also qualified as a parachutist and he'd taken easily to the training in folboats. He was ready for any eventuality.

David Gooley joined up in January 1940 and was promoted to the rank of sergeant by the time he was selected for signals training at Bonegilla in April 1942. From there he found a place in the guerrilla warfare school in Victoria and on completion of the course took on the Canungra jungle training school in Queensland. He transferred to Z Special Unit in June 1944.

Doug Warne had been a station hand when he joined up in Dirranbandi on the Queensland and New South Wales border in August 1941 and he'd never knuckled under to army regulations. His mates told him he looked a bit like Errol Flynn and he didn't argue; but he was far less agreeable with the sergeants and warrant officers who tried to tell him what he could and couldn't do. He'd been a private, a corporal, a trooper, a lance corporal; he'd gone AWOL more than once; he'd had more than a few fights and he'd even been hospitalised with acute appendicitis. But he had also become a first-class mechanic: he could fix anything. Give him a job that tested him—like the one he had with Ivan Lyon—and there was no stopping him.

BY NOW Roma Page had returned to Canberra and, like the rest of the loved ones, could only wait and hope. 'At the end of his leave,' she said, 'Bob took me to the Flinders Street Station and put me on the train. He said to me, "I'm not going away again. This is the last time".'

As Ivan had promised, the boys planned to be home for Christmas. But the boys closest to him—Davidson and Page—were not quite so sure.

Davidson told Nancy: 'I must go with Ivan.'

Page said: 'I can't let him down.'

Then, like Nemesis, Commander Branson struck again. The operation was almost cancelled when he committed another breach of security—unforgivable this time—by revealing details of Operation Rimau to an American woman whom he had just met at the Peppermint Grove Hotel in Perth. In response to a question from her about Ivan Lyon, Branson had told her that Lyon was about to set off on a mission bound for Singapore. Fortunately, the woman worked for the American commander Admiral Christie, one of Ivan Lyon's biggest fans, and she immediately informed him about Branson's life-threatening loose talk.

As Rimau was an entirely Anglo-Australian operation, Christie had no particular axe to grind but he summoned Shadwell, Marsham and Lyon and bluntly informed them about Branson's stupidity. Both Shadwell and Marsham thought that the security of the mission had been so badly compromised that it should be called off. Lyon disagreed. The information had gone no further than Admiral Christie, he said, so the real damage was negligible. Marsham blustered that it might be too dangerous for him to pick the team up after they had carried out the raid, but Lyon wasn't fazed, replying quietly that, in that case, they would find some other way back.

Reluctantly, Shadwell gave the go-ahead on 6 September on behalf of Mountbatten and the commander-in-chief of the Eastern Fleet. Three days later Lyon and Chapman went over 'Fremantle Submarine Operational Order No. 1' with Marsham in Shadwell's presence. This scheduled the submarine's role in the entire Rimau mission, from setting the party down at Merapas Island to picking it up again during the night of the 7th and 8th of November. Chapman and Carey would supervise the unloading of the Rimau party, return to Australia with the submarine to organise their 'extraction', then go back into the operational area to ensure that the men were safely recovered. The orders were explicit; there was no room for any misunderstanding.

On the Rimau saboteurs' final night in Australia, a marquee was set up at their base and the men held a farewell party for the crew of *Porpoise*, the Garden Island Naval Base staff and an assortment of friends, including the girls who operated searchlights on a hill overlooking the coastal defence battery. The following day *Porpoise* was made ready for departure and that afternoon—at 12.20 p.m. on 11 September 1944—the mighty submarine sailed into Cockburn Sound with the twenty-two members of Operation Rimau plus the two Conducting Officers on board.

The Sleeping Beauties had finally been loaded into the submarine through the forward hatch and accommodated in empty torpedo compartments, something that Marsham had originally maintained was impossible. This meant that Chapman's J containers, over which hundreds of hours had been wasted, could be used to carry stores on the submarine's hull, thus creating more room on board *Porpoise*. The revised loading procedure enabled Lyon to take all fifteen SBs, as well as 14½ tons of operational stores, eleven folding assault boats, no fewer than four full-strength Boston Mark II radio transmitter/receivers and six walkie-talkies.

There was also a detailed signal plan, though documentary evidence of its existence has been extraordinarily difficult to obtain. In every copy of the Rimau material deposited in the National Archives of Australia—at least five separate filings—the signal plan is referred to as appearing in an appended 'Folio 4' of six appendices. However, in every case Folios 1 to 3 and 5 to 6 are present. Folio 4 is absent.

In each case it appears to have been deliberately removed before the file was deposited. However, by chance discovery of a filing lapse, a single copy was uncovered in an Operation Hornbill folder. Headed 'TOP SECRET, Signal Plan "Rimau" Project' it is dated 12 August 1944. It gives the Call Signs—ACF for the Outstation Rimau, KON for Base Station Darwin. It gives the frequencies day and night. Other details include:

Contacts—the base station will maintain continuous watch between 1300Z and 2300Z on [frequency] 999Z Kc/s and between 2300Z and 1300Z on 1447Z Kc/s.

The outstation may call the base station at any time using the appropriate frequency at the time of day as stated above and the base station will reply on the appropriate frequency.

All times shown on the signal plan are to be considered as 'Z' time (GMT).

Procedure—Commercial procedure only will be used. Plain language will not be used either as messages or as talk between operators.

Identity of Message—The first and second groups of the text will constitute the identity of the message.

Request to Check Enciphering of a Message—The letter 'Y' followed by the identity of a message denotes that the enciphering message is to be checked.

Priority Prefixes—The following prefixes in the preamble will denote priority: B—Important; F—Immediate; J—Most Immediate. The priority prefix will be signalled in the initial offer of a message and again immediately before the number of groups in the transmission of the message.

Cipher—Cipher keys and tables will be handed to OC Rimau prior to departure. He and such of his personnel as he details will be personally briefed in the use of the Cipher.

Signal Plan Walkie-talkies—This is to be arranged between OC Rimau and OC Submarine according to requirements.

This was the Rimau lifeline. It was the creation of Ivan Lyon himself. It provided him and the men whose lives he controlled with a twenty-four hour guardian in Darwin, and through it access to the RAF long-range Catalina flying boats based in Ceylon and India; to the RAAF re-established in Darwin after the Japanese had lost control of the skies over the northern capital; and to the United

States Air Force which now had the upper hand as MacArthur smashed through the enemy defences and landed in the Philippines.

The RAAF had established a list of 'rescue points' in association with the Netherlands Forces Intelligence Service (NFIS) and in mid-1944 they had been working together to revise it. The Director of the NFIS, Lieutenant Colonel S.H. Spoor, wrote to his opposite number in RAAF Intelligence, attaching the current list of places in the former Dutch East Indies where downed pilots—and other allied servicemen—could be rescued by flying boat. There were forty-two points in all, ranging from the Celebes in the north to Timor in the south—a blanket coverage of the Rimau area of operation.

On 18 June 1944 Squadron Leader S. Jamieson, the RAAF Intelligence Officer for North-Western Area (NWA) based in Darwin, wrote:

> Four conferences were held at this section about a month ago when the list of points in NWA was thoroughly revised and cut down by about half. The conferences were attended by Air Force Intelligence Office, Target Officer, Military Intelligence Section representative, Far Eastern Liaison Office representative, Dutch Liaison Officer and Major Kremer (one conference).

The revised list, he says, was then distributed to the appropriate intelligence sections throughout the Allied forces.

Did Ivan Lyon have a copy when HMS *Porpoise* left Fremantle and headed north toward Lombok Strait? Did he even have the codebook that would allow him to make contact with his Darwin base guardian? There have been suggestions that his codebook was found on the bed in his Melbourne quarters after he had departed for Fremantle for the final time. The evidence offered is a statement from the Rimau cipher clerk, Staff Sergeant Mary Ellis, who had worked out the code with Lyon—a one-off code based on a particular page of the book. She says she found the volume after Lyon had departed and identified it as the Rimau codebook.

The story was taken up by Alan Powell in his *War by Stealth* with the statement, 'Probably it was true, as Rimau's cipher clerk suspected, that Lyon had determined that nothing should enable the party to be recalled—but neither could they alter any detail of the return rendezvous arrangements with the submarine.'

Rimau's course was set. There was to be no going back. But not for these reasons.

# CHAPTER 11
# CLOSING IN

AS HMS *PORPOISE* headed north towards the deep green waters of the Java Sea, with an increasingly touchy Hubert Marsham at the helm, the Rimau raiders took stock of their armaments. In addition to the small arms issued to each man they carried Bren guns, 9 mm Sten guns fitted with silencers, hand grenades and an anti-tank gun to take out any enemy craft attacking the junk that Rimau intended to purloin. The key to the mission's success, however, was that none of these weapons would ever be used.

The targets for attack specified in Lyon's orders were Singapore's man-of-war and explosives anchorages, shipping at Keppel Harbour and the Empire Dock, and the wharves at Bukum and Sambu islands. It was a huge, high-risk undertaking, but one that could produce enormous dividends for the Allied cause.

To overcome the Sleeping Beauties' fifty kilometre range limit, the Rimau party would capture a junk off the coast of Borneo and, after loading the Sleeping Beauties on board, anchor it for twenty-four hours in the Bay of Kepala Jernith on the night of 9 October 1944, to allow an officer to carry out a reconnaissance from Subar Island which had served as Jaywick's forward observation post. Two canoes would travel north to the vicinity of Labon Island to find a secret mooring for the junk and another canoe would proceed to Subar to pick up the officer.

Shortly after dark on 10 October the crew would move the junk to an attack base at Labon and the commandos would take to the Sleeping Beauties, attaching limpet mines to Japanese ships, sinking thirty of them and damaging thirty more. They would then scuttle the Sleeping Beauties and the junk in deep water and escape to their base on Merapas Island, one hundred kilometres to the east of Singapore, in the two-man folboat canoes.

Under cover of darkness, *Porpoise* surfaced and raced through the Lombok Strait into the Java Sea at full speed, then travelled under water through Karimata Strait into the South China Sea. It was the same route that the *Krait* had taken the previous year and the Jaywick men on board remarked that it was somewhat quicker this time round.

It was also the first time that a Royal Navy submarine had re-entered these waters since the Japanese had bundled Britain out of its Far Eastern colonies. This was a matter of great satisfaction to Ivan Lyon, but he quickly discovered that it was not a pleasure he could share with the captain. Commander Marsham was psychologically unfit for duty and should never have been allowed to take charge of the drop-off operation. In fact, he was on the edge of a nervous breakdown.

Nevertheless, on 23 September *Porpoise* arrived without incident off Merapas, a thickly wooded island measuring 1.5 kilometres long by one kilometre wide and located at the eastern extremity of the Riau Archipelago. When Marsham surveyed the beaches and coconut plantation through his periscope everything appeared deserted, so at dusk the submarine surfaced and Commander Davidson and Corporal Stewart paddled ashore.

They spent the next twenty-four hours inspecting the island and Davidson drew a map of its main features, including a distinctive tree in which they had slung their hammocks for a few hours sleep. He called it the Hammock Tree. They were picked up by *Porpoise* the following night and reported that Merapas was indeed suitable as a rear base for their operations.

*Porpoise* retired to deeper water for the night but when Marsham brought her back to Merapas the following afternoon to unload stores, he spotted three Malays sitting beside a canoe on the beach. It was thought that the men were probably just visitors and *Porpoise* moved to the opposite end of the island where the Rimaus unloaded their supplies at a secluded beach.

Lyon decided then, however, that instead of leaving the stores unguarded, as previously planned, one of the conducting officers, Lieutenant Carey, would remain on Merapas to protect the stores from passing fishermen and any other itinerants who happened to be in the area. But leaving Carey on Merapas presented Lyon with another problem. It was already clear to him that Marsham would not be capable of making the return journey from Fremantle to Merapas, which meant that Chapman would become the sole officer with responsibility for recovery of the Rimau party. Every man's life would depend on Walter Chapman.

It couldn't be helped.

Lyon buried any misgivings about Chapman's reliability beneath the organisational demands of the unloading exercise. The 14½ tons of stores had to be separated into discreet units for Merapas and the junk they planned to capture. When it was completed there was a little more room in the crowded submarine and that was good for morale. With each passing day the time for action approached and the men were keyed up.

Bob Page had taken effective control of the Australian contingent. He was more approachable than either Lyon or Davidson and became the conduit to and from command. His easy manner and ready laugh worked wonders in the stifling conditions of the sub.

Once the unloading was complete *Porpoise* set off to find a suitable junk to deliver the Rimaus and the Sleeping Beauties to the target areas but for several days she prowled the trade route between the Riau Archipelago and the west coast of Borneo without success. Their luck seemed to change on 28 September when the *Mustika*, an 18 metre, 40 ton Indonesian *tonkan*, or junk, was spotted about fifty kilometres off Pontianak, Borneo.

The *Porpoise* surfaced and the officer of the deck ordered the junk to heave-to. The nine Malay crew offered no resistance when Ivan Lyon and a boarding party took possession of the vessel and herded them into the submarine as prisoners to be taken back to Fremantle. Lieutenant Ross, a Cambridge graduate with first class honours in Natural Sciences and Anthropological Studies, wrote a report on the sortie for Chapman to take back with him.

The master and the other members of the crew had their families at Ketapang. They said they were all married.

Several members of the crew complained of general ill-treatment by the Japanese. They said that a Japanese expected them to make obeisance (*hormat*) in the streets and would hit them over the head if they did not do so. They complained of large numbers of their people in prison, especially chiefs and rajas, of whom many had been killed. Their knowledge of conditions on the Malay Peninsula seemed to be very vague... the master, Mohamed Yuni, told me that Japanese patrol boats were practically non-existent off the Borneo coast and that interception was not frequent. He had not seen an aeroplane for four days.

When the *Porpoise* surfaced alongside the *Mustika* the crew first of all took us to be Japanese and expected us to board and, after inspection, to pull away again. They then noticed that we were wearing berets and had white skins. Their principal reaction was that they had nothing to do with our war and considered that we should have taken a Chinese junk for preference. Their greatest concern was, naturally enough, for their families.

Under the original plan, the crew were to be 'disposed of' but decency prevailed and they were returned to Perth where, after a period in the local jail—for operational security reasons—they were released into the community and, after the war, repatriated to Malaya.

All the Rimaus went on board the *Mustika* and hoisted sail to follow *Porpoise* to deserted Pedjantan Island, midway between the Linnga Archipelago and Pontianak, where the Sleeping Beauties and explosives could safely be transferred. The *Mustika*, however, had no engine and without motorised power the Rimaus were entirely at the mercy of the wind. Almost streamlined compared with the familiar squat shape of Chinese junks, she moved along at 1.8 knots when the breeze caught her two sails. It was some compensation that the Rimaus were able to hitch a tow from *Porpoise* when she surfaced at night, but their inability to move independently of the wind must have been a major concern to Lyon. Even the *Krait* had been more mobile than this.

The two vessels arrived at Pedjantan on 29 September and the next two days were spent transferring all operational equipment to the *Mustika* and making her as seaworthy as possible. Among the equipment were two flags which had been made in Australia especially for the mission, the Japanese Rising Sun and the *Osame Gunsai Kambu*, a flag of similar design but with the addition of Japanese characters standing for 'Shonan Military Administration Headquarters'.

*Porpoise* and *Mustika* parted company at 10 p.m. on 30 September, with the heavily laden junk setting a westerly course for Singapore while the submarine headed back to Fremantle. *Mustika* was not, however, flying either flag. Ivan Lyon intended to give the impression that she was a local boat; the flags would only be waved from the deck if she attracted the attention of patrolling aircraft.

Realising that Carey couldn't be expected to watch over the stores twenty-four hours a day, Lyon headed back to Merapas and dropped off three of the Rimau commandos, Warrant Officer Warren, Sergeant Cameron and signaller Corporal Craft.

The pick-up plan was clear to all parties: the Rimaus would return to Base A on Merapas Island after the strike and would be rescued by *Porpoise* on the night of 7/8 November. If the submarine failed to make contact with them that night, it would continue returning to Merapas every night for thirty nights until 8 December. As necessary, contact would be made with the submarine commander via the walkie-talkie radios.

The six walkie-talkies were seven kilogram backpacks containing thirty-eight batteries each. They were powerful enough to reach the submarine from a considerable distance and there were enough to go round whenever they were separated into groups. Recognition signals were fixed, along with procedures for stragglers. Over the next few days the Rimau party in *Mustika* sailed from Pedjantan Island and made their way to Laban Island via the Temiang and Sugi Straits without incident. Laban, located twenty kilometres south-south-west of Keppel Harbour, was the forward point from which the attack was to be launched.

Singapore was just over the horizon. It had experienced monumental changes since February 1942.

By now the Japanese had settled into their new colony, which they administered through the Shonan Special Municipality with Japanese civilians as executive heads of all the departments. These executive heads could be recognised by the five stars sewn on to a small piece of cloth pinned to their right breasts; the stars were coloured blue, yellow and white and the ranking was in that ascending order. Their full dress uniforms were almost identical with those of army officers. Most were former residents of Singapore and Malaya and could speak quite good English and Malay. Their staff was composed mostly of former employees of the previous Singapore Municipality and the language in all the departments and most of the Japanese commercial firms was English.

The Electrical Department had been taken over by Nippon Hassoden in 1943 but continued to be run by the same staff and under the British system. All food was under price and distribution control by the Japanese but the system had become completely corrupt and a black market flourished.

Labour for military establishments was recruited mainly through advertisements and posters. But there was always an underlying threat of forced labour for new airfields, jungle clearing or conscription to the armed forces. A volunteer force, called *Giyu-gun* and composed mostly of Malays, had been formed for the defence of the island and was trained by Japanese officers on almost the same lines as their own soldiers. Many efforts were made to get the Chinese to join the volunteers or to form their own unit, but without success. By August 1944 the volunteer force was only about one thousand strong.

A few hundred Malay boys, aged sixteen to eighteen, had also been recruited by the *Kempei Tai* and after six months training in small arms, the Japanese language and spying techniques were turned out as informers attached to various military police stations.

The other local military arm, the *Heiho*, was quite separate, though it too was a voluntary movement. It was more of a labour force which in times of emergency could be trained up to military readiness. Again, most of the 8000 membership were Malays. The Chinese wanted none of it.

Singapore's main revenue stream was from gambling, opium and private taxation in that order. So-called 'gambling farms' had been opened at the former Great World and Happy World amusement parks where all forms of gambling were available with unlimited stakes. It was there that the Chinese population made its major contribution, however unwittingly and unwillingly, to the Japanese war effort.

When the leaders of the Rimau raid approached Singapore Harbour they knew a great deal about their target which hadn't been available to Jaywick. Intelligence reports used in their briefing recorded 'a constant concentration of cargo ships and tankers between July and the beginning of September'.

It was customary for the waiting ships to disperse during the day and regroup during darkness in the western approaches to Keppel Harbour. In fact, the Japanese were terrified of Allied submarine activity, though there is no evidence that either the Americans or the British ventured close to the harbour itself.

According to a Japanese army officer, part of the Japanese fleet, including one battleship, two heavy cruisers, three light cruisers and a number of destroyers were *en route* to Singapore Harbour. Seven floating docks had been constructed, three at Tanjong Pagar and four at the naval base. In addition, there was a large graving dock and a large admiralty dock, while a new graving dock was under construction just around the corner from the old one.

Efforts had been made to organise a coast-watching system but it remained haphazard and unreliable. As the Japanese response to

Jaywick showed, they were much more concerned about the likelihood of internal sabotage than the intrusion of a commando force. Indeed, scores of Malay dock workers had been rounded up for questioning in the 'Double Tenth' purge and many did not survive. But the Rimau raiders would discover to their cost that sea patrols around the island maze had been stepped up, with many of the craft manned by *Heiho* volunteers.

It was a dangerous situation. The Japanese had increased surveillance since the success of Operation Jaywick by converting junks and small boats into counterespionage units in their immediate region. They provided extra native patrols with radios. Their coast-watch system was producing some results, particularly when they started offering cash rewards.

The Japanese and their native recruits scrutinised the flags carried on all vessels for indication of the ship's origin and whether it was on officially approved business, in which case the Japanese 'poached egg' had to be shown. In Javan and Malayan waters it had to be accompanied by the Red Anchor on a white background and it is doubtful whether Lyon had been told of this. Although they had two flags in their kit, *Mustika* was flying no flags at all.

IVAN LYON and his men, however, were unaware of this as they went over the attack plan one last time on the night of 9 October. Their only concern was the job at hand: a swipe of the tiger's paw across the pitiless face of the aggressor. They had anchored *Mustika* off Kepala Jernith at the southern end of the Phillip Channel to drop off two reconnaissance parties, one of which would remain in place until just prior to the raid.

Four commandos in two folboats paddled first to Labon, eleven kilometres away, and while two of them returned to *Mustika* to report that the island would be a suitable spot for unloading the SBs, the other two, Bobby Ross and Happy Huston, carried on to Subar Island, the Jaywick observation point a further eleven kilometres towards Singapore where they were to spend the next day spying on shipping in Singapore Harbour. For Huston, it was the second time he had performed this task in thirteen months. He must have been praying that things would go as smoothly this time.

The following morning Lyon moved *Mustika* away from Kepala Jernith towards the cluster of islets off the coast of Batam Island. It was the day of the attack and he had some time to kill.

# CHAPTER 12
# DEATH IN THE AFTERNOON

JUST SIXTY minutes before the Rimau raid was due to begin on the afternoon of 10 October 1944, the crewmen on the *Mustika* were travelling slowly through a narrow stretch of water between Kasu and Sambu islands when they were spotted by members of the Malay *Heiho*. The junk had been forced close to shore by the activity of a Japanese naval task force, including Cruiser Division 16 which was exercising in the area in preparation for the Battle of the Philippines.

There were many warships in the Phillip Channel near Kepala Jernith Bay on the course that Lyon had planned to reach his Singapore targets. It was no place for a lightweight junk loaded down with men, arms, explosives and Sleeping Beauties as enemy destroyers created great bow waves that threatened to swamp her.

Also, a heavy tropical rainstorm—known as a 'Sumatra'—struck that afternoon and tidal currents made navigation hazardous. So it made sense to take shelter and drift in the lee of the tiny islands to wait three hours for the darkness that would cloak their advance on Singapore. Now, in the late afternoon, the wind had dropped and the Rimaus were almost becalmed.

For the last few days the raiders on the *Mustika* had been covering themselves in the brown dye issued to each man in Fremantle so they could pass for native Malay sailors, at least at a distance. It stank and it was sticky. For the Jaywick veterans—Lyon, Davidson, Page, Falls, Marsh and Huston—it was simply part of the drill. But the newcomers were unused to the strictures necessary for survival in enemy territory.

The dye might change the colour of a crewman but it could do nothing for his size and the former architect Major Reginald 'Otto' Ingleton, with his one hundred kilogram bulk, might well have found himself on deck as the *Mustika* drifted slowly around the headland of Kasu and into the villagers' line of sight. He regarded it as his duty to put his architectural sketching skills to the service of his country and the Japanese warships exercising off the port bow might well have tempted him on deck and held him engrossed.

As with Jaywick, the drill was that only three men would be on deck at any one time and when there was a good chance they could be observed the slim, dark-haired types such as Lyon and Page would be preferable.

In any case, *Heiho* Chief Sidek bin Safar spotted something distinctly European on the vessel that demanded further investigation. So he put out in his small motorised barge with his three

Malay recruits and a local Chinese, Ati, who spoke English, to intercept the junk.

Lyon had a plan for just such a development. A Malay speaker, preferably himself, would entice them aboard and they would be taken below. Once captured they could be dealt with according to the needs of the moment—either persuaded to throw in their lot with the raiders or discreetly and permanently silenced as casualties of war.

It was risky but it was infinitely preferable to the alternative— the abandonment of an enterprise that had been months in the planning and which carried the hopes of an empire teetering on the brink of dismemberment. For once the empire fell apart it could never again be reassembled; its separate parts would take root in the soil of self-determination and the days of glory would all be in the past.

However, the Lyon plan was never given a chance. When the sound of the approaching motorboat reached the *Mustika* at approximately 1700 hours Tokyo time—1530 in Singapore— someone on deck panicked and, perhaps mistaking the launch for a Japanese patrol, began firing at the men in the approaching vessel. As the shots echoed across the water, they sounded disaster for Rimau. But there was still something to be saved if all of the approaching *Heihos* could be accounted for—a Bren and five Sten guns opened fire from *Mustika* and in a moment the three *Heiho* privates were dead. Ati leapt overboard followed by Sidek bin Safar and they protected themselves from the hail of bullets behind the barge. Slowly they made their way ashore.

They had something to report.

Immediately after the shooting, villagers watching from the shore saw the *Mustika* move into deeper water about one hundred metres from the drifting barge. Aboard the junk the emotion would have been overpowering. Every member of the team had driven himself through the most demanding physical and psychological pain barriers over the past several months. For the men it was the most dangerous mission they would ever undertake, no matter how long they lived.

For Bob Page, it was the chance to strike back at the evil men who had taken his father into captivity and visited upon him the most terrible agony and humiliation. And now, suddenly, the fifteen Australian soldiers who had come to depend on him were themselves exposed to the real possibility of capture and worse.

For Ivan and Donald, the sons of empire, it was a fierce and shocking blow. But there was so much to be done that the time for recrimination would have to be postponed. And there was still a chance to strike a blow at the Japanese.

Action was the answer, action sharp and swift.

'We haven't come all this way,' Ivan believed, 'to just give up at the first hurdle.' It simply wasn't part of the Lyon character. Even as he helped with the furious loading of the ten folboats and a large rubber craft carried on deck to hold a large quantity of supplies, a plan was forming. Limpet mines and the two Japanese flags were among the goods that went into the rubber boat. By the time the men had taken to the folboats and the *Mustika* had been scuttled with a powerful explosive, smashing the Sleeping Beauties to smithereens, the new plan was full-blown.

Ivan Lyon, Don Davidson, Pat Campbell, Doug Warne and Clair Stewart would paddle the rubber boat to Subar, where Ross and Huston were still keeping watch on Japanese shipping. Three of the folboats, under the command of Lyon, Davidson and Ross, would then continue the operation, dashing into the harbour before the alarm could be raised, mining their targets in the tried and true methods of Jaywick, then reassembling on Pangkil Island in the Riau Group.

Depending on circumstance, one team would strike out to attack the Japanese fleet anchorage in the Riau Archipelago south of Bintan Island, where some really big fish awaited. Meanwhile, the twelve other Rimaus under the command of Bob Page would make for Base A on Merapas Island and be reunited with Carey's four-man caretaker party. The fightback had begun.

The magnitude of the Rimau raids on Singapore is difficult to assess but some facts are undeniable. A series of explosions rocked Keppel Harbour and its environs on the night of 10 October 1944, several hours after the Rimaus were spotted. Villagers in islands scattered around the harbour entrance reported hearing blasts that night but Japanese Navy records, which list combatant and non-combatant ships sunk or damaged in the immediate region due to Allied activities at that time, do not mention any casualties. The only damage noted was that sustained by the heavy cruiser *Aoba* while tying up alongside another ship the following day.

There seems no doubt, however, that Ivan Lyon pressed on with a conventional limpet mine attack on the harbour and blew up three ships. A Japanese signal was later intercepted naming Lyon and referring to the sinking of the ships, and there are three unexplained wrecks off Singapore on Admiralty charts.

More importantly, however, the Japanese have admitted that they demolished all wrecks that were obstructing wharves and waterways around the harbour that night—a huge, noisy undertaking that would have provided perfect cover for Ivan Lyon and his fellow saboteurs to slip in unnoticed and place limpet mines on Japanese ships while their guards were distracted by the sound of authorised explosions.

Claims that the Rimaus caused serious damage to Japanese shipping also gain weight from the fact that the men virtually disappeared for almost four days after being unmasked. They went on the run off Kasu Island in the Riau Archipelago at dusk on 10 October—a Tuesday—but apart from a vague report that in midweek some white men were seen on Batam Island, just south of Singapore, there were no definite sightings of them until Saturday 14 October 1944 when they were spotted on Pangkil Island. A Malay informant named Raja Mun noticed white men on the island and reported them to the Japanese authorities. He received twenty dollars for his pains.

The following day in Australia the first Japanese naval message was intercepted by the Ultra code-breakers. From the commander of Special Base Force 10 in Singapore to his unit commanders in the region, it read:

About twenty people including Caucasians have been engaged in a defensive stand in the northern part of Riau Archipelago since the 10th of October. They penetrated by means of (unintelligible). Thenceforth they dispersed using sampans and rubber boats and are continuing to infiltrate into every part of the Riau Archipelago. The penetration into Pangkil, four miles east of Kurus, has been confirmed. Even though the Army is at present searching them out, maintain strict watch in Riau Archipelago and Bulan Straits.

The implications could scarcely have been clearer to the SOA controllers in Melbourne: Rimau was in deep trouble. The lives of twenty-three British and Australian soldiers were in peril. Something must be done. But what? Apparently they were scattered across the Riau Archipelago. That was a good tactical move from Lyon—throw the enemy into confusion and scatter the defensive forces ranged against him. But until they had reassembled and made contact themselves there was little that SOA could do to assist.

The chances were that the Rimaus would follow the plan and, by roundabout routes, make for Base A at Merapas. And that was where the submarine would pick them up. It was up to the men of Rimau to hold out until then.

Once the Japanese had been alerted to the presence of Allied commandos in the Kasu area, however, an infantry company of one hundred men under the command of Major Fujita from Singapore Garrison was thrown into the hunt. According to entries in the Japanese War Diary, Fujita's resources included the Third Vessel Transport Headquarters, one patrol boat, five motorised landing barges and members of the *Kempei Tai* water police. Divers were also sent down off Kasu Island at the site where the Rimaus blew up the *Mustika* with the Sleeping Beauties in her hold, but nothing was recovered.

Meanwhile, the violent methods of the Japanese search parties created havoc among Malays and Chinese in the area and, as well as force, money was used to bribe villagers into parting with information. Japanese desperation to capture the Rimaus reflected the fury and frustration felt by occupying troops in Singapore over the progress of the war, even though they had no way of seeing the overall picture.

It did not look promising. A top-level committee in Tokyo had secretly reported to the Japanese High Command that Japan could not possibly win *Dainiji Sekai Taisen*, as they called World War II, but there was no agreement between the warring army and navy factions about how hostilities might be ended.

Despite propaganda broadcasts to the contrary, it was clear to many members of Japan's fighting forces scattered the length and breadth of South-East Asia that the spectacular victories of 1941 and 1942 were not being repeated in the equatorial spring of 1944— 'Victory Disease', which had seized the Japanese at the outset of war, was very much an ailment of the past.

Japanese forces on Formosa witnessed just how badly the war was going when American bombers staged a massive raid on 12 October 1944. Bombing continued for three consecutive days during which five hundred Japanese aircraft and forty Japanese warships were destroyed for the loss of eighty-nine American aircraft. Many of the Japanese pilots who were killed had only recently completed their training and had been sent to Formosa as Japan's supply of experienced pilots dwindled to crisis point.

The following day MacArthur left Brisbane for America's operations at Leyte, the central Philippines island. Neither he nor his oriental court cared a jot for Singapore and he quickly forgot the land that had welcomed him as a hero. He never returned to Australia.

# CHAPTER 13
# ON THE RUN

LEAVING DON Davidson, Pat Campbell, Happy Huston and Doug Warne on Pangkil Island, Ivan Lyon crossed the Riau Straits with Bobby Ross and Clair Stewart in three of the folboats as daylight faded on 15 October. He was heading for Soreh Island, a flat, egg-shaped outcrop one kilometre long and four hundred metres wide. Rimmed by white beaches and cloaked in palm trees from end to end, it was a marvellous position from which to observe the Japanese fleet anchorage.

The Rimaus were spotted by Abdul Latif, a Malay whose job was to tend the island's coconut plantation and extract its valuable cooking oil. Latif saw the commandos not far from the hut he shared with his wife and child. They wore shirts and trousers in khaki and green and carried Sten guns and pistols.

The presence of the Rimaus on Soreh confirms the belief that Lyon's sabotage team were not retreating directly to Merapas Island after losing the Sleeping Beauties. 'Anyone heading directly back to the submarine rendezvous [at Merapas] wouldn't have been paddling down the middle of the Riau Straits, which was swarming with Japanese naval vessels and highly dangerous,' says Clive Lyon. 'My father would have taken a route further to the north unless he was hell-bent on doing more damage.'

He was indeed. But with each passing hour the odds were stacked further against him. Lyon hadn't counted on Raja Mun's perfidy, which Davidson learned about from a friendly Malay named Raja Rool late on 15 October. Davidson immediately ordered Huston and Warne to head for Tapai Island in a folboat, towing the rubber raft behind them. Then he and Campbell went over to Soreh Island in the middle of the night to warn Lyon that they had been betrayed. The warning came just in time. At about 1400 hours that afternoon heavily armed Japanese troops approached the island in a landing barge.

The Rimau party on Soreh Island numbered only five men, but all were fit and able to fight. As the Japanese barge approached, Lyon took a quick inventory of their armaments: five Sten guns with four hundred rounds of ammunition, five .38 revolvers (twenty-four rounds each) and twelve hand grenades.

Obviously he would have liked more ammunition but it was enough to give a good account of themselves. And if they could score a victory over their pursuers it would give them a chance to disband and make for Merapas.

Despite its advantages as an observation point, however, Soreh was a defensive nightmare—completely flat and with little undergrowth, visibility was excellent from shore to shore. Ivan Lyon placed Davidson, Campbell and Stewart in two relatively unexposed positions on the western side of one of the beaches. One was a small depression with a suitable field of fire back towards the island. Don Davidson was in charge of the second position in a trench five metres by three metres and about half a metre deep, with stones packed along the rim. Lyon and Ross climbed one of the few Ru trees scattered among the palms and overlooking the landing site.

At 1500 hours the Japanese barge dropped its ramp and forty to forty-five Malay *Heiho* under Japanese command with NCOs from the *Kempei Tai* water police came ashore with the intention, according to the Japanese, of making a routine search of the island. Only one small party walked towards the ambush sites, while the bulk of the Japanese unit remained in reserve at the landing point. The Rimaus opened fire, inflicting heavy casualties on the advancing *Heiho* and killing their Japanese officer.

The Japanese 2IC and the remaining *Heiho* responded with rifle and machine-gun fire and a desperate battle ensued for several hours, with the greatly outnumbered Rimaus managing to keep the enemy pinned down. When darkness fell, there was no moon to light the scene and, in the next two hours, Stewart was able to slip away from the beach and find a hiding place on the island without being detected.

But there had been casualties. Davidson and Campbell had both been wounded in the firefight so Lyon and Ross set up a perimeter behind which the two wounded heroes could make their escape. One of them even spoke to Abdul Latif and his wife who were sent by the Japanese to see what was happening. As he spoke to them in Bahasa Malay, this was probably Lyon.

Around 2000 hours that night all hope that Lyon and Ross might be able to hold off the enemy and escape the following morning disappeared when another Japanese barge arrived on Soreh with around fifty reinforcements who immediately opened fire on the Rimaus' position. Although running short of ammunition, Lyon and Ross returned fire and the shooting continued late into the night.

Clive Lyon said: 'The odds were not very good but they held them at bay for about five hours in an horrific gunfight. There seems no doubt that right to the end my father was doing more damage. He wouldn't give up.'

When dawn broke the following morning, the Japanese advanced on the Rimaus' position to find two dead men bearing multiple wounds. Ivan Lyon and Bobby Ross had been killed by a Japanese hand grenade.

And even though Don Davidson and Pat Campbell had managed to escape from Soreh during the battle and paddle eight kilometres to the next refuge, Tapai Island, they were in grievous trouble. Beaching their boat around 1500 hours on Monday 16 October, they managed to take shelter under a rocky ledge where they lay down to rest.

Shortly after daybreak on Tuesday 17 October, they were sighted by a Japanese patrol who found them dead from their wounds.

From that moment, Bob Page was effectively in charge of the Rimau mission. As a captain he might be outranked by Major Ingleton, but the men looked naturally to him for leadership. He was the Jaywick veteran. He was the remaining member of the triumvirate who had conceived and run the show. He was the one they turned to. Even before he knew for certain that he would never see Lyon and Davidson again, he nevertheless had to assume the mantle of leadership. He would keep the sentiment for later.

The only survivor in the gunfight on Soreh Island had been Corporal Clair Stewart, who had gone to ground in the darkness. The Japanese had found the Rimaus' three folboats the following morning and, although unable to get off the island, Stewart somehow succeeded in avoiding capture until 18 October.

All the remaining men from the strike party, with Bob Page's group of Ingleton, Riggs, Sargent, Falls, Fletcher, Gooley, Hardy, Marsh, Pace, Reymond and Willersdorf well out in front, were now heading for Merapas, more than one hundred kilometres from the Riau islands where the guard party of Wally Carey, Alf Warren, Colin Cameron and Colin Craft awaited. Huston and Warne, who had abandoned the rubber craft on Tapai after hearing gunfire from Soreh Island, trailed behind.

Travelling was extremely difficult as the monsoon had come early and they had to paddle in their flimsy craft through tropical rainstorms and swollen seas. But at least that gave them some cover from the growing number of Japanese forces joining the search.

When they finally reached Base A, the first priority was to regroup, to assess their capabilities, then to plan the next phase of the escape. Clearly, their best chance lay with the return of the submarine. It was due in three days time—on the night of the 7/8 of November—and the only real question was whether to break radio silence then to let Darwin know their plight or to wait until the submarine came within range of their walkie-talkies.

Lyon had unloaded at least one of the big Boston transmitter/receivers on Merapas with the rest of the stores. Otherwise there would have been little point in leaving Signaller Craft in the party. This is disputed, however, by Sam Carey, now in his nineties, organiser of the aborted Operation Scorpion and brother of Wally who was on Merapas.

Carey writes: 'It astonishes me that you could assume that the Merapas escapees would have a radio to enable them to report to Melbourne. Authors continue to rewrite history according to their imagination.'

Roma Page, however, is certain that Bob Page would have used whatever means were available to save his men, including the use of the radio. 'He knew his responsibility,' she says. 'He would have done anything to save them.'

If they did use the big transmitter, the records have been expunged, along with the copies of Rimau's radio folio. What cannot be doubted, however, is that there were plenty of walkie-talkies on Merapas to make contact with the submarine. And the captain of the sub, Commander Marsham, would be expecting to hear from them in line with the arrangements made when they were dropped off. The remaining conducting officer, Walter Chapman, would see to that. Or so they believed.

As it happened, there had been a change of plans.

WHILE THESE brave men were desperately trying to stay alive in the maze of Riau, further to the east Douglas MacArthur's hour of destiny in the Philippines had finally arrived. On 18 October American warships shelled Japanese coastal defences on Leyte and, two days later at 1005 hours on 20 October, American soldiers began to swarm ashore on two beachheads near the east coast town of Tacloban. At 1300 hours MacArthur, in a uniform bereft of medals, but wearing his trademark sunglasses and soft cap, stepped from the cruiser USS *Nashville* into a landing barge and ordered it to head for Red Beach, scene of the heaviest fighting.

Fifty metres out from shore, the barge ran aground. The ramp went down and MacArthur, flanked by members of his staff including Richard Sutherland and George Kenney, was photographed striding through the churning surf. Once safely on shore, he announced: 'I have returned.' Hollywood could not have done it better.

Some 132000 US troops came ashore on that first day but although there was little fighting on the beaches, the Japanese garrison of 80000 troops had no intention of surrendering. The following day the cruiser HMAS *Australia* became the first Allied ship to fall victim to a *kamikaze* air attack. She was badly damaged and had to withdraw from the area.

Three days after the landings had commenced, three Japanese naval forces totalling almost the entire Japanese fleet attacked the invading force in what turned into the greatest sea battle in history: the Battle of Leyte Gulf in which the Japanese lost thirty-six warships totalling 300000 tons, compared with American losses of six warships totalling 37000 tons, including the carrier *Princeton*, which was hit by a single bomb and sunk with the loss of more than five hundred men. US planes retaliated with a massive air strike against the giant 72 800 ton Japanese battleship *Musashi*, sinking her with thirteen aerial torpedoes and seven bombs and killing more than a thousand Japanese sailors.

When the smoke cleared, the Japanese still had a few fighting ships afloat but their main hope of protecting the Home Islands now lay with the their new weapon: the 'divine wind' squadrons— the *kamikazes*.

On the great strategic map the Japanese were in desperate straits but in a tiny sideshow in the South China Sea an equally desperate human drama was under way. While the world watched as the rolling Allied tide swept the Japanese back toward their island home, no one, it seemed, was much interested in the fate of Bob Page and his band—least of all the man with the principal responsibility for getting them home safe and sound.

# CHAPTER 14
# THE FIRST BETRAYAL

AS SOON as *Porpoise* had arrived back at the submarine base at Fremantle on 11 October, it was obvious that the stricken Marsham would have to stand down from his command. In fact, he asked to be relieved of duty and Captain Shadwell, seeing the state he was in, unhesitatingly agreed. The vital rendezvous with the Rimau party was passed to HMS *Tantalus*, captained by Lieutenant Commander Hugh Mackenzie of the Royal Navy.

Hugh Stirling Mackenzie—nicknamed 'Rufus' or Red Mackenzie, to distinguish him from another submarine commander, Black Mackenzie—was born on 3 July 1913 at Inverness. He had gone to Dartmouth as a cadet in 1927 and joined the submarine service in 1934. His latest command, *Tantalus*, was a modern T-Class hunter submarine of 1090 tons, with one four-inch gun, and ten 21-inch torpedo tubes, capable of a top speed of fifteen knots. Mackenzie was furious at having been ordered to abandon his patrol duties to pick up a bunch of adventurers from some commando outfit.

Indeed, the figure of Mackenzie, who died an admiral, knighted for services to the national defence, looms over Rimau like a malignant shade. Prior to Rimau he had been on patrol in the Malacca Straits since April 1944 and was fiercely impatient to score some 'kills' on enemy shipping.

He had not had a happy war. Some unseen force higher up the chain of command seemed to keep shutting him out of the action. His record suggests, however, that while he entertained no doubts whatsoever about his own abilities and good judgment, it was not an attitude shared by the Lords of the Admiralty at the time.

At the outbreak of hostilities in 1939 Mackenzie was a lieutenant serving at Fort Blockhouse, Gosport, in the submarine reserves. The two reserve vessels *Oswald* and *Osiris* were quickly recommissioned and, with a crew of reservists, took on stores and headed for the Mediterranean.

Mackenzie joined *Osiris* as first lieutenant and when they reached Alexandria it was only to find that the First Flotilla had left for home waters and *Osiris* was the only British submarine left in the Med. She began a patrol off the Dardanelles but there was no enemy activity.

Mackenzie said later: 'It was very frustrating knowing most of my contemporaries were in home waters and starting to fight the war. I longed to get back into a more operational role.'

When Italy came into the war in June 1940, however, British submarine strength had been reinforced with newer boats, the O/P classes from the China Station together with the depot ship, HMS

*Medway. Osiris* was shunted off to the Aegean but there was nothing doing there either. The next posting was to Malta but the only action Mackenzie found was as a target of high-level Italian bombers.

'We then had a patrol in the Adriatic,' Mackenzie said, 'which I felt was the submariner's dream. There was a constant flow of shipping between the south of Italy and Albania to prosecute the war in Greece and we had lots of targets.' Unfortunately, they had only one 'kill', a small convoy escort, and shortly afterward his captain sent him home the long way—via the Cape of Good Hope—to begin his commander's qualifying course. This he passed with no particular distinction and was then listed as a 'spare CO'. When his first command arrived he was dismayed to discover it was of a World War I vintage *H31* submarine operating from Londonderry in Northern Ireland.

Moreover, as he prepared to take his new command down the river to sea for escort training exercises, he ran into an incoming cargo ship on a routine run from Glasgow to Londonderry. Mackenzie claimed that only his seamanship prevented his vessel being cut in two. He achieved this, he said, 'by actually running into it'. So it was off to Belfast for repairs and Mackenzie relinquished command. Once again, he was a 'spare CO'.

In April 1941 another World War I veteran, *H43*, was entrusted to him. After a refit at Sheerness, he took her to the north of Scotland where he played target in training exercises for the northern coastal command. Later that year he was again removed from his ship to join a mine-laying submarine which took him back to Alexandria, once more as a 'spare CO' in the First Flotilla which had now returned from home waters.

There were three spare COs in HMS *Medway* and he was detailed to act as assistant to staff officer, operations, who controlled the disbursement of submarines within the flotilla—a desk job. But he made the best of it: 'I was among a lot of old friends and it was a very happy time,' he said, 'marred only by the high rate of loss.'

Finally, he took command of a vintage vessel, HMS *Thrasher*, in late 1941 and was soon off on patrol. 'It was quite a nerve-wracking experience,' he said. 'We got into a minefield but managed to wriggle our way out. We saw no major shipping except a schooner which wasn't worth a torpedo, so we came on the surface and fired our gun. She blew up in a sheet of flame, so was obviously carrying fuel.'

His luck held when *Thrasher* was attacking an enemy ship and two bombs dropped from an escorting aircraft actually hit the submarine but failed to detonate. As Mackenzie tells the story, he was at first unaware that he'd been hit. They heard a bang or two but

no great damage was done and we got away. Much later that day, we'd been told to move our patrol position to the Gulf of Taranto when we ran into a slight swell. I was asleep in my bunk at the time and was woken by something going, 'bonk, bonk, bonk', rattling in the casing. I told the officer of the watch to send someone down to see what it was. I received an alarming report back. One bomb was lying on the fore-casing just under the gun and there was a hole under the casing by the gun which seemed to indicate that something had gone into the casing which might be causing this noise...sure enough, there was a 100 lb bomb.

I sent for the First Lieutenant and the Second Coxswain who were responsible for the housekeeping of the casing and told them to drag the first bomb up to the bows and get a sack and lower it over the side.

The first lieutenant, Lieutenant Roberts, and Petty Officer Gould, the second coxswain, did just that, manhandling the bomb into the water while Mackenzie went full astern. Then Roberts and Gould climbed down into the casing and manoeuvred the second bomb to the forehatch, dragged it forward and dropped it overboard. It took forty minutes and all that time the two men knew that Mackenzie might have to dive the submarine and drown them both.

Mackenzie's curious idea of duty was such that all he said in his report about the men's heroism was, 'I should like to bring to your notice Lt Roberts and PO Gould for their excellent conduct when acting as "bomb disposal party".' When he returned from patrol, however, he was ordered by his commander-in-chief, Admiral Sir Andrew Cunningham, to make full recommendations for an award for Roberts and Gould.

'Several months passed, and with them several exciting patrols,' Mackenzie recalled. 'The events of February 16/17th 1942 were almost forgotten when we were shaken, I think that is the right word, by the news that Roberts and Gould had each been awarded the Victoria Cross. A great personal honour to themselves and as they and I felt, also to their fellow submariners.'

In June that year *Thrasher* sank Mussolini's yacht *Diana* (Il Duce was elsewhere) but in August she was almost sunk just north of Port Said. 'We were attacked by a Swordfish aircraft of our own side,' said Mackenzie. *Thrasher* just made it back to Alexandria in a sinking condition. Mackenzie himself was awarded the DSO and Bar for his six war patrols in *Thrasher* when he was credited with sinking 40000 tons of enemy shipping.

Once again he lost his command and became a spare CO, but this time filled the empty hours quite agreeably, appearing in a propaganda film at Elstree Studios and giving the occasional public talk about the incident of the two unexploded bombs.

Then in April 1943 he was sent up to the shipbuilding yards of Barrow-in-Furness to take command of *Tantalus*, which was just coming off the line. A month later the ship was commissioned and crewed. There followed the usual intensive working up on the Clyde and Scapa Flow before a first operational patrol up to Spitzbergen.

*Tantalus* was then assigned to Far Eastern station with the submarine flotilla at Trincomalee, Ceylon. Much to his chagrin, however, he was ordered back to Portsmouth Dockyard to increase the ship's range by having the ballast tanks converted to fuel tanks. This took until the end of the year.

Rufus Mackenzie finally sailed for Trincomalee in February 1944, then on to the Malacca Straits in April. But even that didn't satisfy the restless warrior. 'It was very shallow, hot, dirty water,' he said, 'difficult navigation with sandbanks everywhere and very few targets.' And as if that were not enough, on many of his patrols he was burdened with the landing of 'agents'.

'They were usually dropped off the west coast of Malaya,' he said in a taped interview which was uncovered at the Imperial War Museum. 'One went close in shore and landed them by folboat. We nearly always managed to land them successfully but seldom picked them up and nearly always got surprised by Japanese forces when we tried to reach them.'

For the next few minutes of the interview Mackenzie expatiated on the subject of Japanese torture to wring from the agents the details of their pick-up arrangements. 'Not many of them came back,' he said. 'They were mostly British who had been out in Malaya before the war; some Chinese. Our next task...' And here Mackenzie addresses the interviewer, 'May I interrupt here?'

An electronic expert has stated that 'whatever was spoken thereafter was subsequently wiped'. The evidence suggests that this was done either by Mackenzie himself or at his behest. 'Our next task' was the retrieval of the commandos on Operation Rimau.

The foregoing, however, is more than sufficient to provide a picture of the man responsible for the fate of the commandos and the frame of mind he brought to the task. When *Tantalus* set sail from Fremantle on 16 October, Mackenzie's orders for rescuing the Rimau party were absolutely specific. They are contained in Fremantle Submarine Operation Order No. 1, dated 9 September 1944:

Approximately on D/58 [7 November] the submarine, or another detailed to take *Porpoise*'s place, will return to Merapas

Island for the purpose of rescuing the operational party of 22 men [*sic*]. In the event of the pick-up failing to materialise about the date given, namely D/58 [7 November], the operational party will remain there until D/88 [7 December], after which date they will make such alternative arrangements as are possible to escape.

If that left any room for doubt, Mackenzie was also given written orders stating that 'subject to patrol requirements, HMS *Tantalus* will leave her patrol at dark on 7 November and proceed to the vicinity of Merapas island'.

Moreover, Major Chapman was on board *Tantalus* with an assistant, Corporal Ronald Croton, and if anyone knew how vital it was for the submarine to arrive at the appointed time it was Walter Chapman.

Armed with seventeen torpedoes, *Tantalus* entered the Java Sea via Lombok Strait on 20 October and Mackenzie started scouring the waters through his periscope for Japanese ships.

THE INTREPID Major Fujita had been ordered by his superiors not to return to Singapore without his captives. Acting on a tip-off from a Japanese patrol investigating rifle fire in the area, he caught up with the Rimaus on Merapas Island, where Bob Page's twelve-man party had been reunited with the four caretakers. Huston and Warne also turned up safely from Tapai, giving the Rimaus a total strength of eighteen. Fujita sent a unit to attack Merapas Island in force on 4 November 1944, three days before the *Tantalus* was due. Under Page's orders, the Rimau team split into two groups and took cover. Late in the day Fujita's 2IC, Captain Sungarno, had the misfortune to encounter one group and was shot dead. Lieutenant Orzawa, Sungarno's subordinate, called for reinforcements and Fujita himself arrived with them to supervise the attack next morning.

By then, however, Page and nine of the surviving commandos— Ingleton, Falls, Fletcher, Gooley, Hardy, Marsh, Carey, Warren and Huston—had escaped by folboat to nearby Mapor, a much bigger island some eight kilometres to the north-west. But the second party—Warne, Craft, Pace, Reymond and Willersdorf, under the command of Lieutenant 'Blondie' Sargent—lost contact.

They stayed under cover for another night, then stole two sailing *koleks* which some Malays had moored off Merapas while tending the island's coconut plantation. They headed for Pompong in the hope of pirating a junk and sailing to Australia.

But they had to leave without Gregor Riggs, the cherubic young naval officer who had accompanied the Sleeping Beauties to Australia without any idea where he might end up; and without twenty-one-year-old Colin Cameron. Cut off from their comrades, they were killed by the Japanese on Merapas Island. Both men had created a diversion to enable the others to escape. According to a witness, Abdul Rachman Achap, Riggs ran the length of the island with the Japanese in pursuit and was finally shot three times in the chest. The Japanese, impressed by his heroism, buried him on Merapas in a grave marked by a cross.

The Rimaus also had to abandon a substantial quantity of stores and most of their radio equipment, smashing the big transmitter rather than letting it fall into enemy hands in working order. They also left behind Wally Carey's diary, Otto Ingleton's sketchpad, Bob Page's camera and the two Japanese flags.

These items were taken to Singapore where an interpreter attached to the army's intelligence branch, Hiroyuki Furuta, was already translating the neat notebook that had been retrieved from Donald Davidson's body. Together with Ingleton's sketches and the developed film from Page's camera, Furuta's translations provided the *Kempei Tai* with overwhelming proof that they had stumbled on a major Allied operation.

Meanwhile, Page and the main force waited on Mapor for their rendezvous with the submarine on the night of the 7th of November, then sent men across to Merapas on the appointed night to keep watch at the Hammock Tree between dusk and dawn. They returned to report that there had been no sign of the rescuers. It was a bitter blow. Having been forced to abandon the big radio transmitter/receiver on Merapas, Page had no way of knowing there had been complications at the Fremantle end. As far as he was concerned, Commander Marsham and the *Porpoise* were somewhere in the vicinity.

The arrangement was that they would make contact by walkie-talkie. It is difficult to believe that Page would abandon that lifeline, even in the most extreme circumstances. But if it had been lost in the heat of battle, he had the consolation of knowing that Chapman would be aboard to guide Marsham to the pick-up point. If he had managed to keep one last walkie-talkie then we may be sure that in the extreme he would use it to contact his rescuers to tell them of the Rimaus' new position. If indeed he did so, it was in vain. No walkie-talkie could possibly have reached Lieutenant

Commander Rufus Mackenzie; for the *Tantalus* was many kilometres from the rendezvous. Mackenzie was hunting 'targets' in the South China Sea.

HAVING PASSED into an area he fondly hoped would be a happy hunting ground, Mackenzie spent most of the time at periscope depth searching for Japanese supply vessels. He had no success for seventeen days, then he finally sank a small Japanese merchant ship, the *Taga Maru*. When 7 November arrived, *Tantalus* still had fifteen torpedoes on board and Mackenzie decided to scrap the night time 7 November pick-up date and continue patrolling for another fourteen days until 21/22 November.

He justified this action by claiming that his orders said the Rimau party might expect to be picked up at any time within a month after the initial date. Yet the only room for variation to his written orders was in the phrase 'subject to patrol requirements', which, in view of the absence of the enemy, did not apply. Mackenzie, however, continued to hunt. To add to his frustration, his patrol was interrupted when he was ordered by radio to keep a watch for American pilots who might ditch in the sea after bombing missions over Singapore. He saw neither American aircraft nor American pilots and resumed his patrol with even greater determination.

He had no way of knowing that Japanese sea traffic in the waters off Burma, Malaya and the Dutch East Indies was now restricted largely to junks and that he was, in fact, on a wild goose chase. Nor did he know—for no one from the Ultra operation of Central Bureau and FRUMEL who had intercepted the Japanese messages had told him—that the men who depended on him were in a desperate situation.

Willoughby and the Bataan Gang had moved north with their master on 13 October, but the same rules still applied: nothing could be done to alert the Japanese to the fact that the Allies were reading their telegraphic messages; under no circumstances was Ultra to be compromised.

It is inconceivable that Chapman-Walker would have received the Ultra intercept about Rimau and taken no action, and it is equally improbable that Captain Shadwell saw it either or he would surely have alerted Rufus Mackenzie. It is unknown who actually read the message, mulled over it for perhaps days and then decided it was too hot to pass on to the appropriate commanders. The cover-up on that crucial point is still firmly intact.

While Mackenzie fumed about the lack of targets, American submarines were scoring three of their biggest hits of the war—the Japanese aircraft carrier *Junyo* on 17 November, the battleship *Kongo* on 21 November and the giant carrier *Shinano* on 29 November, the last of which was sunk in Japanese home waters. But a desire to sink enemy ships is no excuse for Mackenzie, who had been sixty kilometres from Merapas Island on the night of 7/8 November. Chapman's actions—or lack thereof—are almost inexplicable.

ON THAT FIRST tense journey in the *Porpoise* to the operational area, Walter Chapman made a native 'joss', or good luck charm, and tossed it off the bridge at night. The next day they found the junk they had been searching for. When they had transferred all the

Sleeping Beauties and stores to *Mustika*, in the lee of Pedjantan Island, Chapman had gone ashore with Lyon, Page, Stewart and four of the Malay crew to explore the area as a possible coast-watching base for the future.

On the eve of their parting he helped arrange for the coxswain on *Porpoise* to bake an ovenful of bread for the Rimaus to take on the junk. He had broken a little finger catching coconuts to load on *Mustika*. He had helped to fix the Merapas rendezvous point under the 'Hammock Tree' during any night from 7 November onwards. He had joined with the *Porpoise*'s crew as Captain Hubert Marsham led them in three cheers for Lyon and his men. He had just time for one last handshake with the leader.

'Best of luck, Ivan,' he said. 'See you at Merapas.'

Lyon replied, 'Well done, Walter, thank you for everything. Don't forget that Hammock Tree.'

After the war Chapman told friends that he took a 'distinct liking' to Rufus Mackenzie when he boarded *Tantalus* for the return journey only four days after reaching Fremantle. Part of the explanation for his role at the rendezvous may be found in Mackenzie's decision, almost immediately, to treat him as a member of the crew required to stand a regular watch. Suddenly, Chapman's task as a Rimau Conducting Officer was compromised. For a character whose natural bent was the role of follower, new loyalties intruded. At sea, a naval captain is the last living despot and Mackenzie was shrewd enough to capitalise on Chapman's weakness.

On 28 October they had passed the island of Mapor travelling on the surface and Chapman could see the outline of Merapas's Wild Cat Hill on the horizon. Then, as Mackenzie resumed his single-minded hunt for 'targets', Chapman was drawn ever closer to his orbit. On the evening of 7 November, with *Tantalus* well positioned to make for the rendezvous, Mackenzie called him in for a 'serious conference'. His message was simple and he put it in simple terms in a subsequent report:

> My main object being offensive action against the enemy, it was obviously improper to abandon the patrol in this state [*i.e.* with fifteen torpedoes still to be fired] in order to pick up the party.
>
> In addition, the orders for the party were that they might expect to be picked up at any time within a month after the initial date, November 8th. For these reasons I decided to delay leaving patrol and carry out the operation until such time as fuel and stores and/or expenditure of torpedoes demanded.

Then in bold hand: 'Major Chapman was naturally consulted and concurred.'

Four days later on 11 November, a few kilometres north-east of Merapas, Mackenzie spied the *Pahang Maru*, an unarmed coastal trader crewed by eleven Malays and one Chinese under the command of a single Japanese soldier. Mackenzie didn't hesitate. He surfaced and, while Chapman recorded the scene with a movie camera, opened fire with the submarine's four-inch gun on the helpless craft.

The first rounds killed the captain and several members of his crew and the next started a fire in the cargo of oil drums which caused the Japanese soldier and the other crew to abandon ship. They were picked up and brought on board *Tantalus*. The Malays were handed over to the captain of a Chinese junk who was fortunate that he hadn't been spotted earlier when Mackenzie was thirsting for a kill. The Japanese was kept on board *Tantalus* as a prisoner of war.

After all these ludicrous shenanigans, with Chapman's military role becoming even less professional as ship's cameraman, Mackenzie patrolled the South China Sea without success for the next nine days. Ironically, he was roaming between Singapore and the Natuna Islands, which were to have been the centre of Hornbill's activities. On 19 November Mackenzie received instructions from headquarters to be on the lookout once again for any American pilots who might ditch in the sea off the Malayan coast. For the second time, Mackenzie mounted a fruitless all-night watch.

*Tantalus* finally arrived off Merapas on 21 November, still carrying the fifteen unused torpedoes and fully two weeks after the desperate heroes of Rimau had been expecting her. At seven o'clock that evening, Mackenzie raised his periscope to study the lie of the land.

Much later that night, Chapman and Corporal Croton, the dark-complexioned Australian bushman turned commando, loaded their folboat with emergency rations and silent Sten guns and pushed off about four hundred metres from shore. They headed for the Hammock Tree. Chapman, however, was frightened by the sound of the surf and tracked the canoe away from the area and around the point to calmer waters. When they landed it was after 1 a.m. and, as they made their way across the slippery rocks, Chapman's strength quickly ebbed. Never an athletic figure, he had been cooped up in a submarine with only a single four-day break for more than two months. And now, suddenly clear of the overbearing Rufus Mackenzie and with the prospect of a confrontation with, at best, an angry Ivan Lyon, his legs turned to jelly.

Drenched with sweat, slime and sea-spray he was scrambling over the slippery black boulders at Dead Coral Beach, falling, hurting himself, fighting back waves of nausea. He didn't want to be here. He wanted to stop, to go back, to leave. Croton raised his Sten gun.

'There's a job to do,' he said.

Chapman's panic attack subsided. He switched on a torch to light the way. Croton ordered him to turn it off. He did.

With Croton's help, he made it into the grove of trees beyond the beach and there they rested—Croton dozing, Chapman in an exhausted sleep—until first light.

When they finally reached the Hammock Tree, they found the area deserted. Under a bush, Croton discovered some pieces of silver paper, probably chocolate wrapping, but that was all—no tracks, no other signs of habitation whatsoever. They climbed Wild Cat Hill behind the rendezvous point but that brought no further clues so they returned to the flats and at the edge of a swamp found two waterholes dug out with dixie tins which remained as balers. Ration tins had been discarded nearby and on a tree branch they found a sweat rag and a bandage.

They followed a path from the waterhole and discovered a lean-to shelter about eight metres long and three metres wide. It had a palm-leaf roof and even a flooring from the same material. There were obvious cooking fires and scattered about were large ration tins which were part of the stores unloaded from *Porpoise*.

Other evidence of the Rimau party were empty Three Castle brand cigarette packets and a sign carved on a nearby tree in what looked like Japanese characters.

But they could find neither a message nor any evidence of a fight. After a while, they left the area and walked toward the other end of the island where they saw two or three Malays in the distance, apparently working their coconut plantation. For reasons best known to himself, Chapman decided against approaching them; instead he and his corporal veered off to the other side of the swamp and there they discovered eight one-man shelters, each with Rimau commando cookers with half-cooked food over extinguished wood fires. Two other shelters would have been suitable protection for folboats.

Again, there were no signs of combat.

Chapman was exhausted again and could do little more than wait for the *Tantalus* to show up. When the submarine's silhouette loomed up from the sea at 2000 hours, they were ready with the folboat to return.

Back on board, Chapman reported his findings to Mackenzie who, according to the Rimau Conducting Officer, replied, 'Perhaps we ought to have put in on the 8th. They might still have been there.'

It did not occur to either man, it seems, to return the next morning, round up the two or three Malays and ask them if anything untoward had occurred on the island. Nor did they discuss the possibility of landing a larger boat party that night or returning, as previously arranged, on subsequent nights when a member of the team might have arrived from a hiding place on one of the nearby islands. Nor did they even circumnavigate the island that night looking for signals from the Rimau survivors.

Instead, they sailed away. Mackenzie was on the hunt again, for 'targets'. Indeed, on the 28th, he spotted a small convoy and carried out an attack. His torpedoes missed. The following day he turned for home.

In his report, he records his decision to abandon the Rimau men with monumental hypocrisy: 'It was a very bitter disappointment to Major Chapman and a blow to us all,' he wrote. 'It is to be hoped that the delay in carrying out the operation was not the cause for the loss of this gallant party, but it must be considered a possibility.'

Walter Chapman had a lot of explaining to do. *Tantalus* had just berthed when he and Croton were whipped off the dock to SRD headquarters on Garden Island for debriefing. As the officer in charge of the pick-up party, Chapman's version of events was accepted as gospel over the word of a mere corporal, yet his first report on the abortive mission, dated 12 December 1944, was dishonest in every important detail. He did not admit that Mackenzie had consulted him about the delay in the pick-up, nor did he mention that Croton had threatened to shoot him.

Knowing that his SRD superiors would never see the original, Chapman even retyped Mackenzie's two-page report and attached it to his own as 'Appendix 1 to report of sixth war patrol of HMS *Tantalus*'. Whereas Mackenzie had written, 'It is to be hoped that the delay in carrying out the operation was not the cause for the loss of this gallant party, but it must be considered a possibility,' Chapman typed, 'It is to be hoped that the delay in carrying out the operation was not the cause for the loss of this gallant party, but it is, unfortunately, very possible.' The change indicated that Mackenzie was accepting responsibility for the fate of the Rimau party.

Chapman did, however, faithfully reproduce Mackenzie's final paragraph:

Major Chapman deserves more than a word of credit; his co-operation, advice and assistance in all matters have been invaluable. After thirty-one days at sea in *Porpoise* and then only four days in harbour before joining *Tantalus* one might have thought he would be rather tired of submarines. The reverse appears to be the case and his pleasant company has been a great asset.

Chapman's main concern was to make SRD believe that even if the pick-up party had arrived on 7/8 November, it would have been too late to rescue them. He maintained that mangoes, coconuts, bananas, palm leaves and decaying food found on Merapas Island were at least two weeks old. His thorough search, he claimed, had proved that the Rimau team had abandoned the island some time earlier and that they were nowhere near it. The most likely scenario, according to Chapman, was that 'Lieutenant Carey was taken off the island by the enemy, his presence having been given away by the Malays, before the main party started arriving. The main party was then picked up individually as they arrived on the island. The enemy removed the stores at the same time as removing Lieutenant Carey.'

This was pure conjecture and it couldn't have been further from the truth. Bob Page and the other Rimaus were safe on the next island, Mapor, and as the orders had decreed Page had maintained a picket on Merapas from dusk to dawn each night. They had missed the submarine on the night of 21 November because Mackenzie, ignoring the careful instructions in his orders, had surfaced *Tantalus* on the wrong side of the island. Then Chapman and Croton had not arrived at the Hammock Tree until after daybreak on 22 November.

By that time Page's sentries had already returned to Mapor and reported that there had been no sign of the submarine or the rescuers. The watchers also missed Chapman and Croton that night when *Tantalus* arrived to collect them because the pick-up point was out of sight on the southern side of the island.

So Bob Page waited on Mapor Island through the last week of November and into December. The sub had to come. He never believed that the powers-that-be would callously abandon him and his comrades to certain death. He could never conceive the mindset of a Rufus Mackenzie. He could never believe that Walter Chapman would let him get away with it.

# CHAPTER 15
# THE SECOND BETRAYAL

TO JOHN Chapman-Walker, Jock Campbell and the other men at SRD headquarters in Melbourne, it appeared that the Rimaus had inexplicably disappeared from the face of the earth. Their only means of communication had been by radio and, having been forced to abandon their transmitter on Merapas Island, they had gone missing without making radio contact with Australia.

The Official History of the Operations and Administration of Special Operations Australia (SOA) conducted under the cover name of Services Reconnaissance Department (Volume III, dated March 8 1946), contains the following section on communications:

In August 1944, signal planning was commenced for the Rimau operation which consisted of a penetration of Singapore Harbour with the object of destroying shipping. The only communication required was the facility for calling Leanyer station [Darwin] on 24-hour emergency listening watches to arrange rendezvous for pick-up after completion of the mission. Two signals personnel accompanied the party. No signals were heard from the party and it has since been ascertained that the entire party was captured before attaining its objective.

It is somewhat misleading. As we have seen, the radio schedule was prefigured on a two-way traffic of messages between Darwin and the Rimau's big Boston transmitter/receivers. The arrangements for submarine rendezvous would be made between the ship and the commandos via walkie-talkies when the submarine was in the area.

Nor was there any condition in the arrangements that contact should only be made after the mission was completed. The conclusion is inescapable that, at the least, the official history has been economical with the truth.

Nor does it mean Allied Command at the time was ignorant of their plight. On 22 October MacArthur's Central Bureau intercepted a Japanese message on their Ultra network from Singapore station to Tokyo: 'We discovered a *tonkan* (junk) of about 100 tons acting suspiciously and were about to (board) it when we were fired on by the crew which had several white men in it. Three men were killed and after that (unintelligible) to nine enemy rubber boats.'

Taken together with the earlier intercept it would have been clear to the SRD controllers that Rimau was in trouble. Instructions could have been relayed to Mackenzie to have him waiting in the vicinity of Merapas by the time Page and his men arrived there on

4 November. The intelligence could and should have been transmitted to the men waiting on Merapas. If it was not, then it is understandable the official historian would wish to gloss over the fact.

It now seems clear, however, that SRD were not told. Either a decision was taken that Ultra could be compromised by the 'dirty tricks boys' or the in-fighting between the various intelligence units had become so poisonous that communication between them was itself deeply compromised. The idea that the Bataan Gang surrounding MacArthur deliberately made no attempt to keep their British allies informed would be impossible for the official historian to document.

On their return to Fremantle in *Tantalus*, Mackenzie, Chapman and Croton were unable to shed any light on the Rimaus' disappearance except to state that there had been signs of occupation and a hasty withdrawal from Merapas at some stage before *Tantalus*'s arrival on 21 November and that some Malays had been present on the island when Chapman and Croton had gone ashore.

Chapman completed and submitted his report—an extraordinarily sanguine document in which he hails the journey as a great achievement, the *Tantalus* having been on a fifty-three-day patrol covering 11 600 miles, 'an endurance record for a British submarine'.

Chapman-Walker's response to the loss of the Rimau party is inexplicable. He *must* have known from Shadwell around 22 November that Chapman had failed to find the Rimau party on Merapas Island and that Mackenzie was leaving the area without any intention of returning. Yet there is not one scrap of evidence to show that he attempted to countermand Mackenzie's decision, or that he took his case to a higher office and pressed for a wider search for his men.

All attempts to help the men of Rimau might have ended there if Colonel Jock Campbell, who would soon take over the command of SRD from Chapman-Walker, hadn't read through Chapman's report with mounting disbelief. It just didn't add up.

He knew Lyon of old—they were thick as thieves—he knew and admired Davidson and Page; and he knew that none of them was the sort to give up without one hell of a struggle. He ordered a new operation to be drawn up—Rimexit—and planning began immediately.

The first priority was to do what Chapman and Mackenzie should have done: 'extract' the Malays on Merapas and interrogate them about what had happened to the Rimaus on the island. The Rimexit party would consist of two officers and three operatives, including one Malay if required by the leader. They would have food, supplies and medical equipment to maintain them for seven days. They would be armed with silent weapons and travel in a folboat and one ten-man rubber boat, both fitted with silenced outboard motors.

A submarine would take them to Merapas where a landing would be made and the Malays seized, 'rendered harmless if necessary and taken back to the landing point'. From there they would rendezvous with the submarine and the interrogation would take place either on the island or aboard the ship. Much would depend on what they learned from the Malays but the submarine commander would be left in no doubt that his overriding mission was the rescue of the Rimau commandos. The plan stated specifically 'Submarine commander to be requested to break wireless silence as early as possible if sortie results in firm information being obtained as to whereabouts of Rimau party.' They could make for one of the RAAF rescue points where a flying boat could land safely and fly them home.

Planning proceeded through December. By now the relatives of the Rimau men were becoming anxious. Roma Page said:

> When they didn't come back by the sixth of December I began to worry. He'd said December 6, some time after that.
>
> But then I got a telegram saying he was missing...look at me, I'm weeping, after all these years. I promised myself that I wouldn't but he was such a fantastic man...please excuse me. It was fifty-seven years ago and I'm still weeping.

Nancy Davidson was more decisive. Roma Page said: 'When they didn't come back when they were due, she just went back to England. I think she knew.'

Then suddenly Project Rimexit was put on hold. Finally, some Ultra messages filtered through the net—not from the Americans, however, nor even from the Australians in Central Bureau, but the British Force 136 at Kandy. They received some decrypts of intercepted Japanese coded signals dated December 1944/January 1945. The messages disclose that Operation Rimau had come to grief.

THE SITUATION on the island chain had become steadily worse for Page and his commandos. Once the 7 December deadline passed without the return of the submarine there was nothing left to do but to strike south. Between them and the safety of Australia was three thousand kilometres of enemy-held territory, an island chain dangling like a string of pearls down to Timor and across the Arafura Sea to Darwin.

It seems Page's contingent grouped themselves into three boat parties—Page, Falls, Gooley and Fletcher in one party; Ingleton, Hardy, Marsh, Huston, Carey and Warren in another.

Blondie Sargent's contingent headed south in two purloined sailing vessels—native *koleks*—with Sargent, Craft and Reymond in the first and Willersdorf, Pace and Warne in the second.

They were seen on several islands, probably trying to retrieve food and other stores hidden during Jaywick. Eyewitnesses reported six men on Sebangka Island in the Lingga Archipelago and also in Pedjantan, where they had transferred their stores from *Porpoise* in September. Then, it seems, the *kolek* parties assembled on Pompong Island and went hunting for a junk they might commandeer, either forcing or persuading the crew with promises to sail them to Australia. And in these desperate times they would certainly have contemplated doing away with them and sailing south themselves.

By now, however, the monsoon season was at its height; sea navigation was hazardous and the junks tended to stay in port to wait it out. It soon seemed clear to Bob Page that his strategy of splitting up the Rimaus into small groups and spreading them across the island chain might pay off. They were occupying the largest possible Japanese force in rounding them up and there was always a chance that one or more of the folboats would slip through the net.

On 15 December, however, a Japanese patrol interrogated the Malay settlers on Selajar where Page and his three comrades—Falls, Gooley and Fletcher—were waiting prior to the next dash across the open sea. Using a combination of threats and bribes, the Japanese demanded to know if they had seen any white men. Apparently someone talked—Page and his men were attacked. Falls was shot in the hip and captured but the others managed to escape.

But now their pursuers were closing in. Falls was beaten the day after his capture, then transferred to Dabo Police Station on the neighbouring Singkep Island two days later. By then his leader was also in the net. When the Japanese broke into the hut where Bob Page had taken shelter he greeted them calmly. According to the Japanese account, Page told his interrogator he had surrendered because he was at the end of his tether—wet, hungry and exhausted. And Australia was just too far away.

He was registered at the Dabo Police Station on 19 December.

By coincidence that was the day his beautiful young wife received the telegram that he was missing. Ironically, he was no longer.

David Gooley and Roland Fletcher were also caught on Selajar the following day and were promptly incarcerated with Bob Page at the Dabo lock-up. Further north between the islands of Pompong and Buaja, Ingleton's party ran into a combined force of *Kempei Tai* and *Heihos*. In an exchange of gunfire, the folboat manned by Marsh and Huston was holed and sunk. Marsh swam to nearby Tjempa Island where he hid out with Carey and Warren. Happy Huston, however, was caught in a fierce rip-tide, swept away and drowned. The date was 16 December 1944—just nine days before his twenty-first birthday.

Marsh, Carey and Warren stayed under cover until 27 December when they were discovered by a search party. Carey and Warren, comrades during the long wait on Merapas, were transported to Dabo on 28 December. Marsh was not so lucky. He was singled out for a series of beatings and other more vicious forms of torture and was not admitted to Dabo until the following day. By then, he was in bad shape.

Meanwhile, the part-Maori Bruno Reymond, 'Blondie' Sargent and Colin Craft in one of the *koleks* actually found a junk with a Chinese/Malay crew, hailed it and were taken aboard. That night as they slept, however, the crew had second thoughts, overpowered them and threw them overboard. Lieutenant Reymond had received a massive blow to the head and both he and the young corporal drowned. Their bodies were washed ashore on Maja Island close to the west coast of Borneo.

'Blondie' Sargent was luckier. He clung to a log for ten hours and was finally carried into a thicket of fish traps at Cape Satai where he lay for nearly a day. Local fishermen captured him on 22 December and took him to the Japanese Naval Base unit garrison at Pontianak. He was interrogated there on Boxing Day.

About a mile from Buaja on Gentung Island there was a sharp exchange of fire on 18 December. Otto Ingleton and young John Hardy were in the sights of the *Kempei Tai*. But it was only a brief skirmish—Hardy was wounded in the shoulder about four in the afternoon and they were forced to surrender. They were admitted to Dabo Police Station the next day.

One small group—Jeff Willersdorf, Hugo Pace and Doug Warne—were almost through the net. Lacking arms and provisions, they were sailing their stolen *kolek* along the west coast of Borneo, where they turned south in the direction of Timor.

But then tragedy struck the twenty-four-year-old Warne who contracted fever and soon became delirious. They stopped at Cape Putting to give him a rest and to find some fresh food. After a day they resumed but his condition continued to deteriorate. Finally they realised that if they kept him out at sea he would die. Warne himself asked to be landed and they found a sheltered beach at Kadapongan Island.

Privately, his companions believed there was little hope left for him but he waved them away and they resumed their journey. Willersdorf and Pace stopped on Doang Doangan Island and on Dewakang Island to find food and water and sailed two hundred and fifty kilometres further south, reaching Kaju Adi Island off the tip of Celebes where they rested for six hours.

By now it was mid-January and the captives from Dabo police station had been transported to Singapore where the Suijo *Kempei Tai* took custody of the ten prisoners, holding them at Tanjong Pagar police station for interrogation.

The bashings he'd received after his capture had broken the young Brisbane apprentice 'Boofhead' Marsh and, in conjunction with a bout of untreated malaria, he died soon after their arrival. Clair Stewart, the first Rimau to fall into Japanese hands, had also been badly tortured but he was able to describe the battle of Soreh Island and to confirm the deaths of Ivan Lyon and Bobby Ross and the probable deaths of Don Davidson and Pat Campbell. The other eight commandos in captivity—Bob Page, Otto Ingleton, Wally Falls, Ronald Fletcher, David Gooley, John Hardy, Wally Carey and Alf Warren—had all been subjected to varying degrees of physical abuse.

'Blondie' Sargent, captured near Borneo, had by now been taken to Surabaya on Java and was being held at the headquarters of the Second South Expeditionary Fleet. He too was being interrogated.

No one alive today knows the source of the information the Japanese extracted from the captives and which was revealed in the Ultra messages intercepted by Central Bureau. By 10 January, however, a message from Saigon to Tokyo 'in reference to white uprisings in the Singapore area mentioned in mess. 799 [of 21 October]' is disturbingly knowledgeable:

1. Twenty-three plotters (including 11 English officers led by English Lt. Colonel Rion [Lyon] left Fremantle by English submarine on 11 September. Going by way of Lombok Island along the Borneo Coast they plundered a junk and changed over to it. On 4 October they raided (unintelligible) Merapas Island. Their object was the penetration of our bases and the blowing up of land installations and shipping at anchor.

During the operations on October 10th they were sighted at the Kaso [Kasu] Islands area to the north-west. They were to arrive to attack their objectives in one-man submarines (15 submarines, but we are checking the authenticity of this) and rubber boats; (unintelligible) magnetic delayed action mines about 10 lbs in weight and 120 in number; after an hour these were to explode.

(Unintelligible) were seen in the vicinity... and they got into rubber boats and escaped. After that, pursuing with army and navy co-operating and exterminated them for the most part.

It was a sickening message for 'Jock' Campbell to read. It was so unequivocal—'exterminated for the most part'—and if by chance any were left on the run there was simply no way of knowing where they were or how to reach them.

He lifted the secure phone on his desk. Rimexit was cancelled. If there were any survivors, they were on their own.

As it happened Jeff Willersdorf and Hugo Pace had resumed their epic voyage toward Australia. Along the way villagers gave them food and water as they navigated across the Banda Sea in their tiny vessel. Finally, after travelling three thousand kilometres through enemy-held territory they reached Romang Island, a thousand kilometres to the north of Timor and only six hundred kilometres across the Timor Sea from Darwin. Moreover, they were only two hundred and twenty kilometres from a recognised RAAF pick-up point. They had arrived on Romang Island on 17 January 1945. All they needed was a few days rest and some fresh supplies and they would make that final dash for home. But it was here that their luck ran out. Betrayed by a local village chief, they were captured two days later and taken to Japanese headquarters in Dili.

On 10 February, the Seventh Area Army, Singapore, dispatched a radio message to all chiefs of staff and commanders of base forces in Japanese occupied territories. It was instantly intercepted and decrytped:

We want to punish the sabotage units which infiltrated from Australia and were captured in the Singapore area recently. Although the matter will in each case be left up to the unit concerned, we wish the investigations to be such that no one is left to do harm afterward.

Since it has been sufficiently proved that this group clearly intended to infiltrate and perpetuate [sic] sabotage, in violation of international law and the conventions of warfare, we plan to refer the matter to a military tribunal and punish it firmly and strictly as a serious war crime.

It could hardly have been clearer—for the Rimaus even the most elementary decency could be discarded in their treatment. The interrogators in Dili responded with enthusiasm. Jeff Willersdorf and Hugo Pace were tortured without mercy then thrown into a cell and left to die of their wounds. Warrant Officer Willersdorf succumbed in March 1945 and Lance Corporal Pace in June.

Ironically, Rufus Mackenzie was back in the South China Sea at the time of the latest Ultra interception. *Tantalus* had sailed from Fremantle on 3 January 1945 and, after sinking a variety of small shipping, Mackenzie requested, and was granted, a ten-day patrol extension. On 11 February he sighted the fighting tops of two capital ships, the battleships *Ise* and *Hyuga* escaping back to Japan. Mackenzie tried desperately to get ahead of them, but was hampered by their air escort.

*Tantalus* was unable to attack as she was bombed and forced to go deep. However, Mackenzie was the only British submarine CO to sight Japanese battleships through his periscope. To go with his DSO and Bar, Mackenzie was awarded the DSC.

Meanwhile, the combined chiefs of staff—British and American—had given Mountbatten the formal order to go ahead with the liberation of Burma and, as soon as that had been achieved, to recapture Malaya, open up the Straits of Malacca and invade Singapore. Still clinging to dreams of Empire, Churchill maintained that Singapore *had* to be retaken. He told the Americans that 'a grievous and shameful blow to British prestige must be avenged in battle'.

Back on Kadapongan, Doug Warne woke up to find that his delirium had subsided. Although shaky, he had recovered sufficiently to commandeer a small native boat and take evasive action whenever Japanese soldiers, who had been alerted to his presence, came close. He succeeded in avoiding capture until March when Ultra intercepts indicated that the Japanese sent a naval patrol boat from Banjarmasin, Borneo, to join the search. The sailors tracked him down and arrested him.

His captors took Warne—the last Rimau to be captured—to Surabaya, Java, where their brutality knew no bounds. The Japanese fury at discovering there had been yet another member of the Rimau party on the loose can only be imagined.

Private Douglas Warne died one month later in April 1945, either as a result of untreated wounds in prison or, like other prisoners, left to die at 102 Naval Hospital, Surabaya, after being used as a human guinea pig in an anti-tetanus experiment.

In Surabaya, 'Blondie' Sargent, the hope of the side from the Boomahnoomoonah RSL sub-district, was quite alone. He was not to know that Lieutenant Colonel Charles Locke was writing a letter to his wife in response to the flood of letters she had sent him from the Victorian bush town:

> I very much regret that I have been unable to reply to your earlier letters because of lack of definite information. I am now able to tell you that your husband is posted 'Missing' because with others, he failed to return from an operation against the enemy.
>
> In the absence of definite information we are unable to say your husband is other than 'Missing' but there is no occasion to presume that he has not been taken prisoner by the enemy.
>
> I am extremely sorry that this has happened as your husband is one of our most valued officers. Please accept my sympathy and be assured that any information I can give will be passed on to you at once. I can only say that letters posted by you after 11th September 1944 will not have been received by your husband.

The Japanese flew 'Blondie' from Surabaya to Singapore to join his mates and they were transferred to Outram Road Jail in March 1945.

# CHAPTER 16
# THE RIGGED TRIAL

OUTRAM ROAD Jail offered no surcease from the agony of the ten surviving Rimau commandos. They must have been deeply dispirited. The prison was a relic of nineteenth-century colonialism, a dank and cheerless place where three prisoners were crowded into a tiny cell designed for a single, small Asiatic and, according to the evidence of the men who survived it, the treatment of all prisoners was appalling.

Beatings were routine, either with a sword scabbard or with fists and feet. Guards with a penchant for the national sport of *jujitsu* used prisoners as punching bags as they refined their martial art. They particularly sought out men too sick to work and those condemned to death.

The place was crawling with vermin and contaminated with filth. Disease was rampant, with many cases of beriberi, scabies, malaria, dysentery and others. Many prisoners succumbed. Food consisted of a starvation diet of five hundred grams of rice per day; less if you were on the sick list. And according to a fellow inmate held fifty metres away from the Rimaus, the ten survivors were treated no differently from the rest.

'Blondie' Sargent had joined the militia in November 1938, then transferred to the AIF at the outbreak of war. He had served in North Africa and Syria before returning to New Guinea where he'd been selected for commando work. He was still only twenty-five. His CO, Bob Page, was twenty-four.

Major Reginald Middleton 'Otto' Ingleton, the Londoner, had joined the Royal Marines in 1940 and had volunteered to go to Australia in June 1944 to find action in Z Special Unit. He was just twenty-six.

Captain Walter Carey, the Canberra boy who had gone on to become a plantation owner in New Guinea, had joined the SRD at his first opportunity in 1942. He was thirty-one.

Warrant Officer Alf Warren had joined the AIF as a maintenance man on tanks. He transferred to SRD when he heard they needed a good mechanic. He was thirty-two.

Sergeant Clair Stewart, the West Australian, was the signaller whose work on Rimau—whatever it may have been—went for naught. He had been in SRD since November 1943. He was thirty-five.

Sergeant Roland Fletcher, born in Dublin and brought to Australia by his parents on a migrant ship, had gone straight from training camp to Z Unit. He was twenty-nine.

Sergeant David Gooley, at twenty-seven, had joined up in January 1941 and he, too, went straight from training camp into the commandos.

Able Seaman 'Poppa' Falls had been born in Aberdeen, Scotland, but his people had come to Casino in Northern New South Wales and he'd joined the navy. He was twenty-seven.

At twenty-three, John Hardy was the baby of the group, though he had been on active service since December 1942. He had volunteered for special service with SRD.

They had been through the hell of losing some of their closest friends in armed combat; they had been hunted down through swamps and across seas with only the thin shell of a folboat between them and the raging waters. They had scavenged for food. They had pushed themselves to the limits of endurance and beyond to escape their pursuers. And then, when finally cornered and captured, they had been bashed and ill-treated.

Although isolated from the main prison population, the Rimaus were sometimes seen by other prisoners when they emptied latrines. One Rimau confided: 'We're being treated pretty badly.' One of his mates, he said, had had his feet burned by a Japanese guard. After the war, the commandant of the military section of the jail, one Major Kobayashi, faced charges over the death of no fewer than fifteen hundred prisoners.

Indeed, the fact that the Rimaus were in Outram at all was a significant statement from their captors. They were deliberately separated from the other Australian prisoners of war at Changi and the other POW camps at Towner and Havelock Roads. They had already been earmarked as 'war criminals' in the official dispatch from the Seventh Area Army for having acted 'in violation of international law and the conventions of warfare'. This from a nation that refused to sign the Geneva Agreement; that butchered thousands of civilians in the rape of Nanking; that tortured and killed the men on the Burma railway; that perpetrated the Bataan Death March in which ten thousand American and Filipino troops perished; and that, even now, was involved in another death march to wipe out witnesses to their crimes. In February 1945, as the Rimaus faced their daily torture, two thousand Australian POWs were ordered out of their camp at Sandakan, North Borneo, and force-marched two hundred kilometres to the inland outpost of Ranau. When they reached their destination at the end of June, only six remained alive.

In truth, the Japanese were both enraged and appalled at the discovery that some of the Rimaus had actually been responsible for Jaywick. Suddenly the scores of reprisal killings among the Malay and Chinese population and the murder of at least twenty Englishmen in their 'investigation' into the raid were revealed as criminal acts. They had been committed—without the slightest justification—against civilians. The Japanese were unquestionably 'in violation of international law and the conventions of warfare'— even the barbaric variety practised by the sons of *bushido*.

This boded ill for the survivors. Each man fought his own private battle to keep going, to stay alive, to reach out for that marvellous moment when the ghosts of their loved ones in memory would suddenly take flesh and come within touching distance. They had very little to sustain them. They had each other and that was a help. But as the flesh fell off their mates it was like watching a man slowly dissolve and you knew that it was happening to you too. You could see it in their eyes.

However, there was the war news. And despite the best efforts of their jailers to keep it from them, it was inevitable that word of Japanese reverses would quietly circulate and the Chinese whispers would only make it better as it did the rounds. They could not have known the details, only that the Americans were punching through Japanese defences and heading for the Home Islands.

It was just a matter of time.

In fact, while the campaign for the Philippines was still in progress, US forces were advancing in great strides toward Japan itself. There was already an invasion plan which would begin with landings on the most southerly island of Kyushu. The Americans had taken the Marianas and General Curtis LeMay was sending his B-29 bombers the two and a half thousand kilometres from Saipan to Tokyo throughout the closing months of 1944 and into 1945. To reduce the flight by half the strategic planners in Washington settled on the little volcanic island of Iwo Jima in the Bonin Islands. It was a well-defended Japanese base. General Kuribayashi Tadamichi had exploited the natural caves and had dug tunnels beneath the rough, volcanic terrain. His 20 000 men were prepared to fight to the death.

Day after day before the landing, the island was subjected to intense bombardment by naval guns and air strikes. For the first time, the Americans used napalm in a concentrated fashion. It would later take on a terrible notoriety in Vietnam, as would the then air force commander turned politician Curtis LeMay, who wanted to bomb the Vietnamese 'back to the stone age'.

The result fell far short of expectations, however, against the Japanese on Iwo Jima. They were so well protected that no amount of conventional bombing or shelling could defeat them. So when US Marines landed on 19 February, they encountered fierce resistance. Kamikaze counterattacks sank the light carrier *Bismarck Sea* and damaged other Allied ships. Finally the famous image of the US flag being planted on Mount Suribachi took place on 23 February, though the island was not really secured until the night of 9 March. Iwo Jima cost the lives of six thousand Marines as well as almost all twenty thousand Japanese defenders; but henceforth more than two thousand B-29 bombers were able to land on it on their way to and from bombing missions over Japan.

A new tactic had been found for the raids from the Marianas—instead of high altitude strikes in daylight, low-level bombing runs using napalm brought startling success. The first time it was used—on the night of 9 March—it destroyed almost a quarter of Tokyo's buildings, killed more than eighty thousand people and made one million homeless. Suddenly it seemed possible that Japan might be defeated without an invading ground force. Similar bombing raids were scheduled for Nagoya, Osaka, Kobe, Yokohama and Toyama.

Meanwhile, on 1 March a report based on the Tanjong Pagar interrogations of the Rimau men before their incarceration in Outram Road Jail was referred to the judicial department. It sought confirmation that it was legitimate to classify the Rimau prisoners as spies. The response was affirmative. In consequence, the investigation passed from the *Kempei Tai* to the Judicial Department's Major-General Otsuka. In turn, Otsuka ordered Major Kamiya to prepare a case against the ten commandos.

Still the American advance continued. Okinawa, the largest of the Ryukyu Islands north-east from Formosa, had been regarded

KILL THE TIGER

as the natural stepping stone to Kyushu, only five hundred and forty kilometres away. In March, an air attack destroyed hundreds of Japanese planes but there were at least 75 000 Japanese troops on the island under the command of Lieutenant General Ushijima Mitsuru. The invasion of Okinawa was in fact the largest amphibious operation mounted by the Americans in the Pacific War. For the first time, the British Pacific Fleet, four carriers and full escorts of Task Force 57, took part with the American and Australian navies. It was also the first time that the ground forces of MacArthur and Nimitz had fought together.

Under the overall command of Admiral Nimitz and with Lieutenant General Simon Bolivar Buckner commanding the ground forces, the operation began with the occupation of the Kerama Islets, twenty-five kilometres west of Okinawa, on 26 March. Then on 1 April, some 60 000 American troops landed on the central stretch of Okinawa's west coast, seizing two nearby airfields and advancing to cut the island's narrow waist.

In Tokyo, the government of Prime Minister Koiso resigned on 5 April. On the same day, the USSR refused to renew its treaty of non-aggression with Japan and attacked Japanese positions in Manchuria. A week later President Roosevelt died and Harry S. Truman took over in the Oval Office. The endplay had begun.

But while the Rimaus might have known the broad outlines of the struggle against the enemy, they would not have been aware of another race against time that bore upon their fate. On 30 December 1944 General Leslie Groves, head of the Manhattan Project, reported to the White House that it was 'reasonably certain' that an atomic bomb, equivalent to ten thousand tons of TNT, would be ready for testing by the summer of 1945.

On 25 April 1945—a day on which the Australians in Outram Road would have paused to remember the fallen of Gallipoli—US Secretary of War Henry Stimson impressed on his new commander in chief, President Truman, the significance of the new weapon. 'Within four months,' he said, 'we shall in all probability have completed the most terrible weapon ever known in human history— one bomb of which could destroy a whole city.' He then formed a committee of statesmen and scientists to debate how the bomb should be employed. The committee concluded that the bomb should be used to end the war as soon as possible; that it should be dropped on a military–urban target so as to demonstrate its full force; and that a demonstration or warning should not be made beforehand, lest the bomb lose its shock value.

Major Kamiya, in his judicial function as the prosecutor of the Rimau men, consulted Major General Hidaka, General Commander of the Judicial Department of Southern Expeditionary Force in Saigon on 20 April. No minutes have survived of this meeting but, in view of subsequent events, it appears a decision was taken then that the commandos be denied a fair trial, that the verdict was pre-determined before it began.

On 21 May General Hidaka in Saigon instructed the prosecutor that 'a demand for capital punishment should be judicial'. The trial would take place in about two months.

The first major counterattack on Okinawa by the Japanese had begun on 6 April. It involved three hundred and fifty-five kamikaze air raids and an assault by the *Yamato*, the greatest battleship on the high seas—seventy-two thousand tons and carrying nine 18.1-inch (460 mm) guns—which was also on a suicide mission. The capital ship had only enough fuel for the single outward voyage. The Japanese hoped the *Yamato* would destroy an Allied fleet weakened by the kamikaze attacks. In the event, the *Yamato*, the poetic name for Japan, was struck repeatedly by Allied torpedoes and bombs and was sunk in the East China Sea on 7 April with the loss of 2488 lives.

Equally suicidal was a new Japanese weapon, *baka*, which claimed its first victim, the US destroyer *Abele*, off Okinawa on 12 April. *Baka* was a rocket-powered glider crammed with explosives which was towed into range by a bomber and then released to be guided by its solitary pilot into the chosen target for their mutual destruction.

The US ground forces invading Okinawa met little opposition on the beaches because the Japanese had decided to make a stand out of range of America's naval guns. Their resistance lasted until 21 June when the Japanese commander committed suicide.

At Albuquerque, New Mexico, the scientists and engineers of the Manhattan Project were erecting a steel tower at a site on the Alamogordo air base, one hundred and ninety-three kilometres south of the city. In a few days they would haul up the tower the world's first atomic bomb.

In Tokyo, the High Command was divided. The Militarists were losing influence. Those seeking an 'honourable surrender' were pressing their case to the Emperor. At last, they had his concentrated attention.

224

In Singapore, a sense of urgency suddenly became evident among the Rimau prosecutors. Judicial Major Mitsuo Jifuku, who had legal carriage of the trial, decided not to wait for affidavits from anyone who fought in the action at Merapas on the grounds that 'it would cause further delay of trial' and on 28 June made formal application for the trial to begin posthaste.

His superior officer, General Otsuka, raised no objections. On the contrary, five days later on 3 July 1945 the ten Rimau prisoners were taken from their prison to the Raffles College, Japanese military headquarters in Singapore, to stand trial on charges of 'perfidy and espionage'.

Three judges presided: Colonel Masayoshi Towatari, the aforesaid Major Jifuku and Major Miyoshi Hisada. Major Kamiya was the prosecutor and the findings of the court would be ratified by Major General Otsuka. The men were delivered to the bare courtroom at 1 p.m. There is some evidence that in the days before the trial the beatings ceased and their rations increased. It would have been unseemly if they had collapsed while the sons of the Emperor were meting out 'justice'.

The summary of Operation Rimau, as read to the court, is revealing. The torture of the captives had uncovered the facts with as much accuracy as could be expected from men who knew only what they witnessed. It was, they said:

... a special project of infiltrating into the port of Shonan [Singapore] and by making use of special submergible boat called SB make surprise attacks on and destruct the military ships within the port. This plan was named 'Rimau' project from necessity of security. All the accused persons were selected as members of the party headed by Lt-Col Lyon, British Army, left Fremantle on 11th September on board a British submarine *Porpoise* and arrived at an island called Merapas where they established their base, unloaded necessary rations, signal equipment etc., left Capt Carey in charge of those stores and the rest of the party left the island by the same submarine.

On the sea near Pontiak, Borneo, the party captured a native junk of about 100 tons, towed the same to Pedjantan Island and transferred from the submarine to the junk 15 above-mentioned special submergible boats, special magnetic charges called 'Limpet', arms, munitions, rations etc. and [when] these preparations were completed the party sent the nine Malayan crew of the junk to Australia by the submarine, and started on this junk for Singapore Port on about 25th September for attack. On passing off Merapas Island the party landed Warren and two more members to join Capt Carey and the rest continued their navigation toward Singapore sea area for the mission.

The presiding judge then asked each of the men his birthplace, unit, rank, name and age. An interpreter, Hiroyuki Furuta, was provided.

Then came the charges:

1. The clothing worn by the members of the Rimau Project were green coloured shirts and trousers and also Beret Caps of the same colour but except for the few commissioned officers, the members from the date of departure willingly refrained

from wearing badges to show their ranks, also refrained from using caps and so their appearance was such that it was difficult to recognise them as regular fighting members of either British or Australian forces.

Furthermore, since the day of depart [*sic*] from Pedjantan Island all members applied on them so-called Commando or Demouflage dying stuff and dyed into brown the exposed part of their skin, such as face, arms and legs. In addition to that, Lt-Col. Lyon, Capt Page, the accused person, and six more members were wearing loin cloth called 'sarong', the one used by the native Malayans and continued their voyage on the junk without taking off the Japanese National flag which had been hoisted on the stern by the Malayan crews and whenever the junk was sighted by a Japanese patrol plane or crafts they displayed another Japanese national flag (Evidence No. 1) which they had prepared beforehand and pretended as if the junk was an ordinary civilian vessel crewed by native inhabitants who were engaged in daily works under Japanese military adminis-tration, and with these deceptive activities they succeeded in passing the guarded area and infiltrated into the outlying area of the port of Singapore.

At about 1700 hours of 10th October they reached near Casoe [Kasu] Island about 20 kilometres from port of Singapore where they were sighted by the staff of the observation post of Batang Police Station and the inspecting vessel manned by local inspector Bin Shiapal and four other Malayans approached the junk. On seeing this vessel, Colonel Lyon and other members deducted it to be the patrolling craft of Japanese force and

227

determining quick attack of the craft, launched sudden and
heavy shooting on it by automatic rifles and killed four crews
of the observation post.

After this attack, they felt the difficulty of accomplishing
the task and decided to give up the mission and exploded the
junk and made individual flights toward Merapas Base with a
view to catch at the base the submarine which had been
scheduled to come to the base at the beginning of November.
However, their flights were disturbed and the Merapas Base
was raided by parties of Japanese garrisons and while being
unable to contact the submarine, they continued their flights
and by the time of apprehension of all the accused persons in
December, they encountered with the Japanese garrison on
Soreh, Tapai and Merapas and killed Lt Muraoka [sic] and seven
other army personnels. Thus the party was engaged in hostile
activities without wearing uniforms to qualify them for fighting
and also using the vessel which lacked qualification for fighting.

While some of the details are inaccurate this could be, in part,
due to translation. It is significant, however, that the Japanese noted
the Rimaus had been 'unable to contact the submarine'—either
because they had no means of doing so or, more disturbingly,
because Mackenzie avoided receiving their calls. The Rimaus
originally had six walkie-talkies and it seems most unlikely that
they would have abandoned them all. This lends weight to the view
that Captain Mackenzie either ignored their calls or avoided
receiving them by the simple device of not providing his radio
operator with the designated frequency.

The reading of the charges continued:

2. While acting as above, they contrived to collect information to be reported to their home country and assigned the accused Ingleton for sketching, the accused Page for photographing and Lt Commander Davidson for documentary recording and these three persons reconnoitred in their disguise clothing and conditions of guards of islands south of Singapore, state of administration of ships in those areas, trend of public mind there, strength of Japanese navy crafts operating in Riau Straits, conditions of bauxite mines, also photographed same and engaged in collection and recording of the military information, besides other accused persons, also in their disguised costumes, exerted to collect informations for the same purpose. Furthermore, the accused Carey, while on Merapas Island, made very detailed record of the strength of our fleet operating near the base and of movements of our aircrafts over the area and recorded the same.

Judge Jifuku then took over the prosecution from Major Kamiya. He called Major Otto Ingleton as ranking officer to come forward. 'Is there anything that you should like to object among the charges that were read to you just now?'

Ingleton's response revealed the effects of the confinement and the bashings at Outram Road: 'No, I have no objection. They were quite true.'

Jifuku then led him through the various phases of Operation Rimau, gaining admissions that when in enemy waters he and the others discarded their uniforms and disguised themselves with sarongs and skin dye. He drew from Ingleton his propensity for sketching passing craft and the surrounding islands from the deck of the *Mustika*. Then came the fateful moment when suddenly the patrol boat appeared. For the first time the prisoner showed some animation in his responses:

> Toward the evening of the 10th of October when we approached to a point near [Kasu] Island, we saw a ship nearing us. Coming nearer, we found it a navy patroller and I thought, 'Everything is over.' Other people seemed to have been also surprised and there were shouting at various places in the junk, 'Patroller! Patroller!' Then I heard someone shooting and so I took up my automatic rifle and shot the patroller.
>
> Some people, I remember, were running round on the junk. We shot the ship by four or five of our automatic rifles. The ship seemed to be utterly taken aback on account of our surprise attack and tried to get away by turning round abruptly. I saw several of the crew then either dropped or jumped into [the] sea...I did not know it was an observation boat of the police station. I thought it was a patrolling boat of Japanese Navy... I did not know where Lt-Col Lyon was at that time. I merely shot because I heard others shoot, and not by order of him.

Bob Page was next. Again, the record shows that he 'agreed' that the charges were 'quite correct'. Indeed, there is a sense of fatalism in all his responses. For the most part his phrasing is very precise.

Q: *Is there anything that you should like to differ from all the statements that Major Ingleton had made just now? Or any opinion?*

A: None, except that I once saw Lt-Col Lyon wearing his badge of rank on the junk, but where it was I have forgotten.

Q: *Did you also not use beret cap or badge of rank after off* [sic] *Merapas Island?*

A: I did not use it since we left Pedjantan Island.

Q: *We are given to understand that you were wearing salong* [sic] *on the junk. Is it correct?*

A: It is quite correct.

Q: *Did you bring over that salong* [sic] *from Australia?*

A: I used the one which I found on the junk and so I do not know where it came from. I am inclined to consider that it was the one used by the civilian crew of the junk.

Q: *Did you also shoot at the time when your party attacked the police boat near [Kasu] Island?*

A: Yes, I did. I thought it was a navy patrol ship and I shot it.

Q: *How many times did you fight against the Japanese force after that?*

A: Once on Merapas Island and once on the other island. I am not sure if I killed any of the Japanese troops.

Q: *State the conditions in which you made research on Japanese military affairs and photographed it.*

A: As was stated by Major Ingleton, I took charge of photographing and photographed several sceneries [*sic*] of islands and Japanese fleets as seen from the junk. [It will be noted that suddenly Page has taken to speaking in Japanese/English].

*Q: Are these the photos you have taken?* (Showed him film negatives and prints made with them.)

A: Yes, I took those photos.

*Q: Do you remember this camera?* (Showed him a camera)

A: Yes, that is the camera I brought from Australia. With it I took these photos.

And there the questioning ended. There is no indication as to what the photographs showed, whether 'Japanese fleets as seen from the junk' or 'sceneries of islands'.

Wally Carey followed. The questioning was again concentrated on his mode of dress. Jifuku then asked:

*Q: What were you doing on Merapas every day?*

Carey: I walked around the island and made reconnaissance of it. I also observed the ships and aircrafts passing the island, made note of direction of wind, its strength and so forth, and recorded them in my diary.

*Q: What was your objective in doing that?*

A: Partly because I wanted to keep it as my souvenir of this mission, and partly because I thought it might be interesting to my seniors in the headquarters.

Again, there is room to doubt the veracity of the 'record'. There is no reason for Carey to go beyond the 'souvenir' explanation and certainly not for him to use the Japanese/English construction 'in the headquarters'.

After this witness, the 'transcript' reverts to indirect speech and reports simply that:

> Every accused person was asked by the judge whether he had an objection or opinion with regard to his charges, all answered that the charges were correct and they had no objection.
>
> When asked whether they had brought with them badges of rank, Lt Sargent answered that he had one but had not used it since Pedjantan Island and others answered that they had none since they left Australia.
>
> Asked about use of beret caps and commando [dye], all answered that since Pedjantan and Merapas Islands they stopped use of beret caps and applied commando to themselves.

Similarly, they all supposedly admitted to involvement in 'skirmishes' against Japanese troops and engaging in the 'collections of informations'.

Then, we are told, presiding judge Colonel Towatari asked every accused person whether he had anything that he would like to say, 'either to defend him(self) or for any other purpose. All the accused persons answered that they have done the mission for the sake of their country.'

Major Kamiya then addressed the court, declaring that the guilt of the Rimau men had been 'completely proved' by the 'unrestricted and free statements of the accused persons'. He rehearsed the mission and its purposes. Then with breathtaking hypocrisy, he cited international law such as the Hague Convention of 1907 requiring ships to be properly identified.

The same convention defined a 'spy' as a combatant without proper uniform or badge of rank engaged in the collection of military information.

'The country which capture such persons has right to deal with their violence of regulation of warfare and can punish them as having committed war crimes,' he said. 'I consider that a death sentence should be given to each of these accused persons.'

At the conclusion of his address, Colonel Towatari announced that the court would now consider its verdict. The ten prisoners were escorted, with their interpreter, to another room in the college. It was now 1830 hours, 3 July 1945.

# CHAPTER 17
# KILL THE TIGER

THE CAMPAIGN for Okinawa ended officially on 2 July 1945. For the Allies, it was the longest and bloodiest Pacific campaign since Guadalcanal in 1942 and the death toll was far higher. Taking the island had cost the Americans 12000 dead and 36000 wounded, with thirty-four ships sunk and three hundred and sixty-eight damaged; the Japanese losses exceeded 100000 dead.

Three days after the fighting ceased Australia's great wartime Prime Minister John Curtin died and was buried in the Karrakatta cemetery. He had never fully recovered from a coronary occlusion suffered while returning from his summit meeting with Roosevelt in America in 1944. The inscription on his gravestone read:

> *His country was his pride*
> *His brother man his cause*

Shortly before Curtin's death, US command in the Pacific had been reorganised. His man, Douglas MacArthur, was henceforth to be in command of all army units and also in operational control of the US Marines for the invasion of Japan. Nimitz was placed in command of all navy units. Japan itself lay open to direct assault by land as well as sea and air. MacArthur had a detailed plan—Operation Olympic—to begin the invasion of Kyushu.

Diplomatically, President Truman sought 'unconditional surrender' but he added an inducement. While his terms would mean 'the termination of the influence of the military leaders who have brought Japan to the brink of disaster' they did not mean 'the extermination or enslavement of the Japanese people who would be free to return to their families, their farms, their jobs'.

Against the advice of the State Department, however, he did not include a promise that the Japanese might retain their Emperor, the god-king of their Shinto religion. Accordingly, the Militarists pressed their influence at the Imperial Court and the government began to mobilise the home front to resist an invasion. Two million regular soldiers and a similar number of civilians in the Home Guard would meet the Americans as they came ashore and push them back into the sea by sheer weight of numbers.

At Albuquerque, minor technical glitches had delayed the first test of the atomic bomb but now they seemed to be overcome. J. Robert Oppenheimer, the scientist in charge, had few qualms about exploding it over Japan once the test was successful. 'We did not think that exploding one of these things as a firecracker over a desert was likely to be very impressive,' he said.

But that was before he saw it for himself.

By now Singapore and South-East Asia were isolated from the main thrust of the American advance, thousands of kilometres behind the lines. Yet nothing was being done to usurp the Japanese military control and free the twenty-two thousand prisoners who had been suffering the tortures of the damned. It was more than an oversight. It was a betrayal.

The crack Australian divisions who had retaken New Guinea and were at the peak of their power and efficiency were engaged in a meaningless and wasteful operation in Morotai. MacArthur wanted nothing to divert the world's attention from his progress towards Tokyo. The Australian and British political leadership and general staff who followed cravenly in his wake have much to answer for.

For the men of Rimau, shunted off to a waiting room while their judges deliberated, there was no way of knowing just how close the world was to the end of the nightmare. The Japanese, however, who were playing out the farce of a judicial trial, knew full well that whatever else they might do they must cover their tracks. And here the 'transcript' of the trial becomes particularly revealing. For suddenly in place of the dry, scripted formula comes an extraordinary outburst attributed to Prosecutor Kamiya. It is transparently an interpolation after the event. In view of what followed, it is near to nauseating; but justice demands its retelling:

The valorous spirits of these persons make us remind of the daring enterprise of our heroes of Navy Special Attack Corps who died in May 1942 in their attack on Sydney Harbour. The same admiration and respect that all the Australian Government officials, headed by its Premier, and civilians gave to the heroes of ours, we must return to these real heroes in our presence.

When the deed becomes so heroic its sublime spirits [are] to be respected, and its success or failure become only a secondly matter.

The accused persons stated and thanked me the warm treatment given to them. I hope they have understood by this time that the warm treatment was nothing but an expression of our fighting men's spirits who were inspired with the noble attitude of these heroic martyrs.

These heroes must have left Australia with sublime patriotism flaming in their hearts and with the wholehearted expectations of all the Australian people on their both shoulders. The last moment of a hero must be glorious. It must be historic and it must be dramatic. Heroes have more regards for their reputations than anything else. This is the feeling of the Japanese people. As we respect them, we feel our duty of glorifying the last moment of these heroes just as they deserve, and by our doing so, the names of these heroes will remain in the hearts of Australians and Britishers as real heroes eternally.

Then, we are told:

Major Ingleton thanked [the court] for being called a patriotic hero and also for the cordial way of trial. He further stated that although he had known that deceptive use of Japanese flag, surprise attack from the civilian ship and skirmishes in disguised costume were unfair way of combat but he did not realise until the present moment that they were such grave offence. Now he realised it, he shall humbly accept any punishment that is due.

Captain Page and others stated in the same way as Major Ingleton.

It simply beggars belief. Moreover, the defendants had no legal representation—under Japanese law they were not entitled to any cross-examination of witnesses or any pleas in mitigation or any kind of legal challenge or appeal.

After half an hour's deliberation, the men of Rimau were escorted back into the courtroom. The verdict was 'Guilty', the punishment, 'Death by beheading'.

Three days later on Friday 6 July an order for the execution of all ten men was issued by General Itagaki, the beetle-browed Commander-in-Chief of the Seventh Area Army.

The Japanese lies in the doctored 'transcript' continue:

After the trial all the members of this party were increased of their rations and in accordance with their request they were all received in a small hall so they can freely converse each other. Every other possible means for warm treatment was given and all through these days the attitude of them was really admirable. They were always clear and bright and not a single shadow of dismal or melancholic mood did they show. People concerned were much impressed by it.

The sword is part of Japan's Imperial regalia and part of the samurai tradition. In Japanese mythology, it was used by the storm god Susanoo to save the life of a maiden who was about to be devoured by a dragon. It is one of the creation myths of Shinto, invoked by the emperors to justify their rule.

For the 'honour' of beheading the commandos, however, the Japanese authorities had chosen five guards from Outram Road Jail and the weapons were to be the swords that formed part of their regular uniform and which they regularly used to beat prisoners, either inside or outside the scabbard.

At 1000 hours on Saturday 7 July the Rimaus were taken from their cells at Outram Road and driven to the rough execution ground near a reform school on Bukit Timah Road. They travelled on a small bus with the windows blacked out to prevent anyone catching a glimpse of the doomed soldiers. Their wrists were handcuffed behind their backs and elbows tightly roped to their sides. They were unloaded and dragged through a door at the back of the vehicle.

The Japanese lies continue:

All of them were given cigarettes and rested. Then, in accordance with their request, they were allowed to shake hands each other. They all stood up, shook hands merrily and even laughingly in very harmonious air and bid farewell each other. The sky was clear and it was a very historic scenery.

The beheading of Allied soldiers was regarded as great sport by the Japanese Army and a jeering crowd normally gathered to enjoy the spectacle. The spectators jostled each other for a better view and taunted the victims with crude remarks. When the executioner raised his sword and prepared to strike, cameras clicked excitedly. And when he cried out as he brought the sword down on his victim's neck, there was a great roar from the crowd. But with the war only moments from closure, the mass execution of 7 July was a closely guarded secret and there were fewer witnesses than usual, but still an impressive turnout of top brass.

These included Chief Judge Towatari, Major General Otsuka and Major Kamiya, and the commandant of the military section of Outram Road Jail, Major Shuzo Kobayashi, and his civilian jail counterpart, Major Koshiro Mikizawa. The execution was directed by Major Hisada, and the executioners were Sergeants Nibara, Tsukudu, Okamura and Shimoi and Corporal Hirata.

The lies:

> Major Ingleton representing all the members, asked to the Chief of Prison and Prosecuting Attorney in attendance, Major Kamiya to give his thanks to all the Japanese personnel who were taking care of them by that time. He made special stress on the fact that all of them were deeply grateful for the courtesy and kindness that an Interpreter, Mr Furuta, extended on them for a long time in the past and requested them to convey their hearty thanks to Mr Furuta without fail. He repeated not to forget to give this message to him.

Furuta later claimed that, although he had initially declined to attend the execution on the grounds that he was too closely attached to the victims, he had changed his mind and turned up at Bukit Timah, where he had watched proceedings out of sight from behind a bush. He had, he claimed, seen the men smoking cigarettes, having been temporarily released from their bonds, and chatting to one another. When the moment came for them to be re-tied, they had shaken hands and wished each other 'Good luck'.

Furuta claimed that Ingleton had said: 'We have one regret. This is that we cannot see at this place Mr Furuta who has been so kind to us. We all wanted to thank him once more but I suppose he has his duty. Please tell him we thanked him before we died.'

Furuta claims that, despite that moving testimony, he was unable to leave his hiding place and step forward to say goodbye to his 'friends'. It was only when Ingleton, hands bound behind his back, was forced at bayonet point to kneel at the edge of one of the graves that Furuta, unable to bear it any longer, fled from the scene.

Major Mikizawa, commandant of the civilian section of Outram Road Jail, said the prisoners were blindfolded and made to kneel close to three large graves. The five swaggering thugs chosen as executioners, clutching their unsheathed swords, approached the helpless victims.

One detail in Mikizawa's testimony exemplifies not only the inherent barbarity of the execution but also the bungling ineptitude of the empire's prison service: it took the guards more than half an hour to decapitate the ten servicemen. A Korean prisoner at the jail testified that while he was cleaning the warders' room he heard the five talking and laughing about the execution, drawing their swords to show how they had struck, then wiping their blades. 'They teased Nibara [one of the guards] for being so unskilful,' he said, 'and requiring two or three shots each time.'

The bodies of the Rimaus were thrown into the three graves, one on top of the other, four in one and three in each of the other two. Each man had been stripped of badges of rank and identity disks and there was nothing to indicate who was buried there. Several days later six little wooden crosses were placed on top of the mounds of earth.

The lies:

After execution was over, Major Kamiya reported the whole matter to Major-General Otsuka who, in turn, reported to 7th Area Army Commander and the Chief of Staff, the completion of execution as well as the sublime and glorious attitude in which they met their death.

Nine days later the first atomic test at Alamogordo yielded an explosion equivalent to that of fifteen thousand tons of TNT and stunned Oppenheimer and his colleagues with its elemental power. At that moment Truman was attending the final Big Three meeting at Potsdam and he casually mentioned to Stalin that the United States had 'a new weapon of unusual destructive force'. Stalin said he was glad to hear of it and hoped that the US would make good use of it against the Japanese.

Though little else was agreed at Potsdam, the Big Three did jointly invite Japan to surrender unconditionally or face 'prompt and utter destruction'.

When no surrender was forthcoming, Truman gave the US Air Force on Tinian Island the green light. A specially equipped B-29 Superfortress, the *Enola Gay*, piloted by Colonel Paul Tibbets, dropped an atomic bomb on Hiroshima at 0815 on 6 August 1945. Truman wrote later that he never lost a moment's sleep over his decision.

The second bomb obliterated Nagasaki on 9 August. The following day Japanese radio announced that the Potsdam Declaration could only be accepted if the position of the Emperor was respected.

On the morning of 14 August, more than eight hundred American bombers struck at military targets on the island of Honshu. It was at this point that Emperor Hirohito intervened personally to end the stalemate. He recorded a broadcast to his people, saying that they should 'bear the unbearable' and give up the fight. That afternoon the official Japanese news agency sent out an overseas radio bulletin stating that an Imperial proclamation was soon to be made 'accepting the Potsdam Declaration'.

That evening more than a thousand Japanese soldiers attacked the Imperial Palace in search of the proclamation with the intention of preventing its transmission to the Japanese people, as planned, the following day. They succeeded in assassinating the commander of the Imperial Guards Division but failed to find the recording and were finally repelled.

At noon on 15 August a Japanese radio announcer asked all listeners to stand 'respectfully' in front of their radio sets. The familiar strains of the Japanese anthem were played, followed by the high, reedy, unfamiliar voice of the Emperor—the first time his subjects had heard him speak—reading his proclamation.

The enemy, said the so-called 'Voice of the Sacred Crane', 'has begun to employ a new and most cruel bomb, the power of which to do damage is incalculable, taking the toll of many innocent lives'. This was the reason 'why we have ordered our government to communicate to the governments of the United States, Great Britain, China and the Soviet Union, that our Empire accepts the provisions of their joint declaration.'

The war was over.

THE COVER-UP of Japanese war criminals started at the top. After presiding over the Japanese surrender aboard the USS *Missouri* in Tokyo Bay on 2 September 1945, MacArthur resisted pressure to haul Hirohito before a war crimes tribunal on charges of crimes against humanity, believing that would interfere with his plans to introduce a new Japanese constitution.

He had decided, without any solid basis in fact, that Japan could only be held together if Hirohito continued as emperor. Otherwise, he believed that the Japanese would follow the same path to Communism as China had taken under Mao Tse-tung. MacArthur lied to President Truman when he reported that Hirohito's alleged participation in war crimes had been fully 'researched'. Truman, knowing no better, believed him.

Because it suited his purposes, MacArthur swallowed Hirohito's claims that he was merely a constitutional monarch who had intervened only twice in Japanese politics: once to crush the attempted putsch by young turks in 1936, and again in August 1945 to enforce Japan's surrender. As a result, the Emperor was neither arraigned nor called upon as a witness at the Tokyo war crimes trials of 1947–48.

Hirohito, in whose name the Pacific War had been waged and whose divine status had been invoked to justify the inhuman treatment of Japan's enemies, her prisoners and the nations she enslaved, renounced his divinity and posed for photographs beside MacArthur, the new Mikado. Instead of being hanged as a war criminal with the blood of millions on his hands, he was portrayed as a harmless marine biologist with a Mickey Mouse watch.

MacArthur, now virtual dictator of Japan, had taken upon himself without any legal and certainly no moral authority to deny the heroes of Rimau and millions of other war dead their right to natural justice.

The blame for Japan's war crimes was placed at the highest level on the Militarists who had supposedly hijacked power in the aftermath of World War I and used the imperial throne to achieve their ends. The Tokyo war crimes trials arraigned twenty-five senior Japanese commanders and politicians. Just seven, one of them Tojo, were hanged.

In mitigation, most of the defendants argued that they had acted to turn the tide of Western imperialism in Asian countries where Britain and other European powers, and also America, had plundered at will for more than a century. The full extent of Japanese atrocities in China was not revealed because the 'international' tribunal was more concerned with offences committed against Westerners than Asians and also because Chiang Kai-shek, whom the Americans still recognised as China's leader, had no interest in pressing charges about events that had occurred in mainly Communist-held territories. Therefore, the perpetrators went unpunished.

General Slim, the victor of Burma, put the issue of 'honour' into perspective when he said: 'There can be no excuse for a nation which as a matter of policy treats its prisoners of war in this way, and no honour to an army, however brave, which willingly makes itself an instrument of such inhumanity to the helpless.'

In November 1945 Roma Page learned that Bob would not be coming home. She was with his mother, Anne, and the very next day there was a notice in the paper. His father Harold too had died a prisoner of the Japanese.

Roma said: 'It didn't seem fair.'

# CHAPTER 18
# THE FINAL BETRAYAL

NEWS OF THE Japanese surrender created panic among the empire's formerly invincible sons. The men who had dishonoured themselves and their nation in Singapore were in desperate fear that they would be held accountable for the crimes they had committed against civilians and prisoners of war during the previous four years. They took swift action to prevent detection.

Most documents relating to the Rimau team and to seven American airmen who had been executed eleven days before the surrender were burned. In the case of the Americans, the cover-up went obscenely further. These prisoners had been executed at a naval base on Singapore Island and their bodies buried at Niyusun airport. On 15 August 1945, the day of surrender, their executioners drove to the airport, dug up the airmen, brought them back to camp and cremated them on a big fire in the barrack square. The ashes were then thrown into the sea.

'The flames did not attract undue attention,' says an eyewitness, Oka Harumitzu, one of the Japanese cooks at the base, 'as there were fires lit at all the different naval and military establishments at that time to burn all military documents and records before the Allied forces arrived.'

General Itagaki suppressed news of Japan's surrender for four days, thus giving his henchmen valuable time to cover up their atrocities while enjoying the powers of an occupying army with the local population rather than enduring the odium of a defeated nation.

MacArthur's egomania for pomp, ceremony and publicity also helped the miscreants to escape. He ordered that no landings could be made in any of the occupied territories, including Singapore, until the surrender document had been signed in Japan. The British force for the reoccupation of Singapore—Operation Zipper—was already steaming through the Straits of Malacca at full speed when the order was received on 19 August and had to slow down and bide its time, giving the Japanese several more days to destroy evidence, falsify reports and murder witnesses.

When Mountbatten protested to MacArthur, he was told: 'Keep your pants on.'

Mountbatten replied: 'Will keep mine on if you take Hirohito's off.'

But MacArthur was unrelenting.

Unfortunately for Mountbatten, he had been in London making a nuisance of himself at the War Office between the bombings of Hiroshima on 6 August and Nagasaki on 9 August. Brooke noted in his diary: 'Seldom has a Supreme Commander been more deficient of the main attributes of a Supreme Commander than Dickie Mountbatten.'

Mountbatten's love of pomp equalled that of MacArthur but he had taken it further: his headquarters were in the colonial governor's summer residence in the hills outside Kandy where a vast staff numbering some 7000 were at his beck and call. Clearly, MacArthur did not take him seriously, even when he wired him that 'the delay might mean the difference between life and death for prisoners of war at starvation level'.

The Japanese had taken nearly 200 000 Allied prisoners of war, the majority captured in the first six months of hostilities when Hirohito's armies overran Hong Kong, Malaya, Singapore, the Philippines, Sumatra, Java and Burma. Many did not survive. Of 35 000 members of the American and Filipino forces captured in the Philippines in 1942, 10 000 died on the Bataan Death March and many more in Japanese prison camps. More than 12 000 of the 60 000 Commonwealth POWs who worked on the Burma railway did not survive its completion.

To his credit, Mountbatten ignored MacArthur's embargo in Thailand and ordered British paratroopers to be dropped near the location of known concentration camps. They were instructed to keep watch from the jungle and to intervene at the first sign that the Japanese were massacring prisoners. Agents in E Group of Force 136 had located most of the two hundred prison camps through the SEAC area and arranged airdrops of doctors and 650 tons of food and medicine. But that was all. Britain's reconquest of her Asian colonies was, in the end, a terribly decent affair played according to the rules.

At first light on 2 September 1945 British Navy minesweepers cleared a channel through the Japanese minefields and next day the cruiser HMS *Cleopatra*, flagship of the Commander-in-Chief East India Fleet, Admiral Sir Arthur Power, accompanied by HMIS *Bengal*, arrived in Singapore. The British were back. On 4 September Rear Admiral C.S. Holland, flying his flag in the cruiser HMS *Sussex*, and Rear Admiral J.A.V. Morse, flag officer designate Malaya in HMS *Kedah*, arrived escorting the convoys carrying 5th Indian Division and XV Corps Headquarters from Rangoon.

At 6.45 that evening the Japanese delegates, General Itagaki and Vice Admiral Fukudome were brought on board *Sussex* where they signed a document surrendering Singapore and Johore and handed over charts and maps showing the position of all minefields in Malayan waters and the distribution of all Japanese forces under the command of Seventh Area Army and Tenth Area Fleet.

The Japanese delegates gave the strength of their forces in Singapore and Johore as 50 118 army and air force and 26 872 naval personnel, including the naval air arm. The Japanese said that all Allied prisoners of war and civilian internees were in camps under the control of their own officers.

Allied reoccupation began at 11 o'clock the next morning when the first troops of the Fifth Indian Division were disembarked. The following day two Spitfire and two Mosquito squadrons, which had reached Penang on 3 September, roared overhead on their way to Tengah and Seletar airfields on Singapore Island.

Headquarters XV Corps disembarked on the ninth and moved into Fort Canning, formerly the headquarters of Singapore

Garrison until the disaster of 15 February 1942. Then on 12 September at a ceremony in the municipal buildings of Singapore City, Admiral Mountbatten accepted the surrender of all the Japanese forces in South-East Asia. Outside in the quadrangle a Union Jack was hoisted to the strains of the British national anthem. According to Bill Slim, subsequently governor-general of Australia, it was the same flag that Percival had surrendered to Yamashita three-and-a-half years earlier.

The victors' first priority was to save the lives of the thousands of starving, ill-treated prisoners of war who had just been liberated from Japanese camps and prisons. Many of those who had been the victims of Japanese barbarity or witnessed atrocities were shipped home before their testimony could be taken. Others gave evidence to investigators on board ship, but would never return to identify the guilty men.

Mountbatten was also quick to recognise the needs of Empire but, in so doing, provided a loophole through which many war criminals would be able to wriggle to safety. He issued an order to all British commanders that:

the Japanese should be tried on criminal charges only, that is to say brutality, etc… that no one should be charged unless there was very strong *prima facie* evidence that he would be convicted on evidence which could be clearly seen to be irrefutable… *nothing would diminish our prestige more than if we appeared to be instigating vindictive trials against individuals of a beaten enemy nation* [our italics].

In Singapore, British and Australian investigating teams started a massive hunt for missing servicemen whose fate was unknown, most notably Allied airmen who had simply vanished after capture. One of the investigating officers, Major Cyril Wild, who had spent the war as a Japanese prisoner, was given the task of discovering the fate of some of these fliers. It was during the course of his investigations that he heard about an execution which had taken place at Bukit Timah just two months earlier in July. Further inquiries in the area led him to Outram Road Jail where he questioned Major Mikizawa, commandant of the jail's civilian section. Mikizawa had watched the execution of the Rimaus out of prurient curiosity and, terrified that he might be held responsible, decided that his best chance of avoiding blame was to co-operate. He took Wild to Bukit Timah and pointed out three mounds of earth with six rudimentary crosses which contained, he said, the bodies of Chinese prisoners and 'one or two Europeans' whom he had seen being executed. He would say no more and Wild was unable to get permission to have the bodies exhumed on such flimsy evidence.

Fortunately, there was one witness who was able to help the British investigators, including Wild, to reconstruct something of what had occurred. The Malay Amir Silahili, traditional ruler of the Riau Archipelago, had been instrumental in saving nearly one thousand refugees during the evacuation of Malaya and Singapore and transporting them to safety via Sumatra. Silahili had been deposed by the Japanese and detained on Singkep Island in the Lingga Archipelago.

He escaped in September 1945 and arrived in Singapore just a few days after the return of the British. He made contact with the unit which had been detailed to investigate war crimes and told them about the Europeans who had been captured in the Lingga Archipelago and taken to Dabo Police Station on Singkep before their transportation to Singapore.

From this clue a partial picture of the fate of the Rimau commandos began to take shape. Captain J.J. Ellis of SRD had already been dispatched to follow up leads in the Riau Archipelago and Lingga group. The next information came from the interpreter Furuta, who was first interrogated by 'E' Group South on 21 October. As we now know, his testimony must be treated with very great suspicion. For example, he confirmed the death of four white servicemen on the islands of Soreh and Tapai. Referring to the Soreh killing, he said: 'The Japanese made very fine graves for them.' But according to a local living at Soreh the Japanese stripped the bodies of Ivan Lyon and Bobby Ross and left them to rot where they had fallen.

Moreover, it seems clear that Furuta was the author—probably at the behest of his superiors—of the interpolations in the trial 'transcript'. One passage in particlar, quoted earlier, contains his signature:

Major Ingleton representing all the members, asked to the Chief of Prison and Prosecuting Attorney in attendance, Major Kamiya to give his thanks to all the Japanese personnel who were taking care of them by that time. He made special stress on the fact that all of them were deeply grateful for the courtesy and kindness that an Interpreter, Mr Furuta, extended on them for a long time in the past and requested them to convey their hearty thanks to Mr Furuta without fail. He repeated not to forget to give this message to him.

It is the *repetition* within this passage that gives him away.

At the time, however, Major Wild displayed an extraordinary capacity for obtuseness. Wild and his slightly more perceptive Australian colleague, Lieutenant Colonel L.F.G. Pritchard, questioned Furuta who said he had spent time with the Rimau men during their stay at Outram Road Jail 'on several occasions'. He gave an outline of the mission consistent with the transcript. He then added two details. Corporal Clair Stewart had given him a message: 'I hope my wife will excuse me for not saying a special goodbye when I saw her the night before I left for the operation. I did not want to worry her with my danger.'

So too, he said, had Bob Page: 'I trust my father will approve the way I took in giving up my studies and joining the army.'

The words might well have been used by both Stewart and Page in those dreadful days as their death approached. But the suggestion that they were the final words of condemned men is an obscenity. It was simply Furuta's way of ingratiating himself with his interrogators, of suggesting that he shared not just the goodwill but the confidence of men in their most intimate and terrible moments.

Although he was a fluent Japanese speaker, Wild's choice as an interrogator was deeply flawed. He had been the officer carrying the white flag in Percival's surrender party in February 1942 and he had spent his incarceration expiating his own shame. The Japanese put Wild to work on the Death Railway with F Force, an Anglo-Australian POW group which lost 3100 out of 7000 in seven months. Wild was one of the survivors who was returned to Changi where he was liberated in September 1945. He had witnessed Japanese brutality at first hand but chose to see it as an honourable expression of the soldier code. The Japanese could not be held responsible for staying faithful to the memory of the knights of *bushido*. When it came to pinning the blame on his erstwhile captors, Wild applied the suggested Mountbatten formula and found there was no case to answer.

His questioning of Furuta does not bear the description 'interrogation'. He asked: 'What was the meaning of the word "Perfidy" in the charge against Major Ingleton and the nine Australians?'

In a long-winded reply, Furuta suggested that it had to do with their being out of uniform. Wild said,

Speaking of 'perfidy', would it surprise you to know that at the beginning of the Malayan campaign, in December 1941, it was the exception to see a Japanese soldier in uniform? I was in that campaign and the Japanese come [*sic*] over the border into Perlis and Medah wearing Malay and Chinese dress, or cotton singlets and shorts.

Furuta:

I am astonished to hear it. I wish I had known it at the time. I might have been able to help them in their defence. They were heroes and I tried to help them, by speaking to many people, some of them big people. I even dreamt of trying to help them to get away from the Water Police, when they were well treated and lightly guarded.

I dreamt of helping them to get to Changi where they might have been hidden away by the prisoners of war. They were heroes, sir. Even the court was reluctant to condemn them and said that they were heroes.

Wild fails to note that the Rimaus were permitted no defence whatsoever. He then adds a parenthesis:

(Furuta also insisted that the party were always well treated by the Water Police, and were allowed special privileges, including hot baths every second or third day. The interrogators believe that this is true, and that Furuta himself went out of his way to help them on many occasions. It was clear that the whole party had impressed him, *especially Capt. Page.*)

Some years after the war, the Page family in Canberra asked the Reverend Hector Harrison, Moderator of the Presbyterian Church in Australia, to seek out Furuta during a trip to Tokyo. Harrison made arrangements to meet him several times—Furuta never kept the appointments. Captain Page's great friend would not do his family even that small courtesy.

Wild continued his investigations by asking General Otsuka and Major Kamiya about 'perfidy'. He reported:

I asked General Otsuka if a soldier could be executed for espionage under Japanese law if he was captured in battle wearing the uniform of his country. He answered 'No'. Major Kamiya then said they were wearing green shirts. I asked if they were the same colour as that which I had on (jungle green). He hesitated and then answered, 'Yes, but they had no badges'. I told him that we had excellent evidence that they were still wearing badges of rank when they were executed.

This 'excellent evidence' appears to be the indirect report by Wild of a conversation with a pair of former Korean POW guards, Noh Bok Kun and Kim Hyong Soon. They were prisoners in Outram Road Jail for undisclosed offences who claimed to have seen the Rimau men in the prison. They told Wild that some (the officers) wore 'two white cotton bands on their shoulders' while 'three had inverted chevrons on their sleeves'. In Wild's own words, however, the Koreans admitted they were speaking about 'airmen' and he reports that they left for the execution in 'two trucks' in a mood of jollity, 'laughing and talking and shaking hands with one another'. They were almost certainly referring to the massacred American fliers.

It seems, however, that the army declined to accept Wild's 'excellent evidence'. On the contrary, the Australian Minister for the Army, Cyril Chambers, would later write to Mrs J.S. Hardy, mother of the youngest man in the group, John Hardy, in response to her questions about bringing the lad's killers to book:

Dear Madam,
    Information to hand shows that the party, *on their own initiative* [our italics], disguised themselves as natives and

concealed all outward appearances of being soldiers or members
of the Armed forces...Ultimately the Japanese captured your
son and nine others and they were taken to Singapore and
according to information obtained...by being dressed in non-
military attire these intrepid Australians *voluntarily deprived
themselves* [our italics] of the right to be treated as prisoners
according to the custom and usage of war...

However, on 23 October—two days after the Furuta 'interrogation' and having read the field reports from the newly promoted
Major Ellis—Pritchard was satisfied he knew enough of the story
to make a recommendation to his headquarters:

The original copy of the proceedings of their Court Martial on
a trumped-up charge of 'Perfidy and Espionage' has been
obtained. The three judges who presided at the Court Martial
were Col. Masayoshi Towatari, Maj Mitsuo Jifuka, Maj Miyoski
Hisada.
    These men will be arrested.

General Otsuka and Major Kamiya were already in custody in
Raffles College. One of the executioners—Hirata—had committed
suicide at Outram Road Jail. The others were also being held.
    'As far as this HQ is concerned, it is felt that this case is now
complete,' Pritchard concluded.
    Meanwhile, the bodies of the ten murdered Rimaus had been
dug up from their graves at Bukit Timah and forensic evidence
showed that their deaths had been anything but 'heroic'. Captain

Roderick Ross of the Royal Army Medical Corps, who examined the bodies, reported that some of them had been hacked to death. Clive Lyon says: 'The idea that it was a clean, bushido-type operation is absolute balls—it was a horrible business. Yet it was decided that no criminal behaviour was involved and no awkward questions were asked.'

Enter the lawyers. The war crimes section of the British command came into the proceeding on 7 January 1946 with 'guidelines' at the request of the Australian authorities who sought to take the matter further. They said:

It is advised that where, upon investigation, it appears that a prisoner has been regularly tried in accordance with Japanese law for an offence and has been sentenced to death, it is not considered that the person or persons constituting the Court or the person who carries out the sentence can be regarded as war criminals.

This is so even if the victim was beheaded for the purpose of carrying out a sentence of death. If, however, the person or persons who execute a warrant issued in due form, exceed its authority and inflict some form of punishment other than that awarded by the Court, such an act would be illegal and may amount to a war crime... No hard and fast rule can be laid down as to what constitutes a fair trial as different countries adopt different codes or rules governing their trials. It is essential to consider the whole of the surrounding circumstances and to make a decision on general grounds...

If any proceedings on the face of them are palpably unfair, the convening authority may be regarded as being quite unmindful of the rights of the accused or culpably negligent in confirming the sentence. In such a case it is considered that a charge would lie against the authority and the members of the Court upon whom there was a duty to ensure that the trial was fairly carried out.

This was no great help. The trial was palpably unfair but was it in accordance with Japanese law? This is highly debatable. But then a week later came a more definitive ruling from London:

The policy of the British war crimes section is not to bring to trial any suspect unless the evidence is such that a conviction is virtually certain. The reasons behind this policy are, firstly, there are so many cases of a serious nature which can be conclusively proved that it will be at least several months before these can be disposed and, secondly, more than a very small percentage of acquittals would have a bad effect on public opinion.

The problem with gaining a conviction in the Rimau case was that all the Allied witnesses had been executed. Only the conspirators remained and by this time Furuta had so ingratiated himself that he was being employed in the war crime trials of others as an interpreter/translator. That in itself, however, would not have prevented the trial.

The sad truth was that by then no one among the Allied forces wanted the full story of Operation Rimau to be publicly revealed. They all had something to hide.

**The British Establishment** would not have welcomed the revelation that they were *the* motivating force behind an effort to reassert their colonial rights in South-East Asia—at least, not one that ended so badly.

**The Americans** would not have wanted it known that, having been provided with information by their Ultra code-breakers that the Rimau team were in dire trouble, they failed to provide the means to rescue them.

**The British Navy** would have found it insupportable to have the actions—and the failings—of its Captain 'Rufus' Mackenzie publicly revealed. After the war, as Vice Admiral Sir Hugh Mackenzie, he became Chief Polaris Executive and a figure of enormous importance in NATO.

**The SRD** would not have wanted it known that it had bungled its biggest mission. When they learned that the men of Rimau, whom they had abandoned in January 1945, had lived another five agonising months, their shame and anguish must have been palpable.

Even more shaming is the fact that the Rimau cover-up which has been in place for the past sixty years can be traced right to the top of the Australian High Command.

# CHAPTER 19
# NO DISCLOSURE

WHILE THE WAR was still raging in January 1945, Australia's top brass—General Blamey, General Northcott and Brigadier J.E. Lloyd—held a secret meeting with Colonel Chapman-Walker to discuss the ramifications of the Rimau case. It seems that their most pressing concern was to establish whether the commandos had told the enemy anything that might have compromised existing operations. They concluded from the Ultra intercepts that someone on *Mustika* must have panicked and opened fire, leading to the mission being aborted, and that information had subsequently been given to the enemy.

Chapman-Walker would be replaced by Jock Campbell as director of SRD in June 1945 but at this stage he was still running the show and it must have been an uncomfortable meeting for him. However much he had been kept in the dark about the Ultra intercepts up to this point, it is clear that he now knew just about everything.

Blamey and Northcott, who had been instrumental in getting Operation Rimau off the ground in compliance with British wishes, had certainly had this information since late 1944. But it is apparent that their primary objective was to bury Operation Rimau rather than to render assistance to its protagonists. As a result, all reference to information revealed by members of the Rimau party to their captors was deleted from the summary to a Top Secret report which was compiled the following month from intercepted Japanese messages and other intelligence sources under the heading, 'Enemy Information on Inter-Allied Services Dept, Z Special Unit and Services Reconnaissance Department'. The meeting also decided that, in view of the manner in which the operation had been aborted, no medals or honours would be awarded to any of the twenty-three participants.

There wasn't much the Japanese didn't know about Jaywick or Rimau at the end. They even found out that Ivan Lyon was a member of the Strathmore family and that impressed them. Believing that 'Lyon' and 'Bowes-Lyon' were one and the same, the Japanese considered it a high honour that Britain had sent a relative of the Royal Family to fight against them—it was inconceivable to them that a member of the Emperor's family would be asked to bear arms.

There was also the vital issue of Rimau's code and whether Ivan Lyon had deliberately left the codebook behind so that the mission could not be cancelled. This theory, which has been published elsewhere and calls Lyon's professionalism into question, is

264

nonsense. There was no 'codebook' as such, just two copies of the same unnamed volume. The code itself consisted of a few paragraphs chosen from a page in that book in which each letter was given a numerical value. One copy of the book was for Lyon and one for the operator in Darwin who was to listen for their calls.

The fact that Lyon's copy of the book was found in his bedroom by Mary Ellis simply means that he had most likely transcribed the few necessary paragraphs on to a piece of paper, most probably with carbon copies for signallers Craft and Stewart, and officers Donald Davidson and Bob Page. Either that or he might have followed the practice of SOE in London of typing codewords on to a strip of silk which could be sewn into an agent's clothing, thereby making it difficult to detect even in a fingertip search.

Ivan Lyon would hardly have left the 'codebook' in full view on his bed in Melbourne, where it could be found by Mary Ellis, if he had wanted to slip out of Fremantle without it. Moreover, Operation Rimau could have been cancelled at any time through Hubert Marsham from 11 September until he parted company with the Rimau team at 10 p.m. on 30 September. Chapman-Walker and Shadwell did not need Lyon's code to send that radio message to *Porpoise*.

This being the case, why would Lyon have left the 'code' behind knowing it was his only means of contacting Darwin and, apart from the walkie-talkies, communicating with *Porpoise* on her expected return? The answer is that he didn't leave it behind at all and it is slanderous to suggest that he would have jeopardised his men's lives in this vainglorious manner. Clearly, Lyon and key members of his team had handwritten or typed copies of the code in their possession.

Why, then, weren't the radios used to inform SRD of the Rimaus' plight or, at the very least, to find out what had happened to the rescue submarine all through the long November days and nights? And why didn't SRD send any messages to the Rimau men to find out what had gone wrong?

There are several possible explanations. One is that, alerted by Mary Ellis that Lyon had 'deliberately left his codebook behind', no SRD message was ever sent to the Rimau party and the watch for their messages was abandoned before it had even started. In that case, the Rimau party could have radioed a thousand SOSs which were never received, either in Darwin or on board *Tantalus*, because no one was monitoring the Rimau frequency. This seems highly unlikely.

Another possibility is that the commandos sank the three big transmitter/receivers in the *Mustika* knowing that they could still use the one that had been left on Merapas with Signaller Craft. Whether or not they had the time and opportunity to activate it once they returned, on the run, we do not know. Nor do we know of any radio traffic to Merapas from SRD because any transcripts have either been destroyed or remain hidden. The official SRD report says there were none.

The Rimaus, however, told their Japanese interrogators that they had been unable to get in touch with the rescue submarine. Although this point is mentioned in the Japanese retelling of the mission in the trial reports, it should be noted that the Japanese had nothing to gain or lose by recording it for posterity.

There is every likelihood that this is the truth and it gives the lie to this aspect of the Rimau story in every previously published account. The distortion was clearly designed to shift the blame to Ivan Lyon through the time-honoured device of 'pilot error'. And he was in no position to decry those who would betray his memory—not the duped writers and researchers faithfully following the given trail, but the SRD housekeepers who had already sanitised it.

SRD was dissolved in 1946, leaving only inadequate or self-serving explanations to every perplexing aspect of the Rimau story. One typical example is Walter Chapman's reply to Geoffrey Branson's charges about his competence over the wretched J containers.

Chapman noted in his report dated 19 March 1945:

As Branson has now left SRD under a slight cloud and that [sic] his report has been withdrawn by D/U [Chapman-Walker], I would be quite satisfied if my comments could just be noted and no further action taken. I imagine the reason I was not told anything about this in Australia is due to the fact that the Melbourne office wished to allow the matter to drop with Branson's demise.

While it is true that the troublesome Branson had been quietly transferred from SRD, his criticisms of Chapman had been extant since 21 August 1944, some considerable time before his 'demise'. Chapman-Walker had, it seems, simply chosen to ignore the matter until such time as SRD 'housekeeping' required that a response

267

from Chapman should be placed on the record. There was no knowing what cock-and-bull story Branson might circulate after the war about the goings-on inside SRD and the official version had to be credible.

Chapman was also asked to resubmit his report on Operation Rimau. This version, dated 21 March 1945—almost four months before the executions at Bukit Timah—opens with the statement:

> As requested I enclose a copy of my report on the unsuccessful pick up of the Rimau party. This was written a few days after I returned to the submarine from the attempted pick up and contains every bit of information that I gathered on Merapas. *Subsequently some of my conclusions and explanations for some of the evidence I found were altered* [our italics].

While a certain amount of revisionism might have been acceptable to correct mistakes made in the heat of war, the lengths undertaken by the SRD hierarchy to cover their backs over Rimau are inexcusable. Jack Finlay, the SRD chronicler, had been a civil servant before the war and seems to have known the drill. To this end, his superiors promoted in his official report the fiction of a happy band of heroes meeting death with a wave and a smile. That report was circulated to a limited readership in early 1946 when everybody at SRD *must* have known it to be untrue: the Western world, having recoiled from the horrors of Belsen, was still coming to terms with wave after wave of incontrovertible proof that the Japanese were as barbaric as the Nazis.

Yet the report concluded:

The Japanese testify that this group behaved with outstanding courage up to the very end, and viewed their sentence with complete unconcern. In view of the outstanding bravery and endurance of all members of this operation, their efforts to save the secret of their equipment, the casualties inflicted on the enemy during a fighting withdrawal, and the courage with which they met their death, it is recommended that a posthumous M.I.D. (Mention-in-Dispatches) be awarded to all members.

Only two honours can be awarded posthumously, the Victoria Cross and the M.I.D. But the Rimaus were to receive nothing. In his letter to Mrs Hardy, Cyril Chambers said, 'Whilst it is appreciated that your son died bravely on behalf of his country and was engaged on a very hazardous exploit for which he had received special training, you will understand, I am sure, that it is not practicable to bestow decorations on all brave men.'

Then on 29 January 1946 Lieutenant Colonel R.C. Smith, Officer Commanding 1 Australian War Crimes Section (SEAC), accepted the British advice. Having quoted the earlier London ruling, he said in a letter to AMF Headquarters:

Subject to any directions, it is proposed to fall into line with this policy. It is considered that the trial and execution of the ten members of Lt Col Lyon's [sic] does NOT constitute a war crime and it is not proposed to arraign any member of the Imperial Japanese Army in respect thereof unless instructions to the contrary are received from you.

Rimau was to be quietly forgotten.

The cover-up gained impetus from an article written by Cyril Wild in *Blackwood's Magazine* in October 1946. This piece of fiction says:

The Rimau prisoners were treated remarkably well by the Japanese who honoured and respected them. There is evidence that the Japanese were anxious to avoid the death sentence. It was in fact suggested to the prisoners before their trial that they should adopt a humble attitude and plead for mercy. Instead, down to the last corporal and able seaman, they remained resolute and defiant to the last. A young Australian, Captain R.C. Page, who had accompanied Lyon on his earlier expedition also, was asked by the court, 'Did you yourself kill any Japanese soldiers?' He replied in clear and deliberate tones, 'I am an officer in the British army, and I know that my aim was good'.

Not one of them can have dreamt that a single word of his conduct or his fate would ever be known in England and Australia. What, then, was the secret of this cheerful endurance in captivity and of the light-hearted courage with which they met their end?

Nowhere in the court transcript does the quotation appear. Bob Page was a fourth generation Australian. He was, by common consent, the leader of the Australians in the team. He had never joined the British army. But the readership of *Blackwood's Magazine* was British. 'Cyril Wild had read what the Japanese wanted posterity to understand about the executions,' says Clive Lyon. 'His article was the beginning of a myth, a fairy story.'

The weakness in the official case is highlighted by the high command's unquestioning acceptance that the Rimau party had not been subjected to any of the tortures which were part and parcel of the *Kempei Tai*'s known investigating procedures; that, as 'heroes', they had been 'well-treated'. This then leads to the insupportable conclusion that one or more of the Rimaus had imparted information to the enemy for the sake of a hot bath, some clean clothes and a few square meals.

The inference is despicable, all the more so because the Rimau party included the Jaywick veterans Bob Page and Wally Falls, men with a track record of heroism to match any in the Australian pantheon. Furthermore, the SRD controllers should have known from investigators following the Rimau trail from October 1945 onwards that other members of the party who had not been killed in battle or beheaded at Bukit Timah had been so brutally treated by the Japanese that they had died in captivity. Why would the remaining Rimau men have been treated more humanely?

One published account maintains that this was indeed the case because it was 'obvious' to the *Kempei Tai* that the Rimaus were so tough they would not crack under torture. Yet the Japanese equivalent of the Gestapo prided themselves on the results they achieved from beatings, starvation diets and other methods too gruesome to recount here.

Rimau had now entered the public record and the rose-tinted fiction continued. The official historian, G. Hermon Gill, in *Royal*

*Australian Navy 1942–46* (Collins, Australian War Memorial 1968), states:

> All records of the Japanese Military Court, of the Judiciary Department and of translations of interrogations of Japanese *and Korean* [our italics] witnesses, testify to the 'patriotism, fearless enterprise, heroic behaviour, and sublime end of all members of this party'.

Having turned the Korean evidence that the executions were anything but 'sublime' on its head, Gill then quotes Wild's assertions from the egregious Furuta, who was last heard of in Tokyo as the proprietor of a chain of nightclubs. Gill was not alone; the selective release of documents in the intervening years sought to gloss over the hard questions with a *Boy's Own* tale of derring-do. Dick Horton, author of *Ring of Fire* (Macmillan, Sydney 1983) solemnly proclaimed: 'The Japanese regarded their captives as heroes, but that did not prevent them putting them on trial, and eventually beheading them, which, in the Japanese tradition, is the proper ending for brave men and a great mark of respect.' Stephen Harper, in *Miracle of Deliverance* (Sidgwick & Jackson, London 1985), was wrong on both counts when he reported that Ivan Lyon was 'executed "with honour" just over a month before the war ended'.

Even respected SOE historian Professor M.R.D. Foot, a serving officer in World War II and Professor of Modern History at Manchester University wrote in his book (*SOE: The Special Operations Executive 1940–1946*, British Broadcasting Corporation,

1984): 'Rimau was a disaster. All the twenty-eight [*sic*] fine men who went on it, including Lyon, the leader of Jaywick, were lost; and it did not much console those of them who fell alive into Japanese hands that they had the honour of being beheaded, on 7 July 1945, instead of receiving some meaner death.' It is impossible to imagine a meaner death, just five weeks before war's end, than that which befell the Rimaus. These errors remained uncorrected when the book was reprinted by Pimlico, a branch of Random House, as recently as 1999.

However, there were too many anomalies, too much secrecy, too few hard facts to satisfy those who sought to inquire into what really happened. Authors and researchers from Ronald McKie, Brian Connell, Tom Hall, Harold Lander, Lynette Silver and others have progressively unearthed new and disturbing elements.

Lieutenant Colonel G. B. 'Gruff' Courtney, brother of the founder of Britain's Special Boat Service (SBS), claimed in his memoirs that the Americans suspected SRD of being a British 'Trojan Horse' used to regain Britain's former imperial power in the Far East. MacArthur's GHQ tolerated SRD but rendered it ineffective until it could be ignored and, like the Australian Army, diverted from the main activities.

According to Courtney, MacArthur and the Americans were anti-British and jealous of British colonialism. All of SRD's projects were subject to GHQ's approval, and the approval of any air and naval commander whose transport would be involved. GHQ could also prevent an SRD project from receiving adequate funding and consequently kill the project.

In 1990 the Australian Defence Department itself commissioned a monograph from an Australian National University academic, Myriam S. Amar, based largely on the research of Harold Lander. Her most worrying conclusions concerned the role of Ultra:

Many signals were passing between 2 Southern Expeditionary Fleet in Surabaya and Tokyo, Singapore, Pontaniak and Benjarmasin from late October onward. These signals [on the Rimaus' presence] were intercepted by a wireless intercept station and decyphered by Ultra. There are ambiguities in the role and purpose undertaken by Ultra underlined by the fact that these messages [were] not given top priority on arrival.

Equally disturbing is the thought that the code-breakers working in Brisbane were prevented from passing on the raw data immediately because they were confronted by a strong security barrier...The implication of all this is that about 28 October 1944 the submarine *Tantalus* was travelling only a few miles from Merapas. The Commander of the submarine was not warned of the danger encountered by the Rimaus. This story has the unpalatable reality that many of the Servicemen might have been saved.

Moreover, this element of the cover-up continued for decades.

Very few people had a need to know the highly secret aspects of SRD. Intercepted Japanese radio messages were kept in secured areas in Washington and were not released for public access until well after the 1970s...In considering the Ultra secret, it has been alleged that the Allies were aware that the Japanese were shipping many prisoners of war to Japan yet despite this knowledge, the allied submarines continued to destroy Japanese merchant vessels resulting in the deaths of thousands of Allied POWs.

If true, that is a scandal that should, even today, reverberate through the highest circles of the Pentagon and Capitol Hill. Myriam Amar concludes:

The fact that the men of Operation Rimau managed to manoeuvre through tides and currents in Japanese occupied territory commanded superior navigational skills, abilities and great courage. Irrespective of the outcome of the mission, it is to be recognised that these men were not only well trained but strongly motivated heroes.

Why then, we may ask, have they never been so recognised by their governments? Why have their compatriots been kept in the dark? Why have we had to piece the picture together from a hundred scattered sources where they have lain in wilful official neglect? The answer goes to the heart of our story. For only now, sixty years later, can Rimau be seen in its proper context.

At that time—between May and October 1944—Britain was beating the Axis Powers but the cost had already been prohibitive. She was bankrupt. The City of London, once the vibrant mercantile heart of the Empire, was a bombsite. Her financial and commodity markets were in ruins. To survive in the postwar world, Britain had to get her Empire back.

Operation Rimau therefore was the last frantic gesture of an empire which felt itself falling into dismemberment and being overtaken by a new order. The United States of America, which Britain itself had spawned less than two hundred years previously, was now usurping its place on the great stage. Its president, even in his declining days, dominated world politics; his instruments, in the person of his commanders MacArthur, Eisenhower, Patton, King, Nimitz and Marshall were themselves huge, grand figures on the international landscape. They were remaking the global map and they were doing so with barely a by-your-leave to yesterday's men.

In fact, the United States viewed the British claims to empire with a measure of contempt. The memory of British capitulation in South-East Asia barely two years previously was still strong, and when the Americans measured the quality of the British leadership they found it wanting. Churchill they tolerated; he was, after all, half American himself. And he had the gift of the gab; he could rouse British subjects around the globe and bark the bulldog phrase. But in the end his health was rapidly failing; only America could give weight to his doggedness. For example, when Roosevelt insisted that the Supreme Commander of Overlord—the Normandy invasion of Europe—should be an American, Churchill acquiesced even though he had promised the post to Brooke.

To the Americans, George VI was a well-meaning figurehead who should be kept out of power politics, while his cousin, Dickie

Mountbatten, was a self-publicist whose dangerous schemes drove even the British chiefs of staff mad.

The Americans also viewed the politicians Eden, Macmillan, Selborne and many other members of Churchill's War Cabinet as mere remnants of the old Imperial Order. All lost office, along with Churchill, when Clement Attlee's Labour Government swept to power even before the Pacific War had ended. Now it was America's turn and if that meant Singapore, Malaya and Burma found self-determination under *Pax Americana*, so much the better. They owed the British exactly nothing.

For their part, the men who ruled Britain in 1944 believed there was another way to view this latest phase in the exercise of their benign imperial duty. The mission to bring civilisation in its finest European form to the farthest corners of the earth had merely been interrupted. Their Chinese subjects, they knew, had never knuckled under to the Japanese. The Malays, like natives anywhere, had taken the path of least resistance; they could therefore be won back to the colonial master by the exercise of a firm, steady hand. And Britain had a Colonial Service with centuries of experience—bruised and battered perhaps by the ravages of war, but with the corporate memory to rebuild itself in its former image.

All they needed—and they needed it desperately—was the grand gesture that would prove them fit and proper governors to a people who looked up to the white man and understood their place in the scheme of things. At this stage of the war Churchill still wanted to seize the northern extremity of Sumatra and use it as a base from whence to bomb Singapore. But his chiefs of staff would not hear of it and Churchill had to look elsewhere for the great military flourish.

Mountbatten, one of the main architects of the calamitous Dieppe raid in 1942, was always up for another mad scheme, but his record since taking over in Burma had been abysmal. Despite his exalted rank very few of his operations got off the ground; those that did usually ended in disaster; and those that later succeeded owed much to the superb generalship of William Slim.

Little wonder then that Ivan Lyon, the hero of Jaywick, appeared so attractive a prospect when he sought to return to the scene of his triumph. Little wonder that Operation Hornbill was expanded in London even beyond Lyon's expectations in the spring of 1944. It was tailor-made.

But perhaps also, as Hornbill became Rimau and the weaponry started pouring in to fuel a mighty crack across the Japanese shins, the Australians had their own agenda. As we have seen, Curtin and Evatt had no intention of ever leaving Australia's security in British hands again and were already talking about setting up a regional conference with its Pacific neighbours. Australia, after all, was the final target of the Japanese advance. Their northern towns had been pounded by Japanese bombs—Darwin itself no fewer than forty-five times. Japanese submarines had sunk twenty-two coastal steamships. Their midgets had broached Sydney Harbour itself. Thousands of Australian soldiers had died in close-quarter fighting with the aliens who wanted to take their land by force. Thousands more were captured, tortured and carelessly killed. They had their own scores to settle.

But there was still a vestige of Empire in the air. Indeed, Operation Rimau can—and should—be seen as the last Australian military contribution to the notion of a British Empire. It was mounted at Britain's behest, led by British officers and squarely aimed at a very British result. It would be too harsh to say that it failed because it was so British. But there was certainly something thoroughly European that attracted the *Heihos'* attention that fateful afternoon off Kasu Island.

Robert Charles Page and his mates accepted the British leadership because the bonds of history and the bonds of friendship complemented each other. They did not know the burden of expectation they carried from the men in Whitehall, 10 Downing Street and Buckingham Palace. But if they had known they would have accepted it as part of the Done Thing for the time and the place.

As it happened, they were the last to have done so. And they gave their lives for it.

When they were gone, they had no further use. They were an embarrassment to be hidden away, to be quietly buried behind a cloak of official denial and disinformation. But those most closely concerned, the families of the Rimau men, would not let the matter rest. Indeed, in 1947 a distraught Mrs Hardy pleaded with the army minister for the details of young John's companions. Cyril Chambers replied:

It is not in accordance with the practice of the Army to furnish the particulars you desire concerning the next-of-kin of the soldiers who accompanied your son on his mission to Singapore, as the names and addresses of soldiers' next-of-kin are supplied to Army authorities on the understanding that such information will be treated as strictly confidential and will not be divulged in any circumstances.

This difficulty, however, could be overcome if you would forward to the Department two or three letters in sealed envelopes which will be addressed and on-forwarded to the next-of-kin of soldiers with whom your son was associated in the raid. Alternatively, should you prefer, I will arrange for the Secretary of my Department to communicate with two or three of the next-of-kin of sons who took part in this exploit, informing them of your desire to get in touch with them and requesting them to write to you.

Yours Sincerely...


Since then there has been some sporadic connection between the families. Some have come together on occasion as tributes were made and services conducted in the memory of twenty-three young men who stepped forward and accepted a mighty challenge. The passage of time has taken most of their loved ones. Among those who remain—whatever might have been achieved in this present work—there will always be questions.

In February 2001, Roma Page said, 'The cover-up is still happening. Why, oh why, after so long...?'

# EPILOGUE
# JUSTICE AT LAST

IRONICALLY, THE heroes of Rimau *were* avenged. Although none of the Japanese responsible for their execution was charged with that atrocity, justice caught up with most of them for other war crimes. Four of the main offenders went to the scaffold: General Itagaki, Commander-in-Chief of the Seventh Area Army who had insisted on the death penalty; Major-General Otsuka, who had been in overall charge of the Rimaus' prosecution; and the military and civilian commandants of Outram Road Jail, Majors Kobayashi and Mikizawa. Mikizawa was charged over the 1200 Chinese prisoners who had starved to death while in his care.

Major Kamiya, the prosecutor who had manipulated the evidence to make a guilty verdict inevitable, was sentenced to life imprisonment. One of the executioners, Corporal Hirata, had committed suicide before he could be tried, but his four comrades received from five to ten years' imprisonment for other offences.

LIEUTENANT COLONEL Ivan Lyon, MBE, DSO, had died on Soreh Island in the Riau Archipelago in 1944 and was re-buried in Singapore. His wife Gabrielle lived until 1978. Their son Clive's earliest memories were of Japanese soldiers guarding him and other European prisoners in Fukushima internment camp:

> I do remember, unfortunately, that aspect of it. I say unfortunately because some if it wasn't very pleasant. I remember on one occasion I'd broken a window playing in the compound with an older boy.
>
> I'd been hauled in front of the guards and I remember being in the arms of a female warder. Someone was approaching me with a heated poker and trying to find out who had been playing with me and was responsible for breaking the window. I can also remember the American bombing at the end of the war and taking cover in a cellar. We were fairly high up and there was snow and, from time to time, earthquakes. It was cold and horrid.

Gabrielle and Clive were repatriated to Australia where Gabrielle learned of her husband's heroic death. Roma Page remembers Clive as a small boy ringing doorbells in the neighbourhood and running away—elated to have the freedom to do something naughty. Gabrielle was also reunited with her daughter Christienne who had spent the war in Occupied Indochina. Christienne settled in Australia and lived in Canberra for many years until her death.

Clive Lyon returned to England and attended his father's old school, Harrow, and later joined his father's old regiment, the Gordon Highlanders, and spent two years fighting in the Borneo jungles in the 1960s. In February 2001, he received a cheque for £10 000 from the British Government for his incarceration after the Japanese Government refused to compensate British prisoners of war. 'I was born on 12 September 1941 and I should think I was the youngest recipient,' he says.

Ivan Lyon's grandson, Captain Jamie Lyon of the Grenadier Guards, was appointed equerry to Prince Philip at Buckingham Palace. 'The military tradition goes on,' says Clive Lyon. 'I'm glad the interest in Rimau hasn't flagged. It's a story that still stirs people's imagination. It's very comforting that my father and all his gallant companions are still held very much in awe in Australia.'

Bobby Ross was buried beside Ivan Lyon in Kranji War Cemetery, Singapore, in 1946. Ross's mother, Mrs T.S. Ross, of East Grinstead, Sussex, had been informed in a letter from Major George Astley of the SRD, dated Melbourne 17 December 1945, that her son was dead.

Astley wrote:

I can now let you have further information resulting from Japanese interrogations. The Japanese state that Lieut. Ross and Lt. Col. Lyon, the party leader, were killed fighting a Japanese patrol on a small island called Asore [sic] Island, just north of Pangkil Island in the Riau Straits on or about the 10th October 1944...

I feel I must be frank with you and say that in my opinion the details we have received are correct and that there is no chance that Lieut. Ross may have escaped on to the mainland of Malaya or that he is being held in the Dutch islands.

The Ross family are immensely proud that Bobby died fighting at the side of his commanding officer to enable his comrades to escape. 'Greater love hath no man than he who lays down his life for his friends,' says Clive Lyon.

UNLUCKY TO the end, Major Cyril Wild was killed in a plane crash in Hong Kong in 1947.

Major Walter Chapman took his own life on 5 May 1964 after discovering the truth about the Rimaus' fate.

Rufus Mackenzie, however, prospered. After the war, he was made commander of the depot ships *Forth* and *Montclare*, then executive officer of the cruiser *Liverpool*, flagship of the First Cruiser Squadron in the Mediterranean. He was married in 1946 and his wife, the former Helen Bradish-Ellames, bore him a son and two daughters.

Promoted to captain, he commanded the Underwater Detection Establishment at Portland from 1952 until June 1954. From 1954 to 1961 he was in HMS *Dolphin*, the submarine base at Gosport, as chief staff officer to the flag officer (submarines), and in command of HMS *Ganges*, the boys' training establishment at Shotley, Harwich.

Promoted to rear admiral, Mackenzie hoisted his flag as flag officer (submarines) in July 1961, but on New Year's Day in 1963 he was unexpectedly appointed chief polaris executive, with a budget of £350 million and the task of making Polaris operational within five years. Mackenzie was promoted to KCB in 1966, having been appointed CB in 1963. He retired in 1968 and became chairman of the Navy League, and director of the Atlantic Salmon Trust.

Mackenzie had a serious accident in July 1982 when his car caught fire in a motorway collision and he and his wife suffered severe burns. But he lived to complete his memoirs, which were published in 1995 by the Royal Navy Submarine Museum under the title *The Sword of Damocles*. He died the following year at the age of eighty-three.

TWO OF THE Rimau graves in Kranji cemetery remained unmarked until 1990 when the then Governor of Queensland, Sir Walter Campbell, discovered for the first time that his brother Archibald 'Pat' Campbell had died a hero's death on Operation Rimau. At Sir Walter's insistence, the War Graves Commission in London investigated the case. The remains of the two Rimaus had been recovered by the Dutch from Tapai Island and the commission positively idenitified them as those of Lieutenant Commander Donald Davidson and Corporal Pat Campbell.

IN OCTOBER 1994, exactly fifty years after the men of Rimau made their dash for Singapore three thousand kilometres behind the enemy lines, six members of the Australian Defence Force, led by Major Jim Truscott of the Pilbara Regiment, Karratha, Western Australia, arrived to retrace their journey.

It was a physical and spiritual tribute to Ivan Lyon and his men and had the full backing of the Chief of the Defence Force. They would use the army's standard Klepper canoes and 'RIMAU RETRACE', as the exercise was called, would follow the first three hundred and seventy kilometres of the flight from just outside Singapore Harbour to the bottom of the Lingga Archipelago in modern Indonesia.

Major Truscott said:

Ivan Lyon was very much my mentor—an amazing man, a hard player and a fighter to the end. It was a privilege to retrace their major landfalls and speak to several Indonesians who had witnessed or assisted the Rimau operatives. The interest shown in Singapore and by the local people throughout Riau was quite extraordinary.

They started at Batam Island and spent two weeks paddling through the Riau and Lingga groups to the town of Dabo on Singkep Island, where the Rimaus had been beaten and held prisoner. Sometimes they camped in the jungle but more often they were invited to shelter in a house or a spare hut. Occasionally they cooked but more often were invited to share the food of the villagers.

We saw little sign of the Rimau men being on the islands. Most of their hides have been reclaimed by the jungle and the sea. But as soldiers we could still appreciate the folds in the ground which make the difference between living and dying. It was with a mixture of exhilaration and sadness that we traced their silent footprints.

On Merapas they found a rock fort and an empty grave near where two of the Rimaus died.

Whereas the Merapas of 1944 was virtually uninhabited, today a lighthouse on the island is manned by the Indonesian Navy. Brothers in arms, we shared some coconuts and contemplated when war came to Merapas.

They found the days long and it was always a relief to climb out of the canoes, which were very similar to World War II folboats. He said:

While our party experienced none of the disasters which had overtaken the raiding party in 1944 one of our team withdrew after a particularly hard day having aggravated some old injuries—canoeing is like that. Ivan Lyon would not have been impressed, even if our average age of forty-three years was much greater than their youthful twenty-six.

Like most of the other Special Operations mounted from Australia, there has been little recognition of the men who lost their lives on Operation Rimau. The complete story will never be known but one thing is certain—their bravery and endurance is firmly etched in the minds of six Australians.

Before he returned home, Jim Truscott went to Singapore's Kranji cemetery where the seventeen crosses mark the resting place of all the Rimau men whose bodies were recovered.

He said: 'I spoke quietly to Ivan beside his grave.'

# SOURCES

THE AUTHORS are extremely grateful to Roma Page and Clive Lyon for their invaluable guidance through the Rimau story. Robert Macklin interviewed Mrs Page at her Canberra home on four occasions in 2001. She was very generous, not only with her time but also with the reams of documentation that had accumulated over the years. She also read the final manuscript to eliminate errors of perception and transcription.

Peter Thompson interviewed Clive Lyon at his home in Norfolk and was given free run of his extensive archive which included many letters and other documents relating to the life of his father, Lieutenant Colonel Ivan Lyon and to Operation Rimau. Clive Lyon also served with distinction in the Gordon Highlanders and was able to bring a tremendous amount of professional experience to bear in military matters. Having served in South-East Asia, he was also familiar with Singapore and many of the landmarks involved in Operation Rimau.

We are also indebted to the staff at the National Archives of Australia and the Australian War Memorial, Canberra, and at the Imperial War Museum and Public Record Office, London. They were enormously helpful in opening channels to hitherto un-examined areas of the records and never tired of sifting through their vast resources to find documents related to Operations Jaywick, Hornbill and Rimau, some of which had not see the light of day for sixty years. Our friend and fellow journalist Bill Richards, Media and Communications Manager of the Australian National Maritime Museum, Sydney, took Peter Thompson on board HMAS *Krait*, which has been preserved as part of Australia's wartime heritage. Bill's help was vital in our reconstruction of Operation Jaywick.

Finally, we would like to thank John Parker, author of numerous military books, for bringing the Rimau story to our attention and for providing the initial research which put us on the trail of the full, extraordinary saga.

The books we read included:

Alanbrooke, Field Marshal Lord, *War Diaries*, edited by Alex Danchey & Daniel Todman (Weidenfeld & Nicolson, London, 2001)

Allbury, Fred, *Bamboo and Bushido* (Robert Hale, London 1955)

Amar, Myriam S., *Operation Rimau 11 September to 10 October 1944, What Went Wrong?* (Australian Department of Defence, Revised Edition, March 1990)

Ballard, G. StV., *On Ultra Active Service: the story of Australia's signal intelligence operations during World War II* (Spectrum, Richmond 1991)

Beaumont, Joan, *Australia's War 1939–45* (Allen & Unwin, Sydney, 1996)

Bramall, Field Marshal Lord, *The Imperial War Museum Book of the Desert War 1940–42* (Sidgwick & Jackson, London 1992)

Campbell, Rosemary, Heroes and Lovers: A Question of National Identity (Allen & Unwin, Sydney, 1989)

Churchill, Winston S., *The Second World War* (Cassell, London 1959)

Clausen, Henry C. & Lee, Bruce, *Pearl Harbor: Final Judgement* (Crown, New York, 1992)

Connell, Brian, *Return of the Tiger* (Evans Brothers, London 1961)

Cruikshank, Charles, *SOE in the Far East* (Oxford University Press, Oxford, 1983)

Drea, Edward J., *MacArthur's Ultra, Codebreaking and the war against Japan, 1942–1945* (University Press of Kansas, 1992)

Elphick, Peter, *Singapore: The Pregnable Fortress* (Hodder & Stoughton, London, 1995)

Foot, M.R.D., *SOE: The Special Operations Executive 1940-1946* (BBC, London 1984)

Gailey, Harry A., *The War in the Pacific* (Presidio Press, California, 1997)

Gilbert, Martin, *Second World War* (Weidenfeld & Nicolson, London 1989)

Gilchrist, Andrew, *Malaya, 1941: The Fall of a Fighting Empire* (Robert Hale, London, 1992)

Hasluck, Paul, *The Government and the People 1942–45* (Australian War Memorial, Canberra, 1970)

Hetherington, John, *Blamey, Controversial Soldier: a biography of Field Marshal Sir Thomas Blamey* (Australian War Memorial, Canberra 1973)

Horner, D.M., *Crisis of Command: Australian Generalship and the Japanese Threat 1941–43* (Australian National University Press, Canberra, 1978)

Horton, Dick, Ring of Fire (Macmillan, Sydney, 1983)

Howarth, Patrick, *Undercover: The Men and Women of the SOE* (Routledge & Kegan Paul Ltd, London, 1980).

Kirby, Major General S.W. and others, *The War against Japan* (HMSO, London, 1957)

Lauer, E.T., *32ⁿᵈ Infantry Division World War II* (Madison, Wisconsin, 1956)

Long, Gavin, *The Six Years War: Australia in the 1939–45* War (Australian War Memorial, Canberra, 1973)

MacArthur, General Douglas, *Reminiscences* (Heinemann, New York, 1964)

McCarthy, Dudley, *South-West Pacific Area First Year: Kokoda to Wau* (Australian War Memorial, Canberra, 1959)

McKie, Ronald, *The Heroes* (Angus & Robertson, Sydney, 1967)

Maneki, Sharon A., *The Quiet Heroes of the Southwest Pacific Theater: an oral history of the men and women of CBB and FRUMEL*, (United States National Security Agency Center for Cryptologic History, Washington, 1996)

Marks, Leo, *Between Silk and Cyanide* (HarperCollins, London 1998)

Milner, S, *Victory in Papua* (US Army, Washington, 1957)

Moore, J.H., *Oversexed, Overpaid and Over Here: Americans in Australia 1941–45* (University of Queensland Press, Brisbane, 1981)

Morgan, Janet, *Edwina Mountbatten: A Life of Her Own* (HarperCollins, London, 1941)

Paull, Raymond, *Retreat from Kokoda* (Heinemann, Sydney, 1958)

Parker, John, *SBS: The Inside Story of the Special Boat Service* (Headline, London, 1997)

Perret, Geoffrey, *Old Soldiers Never Die: The Life of Douglas MacArthur* (Andre Deutch, London, 1996)

Powell, Alan, *War by Stealth: Australians and the Allied Intelligence Bureau 1942–1945* (Melbourne University Press, Melbourne 1996)

Rivett, Rohan, *Behind Bamboo: An Inside Story of the Japanese Prison Camps* (Angus & Robertson, Sydney, 1947)

Ross Lloyd, *John Curtin: A Biography* (Macmillan, Sydney, 1977)

Silver, Lynette Ramsay, *The Heroes of Rimau from the research of Major Tom Hall* (Sally Milner Publishing, Birchgrove, NSW, 1990)

Smith, Michael, *The Emperor's Codes* (Bantam Press, London, 2001)

Smurthwaite, David, *The Pacific War Atlas 1941–45* (CIS, Melbourne, 1995).

Thomson, Judy, *Winning With Intelligence* (AMHP, Loftus, Australia 2000)

Tsuji, Masanobu, *Japan's Greatest Victory, Britain's Worst Defeat: The Capture of Singapore 1942* (Spellmount, United Kingdom, 1997)

Whitington, Don, *Strive to be Fair* (ANU Press, Canberra, 1977)

From the SOE: Operations in the Far East, the Public Record Office, London, we read the following documents:
—General remarks on the Rimau Pick-up: Major Walter Chapman
—Interrogation of Interpreter Furita (i)
—Interrogation of Interpreter Furita (ii)
—Interogation of Koreans Noh Bok Kun and Kim Hyong Soon
—Interrogation of Major General Ohtsuka and Major Kamiya
—Operation Rimau: Major Walter Chapman's Report
—Report on Patrol of HMS Tantalus

—"Rimaus executed or killed" intercept

—Sir Colin Gubbins' meeting with General Douglas MacArthur (Codename AK 1000)

—SRD Official History of Operation Rimau

—SRD Report on Operation Hornbill

—Statement by Major Fugita

—Statement of the Amir of Senagang

—Statement of headman of Mapur Island

—Statement by Raja Mun

—Statement by Yap Chin Yan

—Translation of Proceedings of Military Court of 7th Area Army (the Rimau trial).


From the Australian War Memorial and the National Archives we read the following documents:

—Address, author unknown, to Wesley Church, Canberra on the unveiling of a window to the Page family

—Brief Account to Australian Intelligence of the Civil Administration in Singapore till Aug 44

—Cables, Department of External Affairs, Canberra to Secretary, Dept of Army, copies External Affairs Officer London, re War Trials of Japanese.

—Correspondence between A. L. Sargent and his sister and the Peechelba Sub-Branch of the RSL; and Lt Col C. Locke, Commander of Z Special Unit and Mrs Sargent

—*Daily Examiner*: 1915 Harold Page promoted to Lieutenant, 1916 Harold Page awarded Military Cross, 1918 Harold Page wrote home,

1919 Harold Page returned to Grafton after three years at the Front, 1919 married Annie Miller Brewster wedding.

—Einstein's Letter to President F.D. Roosevelt

—The End of the Japanese War—report for Australian Defence Forces, February—September 1945

—Hornbill—Balance of Stores for First Sortie—re cables 414 and 446

—Intelligence Report on vessels in Singapore Harbour, June 1944.

—Japanese messages, Dilli to Piroe, Singapore to Pinrang, to Batavia and Tokyo 15 October, 1944, 22 Oct, 26 Dec, 7 Jan, 1945, 9 Jan, 10 Jan, 15 Jan, 20 Jan, 21 Jan, 23 Jan, 25 Jan, 26, to Piru Ken 28 Jan, to Saigon, 29 Jan, Jan, 30 Jan, 2 Feb, 3 Feb, 7 Feb, 12 Feb, 17 Feb, to Saigon and Tokyo 21 Feb, 14 March

—Maritime Japanese Systems of Identification, United States National Security Adviser, declassified July 1978

—Minute from HQ 'E' Group to Flag Officer, Malaya, on missing personnel of Clandestine Party

—Minute Paper on Signals to Overseas Centres from Ultra Sources, 9 March, 1944

—Minute Paper to Lt Col RA Little, on Special Ultra Cypher Office, Melbourne, 3 May, 1944

—Minute Paper on Transmission of Ultra Material to UK, 23 Febuary, 1944

—Most Secret signal on Ultra Nodeco from Lt Col Sandford to Lt Col Little, 22 February, 1944

—Minute Sandford to Little, 19 February, 1944. Investigation of Ultra allegations

—Minute Papers, spy suspected in Canberra, 6 January, 1945

—Modification of Hornbill Plan—SRD—17 July 1944

—One-Man Submarine (Sleeping Beauty)—evaluation by US Navy, 1944—Report on Search for Allied Personnel in Riau Archipelago, October, 1945

—Operation Hornbill—Situation to Date, from Comdr RN S.N.O. SRD to DCNS to 23 June, 1944

—Personal dossiers, Rimau and Jaywick personnel

—Photographs, SOA, for Director, Military Intelligence, AMF Melbourne, 1946

—Report on Aerial Reconnaissance, Bintan Island, 26 Sept, 1945

—Report: Small Operation clandestine party under Lt General Dempsey

—Report from Lieut J.F. Lind-Holmes on Rimau/Hornbill Operations to Commander G.C.F. Branson, RN, 19 September 1944

—Secret Report from Area Intelligence Headquarters, Townsville on Escape Points for aerial pick-up from Group 22, Darwin, 23 June, 1944

—Series of signals to and from Director General of Security, Canberra on suspected on Japanese knowledge of Ultra material, March 1945– Chinese and Russians suspected leaks

—Signal Plan, Rimau Project, 12 August 1944

—Special Intercept Signal Traffic, SOIC from Lt Col Clementson to Lt.Col ADMI, 30 June 1944

—Top Secret Control Procedure, Ultra, General HQ Southwest Pacific Area, 14 March, 1944 from Lt General R.K. Sutherland, Chief of Staff

—Top Secret Report on The Activities of Australian Secret Intelligence and Special Operations Sections, based on information from Ultra sources to 1800 Hours 31 August, 1945

—Top Secret signals, C in C East Indies Station, from Capt 8th Submarine Flotilla. Dec 1944

—Top Secret Telegram from Perth to No 57, for Lieut Campbell—Dec 3, No contact with Rimau, Tantalus returning

—Top Secret 'Y' Communications signal from Chairman Sig. Int. Board London to General HQ Southwest Pacific Area, 11 May, 1944

—Twentieth Century International Relations, The Atomic Decision, 1939–45

—War Crimes message, Chinese in Hatfield case, 10 April, 1946

—Z Operation File, Missing Personnel correspondence, 1944–46

Other documents we read include:

—Hand-written letter by Lord Selborne to General Francis Lyon about his son Lt Col Ivan Lyon

—Letter from Prof Carey to Editor, Canberra Times

—Letter, notes from Roma Page to Robert Macklin, 11 Feb. 2001

—Letter regarding Lord Bruce's injunction to SOA to assist British efforts to reclaim Empire

—Major Cyril Wild's article in Blackwood's Magazine October 1946

—Myriam Amar's Monograph for Department of Defence

—Philip Cornford interview with Tom Hall (*Sydney Morning Herald*, August 27, 1994)

—Prime Minister John Curtin's letter to Governor-General recommending VC for Ivan Lyon

—Rear Admiral Sir Hugh Mackenzie's taped interview

—Sir Hugh Mackenzie's obituary

—SRD account of Operation Jaywick

—Transcript of interviews with Clive Lyon March—July 2001

—War Department copies of Japanese decrypts relating to Operation Rimau

# INDEX

KILL THE TIGER